Grand Canyon Women

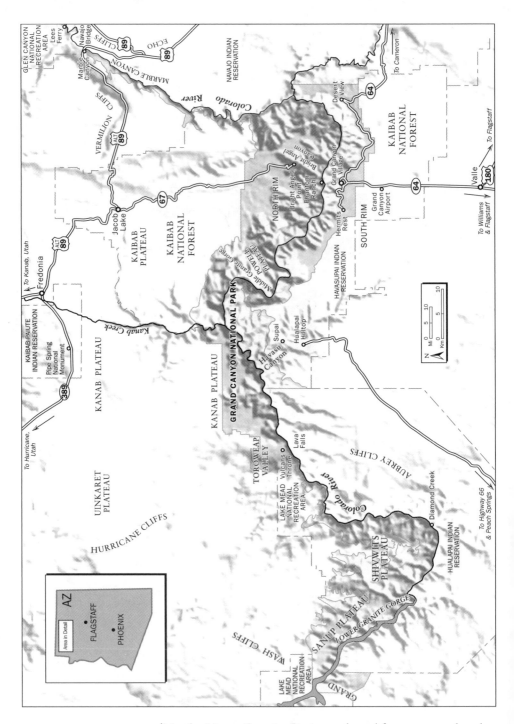

THE GRAND CANYON. (Map by Moore Creative Designs; adapted from map produced by the National Park Service Division of Publications, Harpers Ferry Center, West Virginia.)

LIVES SHAPED

Grand Canyon Women

BY LANDSCAPE

BETTY LEAVENGOOD

PRUETT PUBLISHING COMPANY
BOULDER, COLORADO

Printed in the United States

10 9 8 7 6 5 4 3 2 1

Library of Congress Cataloging-in-Publication data

Leavengood, Betty, 1939–
    Grand Canyon women : lives shaped by landscape / Betty Leavengood.
       p.   cm.
    Includes bibliographical references and index.
    ISBN 0-87108-867-3 (pbk.)
    1. Grand Canyon (Ariz.)—Description and travel. 2. Grand Canyon (Ariz.)—Biography. 3. Women—Arizona—Grand Canyon—Biography.
    I. Title.
    F788.L398   1999
    979.1'32'0082—dc21
    [b]   99-12238
                                           CIP

Cover and book design by Julie Noyes Long
Book composition by Lyn Chaffee
Maps by Tony Moore, Moore Creative Designs
Cover photographs by Eric Wunrow, Toroweap Overlook (North Rim) at dawn. Front cover inset photographs, clockwise from top left, courtesy of the Grand Canyon National Park Museum Collection, Polly Mead Patraw, Elizabeth Kent Meyer, and Gale Burak.

Contents

Acknowledgments

I would like to thank first and foremost all the women profiled in this book who shared their lives with me:

Gale Burak invited me to her New Hampshire home for three glorious autumn days of talking and hiking. In Louise Hinchliffe's lovely home in Sedona, Arizona, she showed me the picture of the Grand Canyon that had inspired her to leave Massachusetts and travel to the Canyon. I met Lois Jotter Cutter first at the Grand Canyon River Guides spring meeting at Marble Canyon in 1995 and later at her home in Greensboro, North Carolina. Denise Traver and I first met at the Rock Springs Cafe north of Phoenix, Arizona; in the spring of 1998, I joined her all-women's backpacking trip to Supai in the Grand Canyon. I spoke with Polly Patraw by phone from her home in Santa Fe, New Mexico. She ended our conversation with, "For 92, I'm doing real well!"

Ruth Stephens Baker and I have enjoyed many lunches after her daily tennis game in our mutual hometown of Tucson, Arizona. I traveled to Durango, Colorado, to meet Louise Teal in the beautiful Strater Hotel. Katie Lee welcomed me to her home in Jerome, Arizona. Patty Knox let a friend and me pitch our tents on her lawn on the South Rim of the Grand Canyon. I met Bernice Reeves and Kitty Marr on several visits to the North Rim. Kitty loaded my group's packs at Roaring Springs on a cross-Canyon backpacking trip, and Bernice saddled my mule for a ride down the North Kaibab Trail. Elizabeth Kent Meyer invited me to her apartment in Glendale, Arizona, and shared her album of her life at the Grand Canyon as a Harvey Girl.

I learned about the other women profiled in this book by delving into the archives of several libraries. Thanks to Diane Grua, Karen Underhill, and Richard Quartaroli at Northern Arizona University's Cline Library Special Collections and Archives for helping me sort through the wealth of material in their collection about women of the Grand Canyon. Colleen Hyde, Carolyn Richards, Kim Besom, and Mike Quinn of the Grand Canyon National Park Museum Collection were unfailingly helpful and cheerful during my visits to the Canyon and in response to my frequent E-mails. Sara Stebbins of the Grand Canyon National Park Library answered many of my "Where do you find . . . ?" questions. Jan K. Davis helped me find the original Phantom Ranch Register at the University of Arizona Library Special Collections in Tucson, Arizona. William Frank of the Huntington Library in San Marino, California, guided me through the extensive Marston Collection.

Others helped track down details. When I learned that Bessie Haley Hyde had attended my high school in Parkersburg, West Virginia, my mother, Gladys Marshall, who lives in Parkersburg, went to the local library and copied Bessie's photos and artwork from the 1924 high school yearbook. A longtime friend, Bill Bee, examined local records, obtaining pertinent information and locating the Haley's Parkersburg home on Oak Street. The late Dan Davis, the first river ranger at the Grand Canyon, told me of his boat trips with Georgie White Clark over breakfast in Tucson.

I also thank all the wonderful people who have hiked the Canyon with me, sharing the beauty, the adventure, the catastrophes, and the fun. There have been many since I first put my hiking boots on the Bright Angel Trail in 1979, but I especially thank Don and Ginny Fisher and Ruth Butera. The Fishers, in spite of the "giving up hiking forever" trip to Thunder River and the sandstorm at Granite Rapids, keep coming back to the Canyon with me. Although Ruth refuses to wear the "My Age Is None of Your Business" T-shirt I gave her after a cross-Canyon hike, she never turns down a chance to return to the Canyon. Her comments, "I bet those are your mules!" and "Are those blue lines roads?" started us on two unforgettable adventures.

Special thanks go to my three children, to whom having a mother who hikes the Grand Canyon seems perfectly normal. My son, Rodney Graham, who as a teenager introduced me to hiking in the mountains near Tucson, has made five trips into the Canyon with me. My daughters, Cheryl and Christy, who share my love of the outdoors and the Canyon, are working to catch up.

I will be eternally thankful for the constant support and

guidance from my editor at Pruett Publishing Company, Marykay Scott-Cicio. She never let me forget that this book would work and kept after me to rewrite, rewrite, and rewrite, until it did!

And my heartfelt thanks to my late husband, John, without whose support this book could never have been written.

—*Betty Leavengood*
Tucson, Arizona

My Canyon Call:
An Introduction

ONE COMES TO KNOW THE CANYON'S DEEPEST ENCHANTMENT
WHEN SLEEPING UNDER ITS STARLIT CANOPY. (Surprise Valley,
1990; photo courtesy of Allyson Armstrong.)

I *FIRST SAW THE* Grand Canyon as the typical tourist. Over spring break in 1970, my husband and I decided to show our seven- and eight-year-old children the Canyon. We were moving from Tucson, Arizona, back east in the summer and wanted to see the Canyon before we left.

Four months pregnant and herding two active youngsters, I don't remember much except the impact of that first amazing view as we approached Mather Point. After driving for miles on the high, flat mesa, we pulled into the parking area—and the earth opened up below. I stared in amazement as postcards became reality and a deep gorge with endless buttes spread before me. I certainly never thought then that I would return again and again to this place, to hike its trails and to write a book about its women.

But I did. Nine years later, back in Arizona, I headed again for the Grand Canyon, this time to meet some friends from Ohio on the South Rim. I arrived a day early to hike. A total novice, I hiked the 4.7 miles down the Bright Angel Trail to Indian Garden, once home to a small band of Havasupai who used the reliable water source to grow crops, but now a Park Service campground.

Sitting in the shade of the cottonwoods, I realized that because I'd started out so late in the day I could not make my way back to the rim before dark. I had to spend the night below the rim at the campground, attempting sleep on a jacket I had in my daypack. The braying of feral burros woke me up at 4:00 A.M.

I started up Bright Angel Trail at daybreak and, without breakfast or snacks to sustain me, had a miserable hike back to the rim. To this day I have never hiked Bright Angel again. When I finally reached the top, a young man asked me to take his picture. He held up seven fingers. "What's that for?" I asked. "I've hiked in the Canyon seven times," he laughed. He offered to take my picture, and at the last second I held up one finger. Now I've run out of fingers.

I returned to the Canyon again about a year later, when some coworkers invited me to backpack to Supai, the reservation home of the Havasupai in the extreme western end of the Grand Canyon. When I hesitated, remembering my first experience, they urged, "The water is beautiful there. You'll love it," and I agreed to join the trip.

Looking back, I've often wondered why I went on that third trip to the Canyon. The beauty called to me, true, but there was also a challenge and an escape. It was a time in my life of personal trauma. My first marriage had just ended in a painful divorce. I had three children and little money. The Canyon provided a temporary escape and gave me a sense of accomplishment that I needed at the

A HAPPY INAUGURAL HIKE, THE FIRST OF MANY IN THE GRAND CANYON. (Bright Angel Trail, 1979; photo courtesy of Betty Leavengood.)

time. I had, in today's terminology, low self-esteem. Hiking in the Canyon gave me a boost. I could do something that many people could not do. I could put one foot in front of the other and conquer some awesome climbs. If I could do that in the Canyon, I could do it in life.

I hadn't formulated these thoughts as my coworkers and I drove from Tucson to Seligman, a small town in the northwest corner of Arizona. After spending a night in a motel, we drove out to Hualapai Hilltop and began the 11-mile trek down. With my borrowed backpack and new hiking boots, I struggled to adjust during the first mile, which dropped 1,100 vertical feet. It became easier as we walked through the nearly level, dry streambed of Hualapai Canyon for 5 miles before entering the riparian habitat of Havasu Canyon where a perennial stream flows out of Havasu Springs.

We stopped in Supai, tribal headquarters and home to nearly four hundred Havasupai, for lemonade and rest. We'd entered another world. Children, dogs, and horses wandered through the village. Women in long skirts entered the trading post. Men gossiped on a bench in front of the post office. Supai is the only place in the United States where the mail is regularly delivered by mule. As we left the village for the 1.5-mile walk to the campground, we saw four Supai men entering a streamside sweat lodge. A little farther along the trail we heard the roar of Havasu Falls. Around the bend, blue-green water tumbled over cliffs 60 feet high. At the base, a deep pool surrounded by white bathtub-shaped pools invited swimming.

We spent three days in the campground, climbing down the cliff below the campground to Mooney Falls, eating frybread, and luxuriating in the travertine bathtubs of Havasu Falls. Too soon we left this paradise, climbing the trail back to Hualapai Hilltop, the final steep climb at its end testing our resolve. Driving back to Tucson, sore legs and all, the talk centered on what part of the Canyon we would explore next.

My next Canyon adventure came only six months after the trip to Supai. My mother called from West Virginia to say, "Your Aunt Ethel and I are driving to Yellowstone, then we're going to Bryce and Zion. We've reserved a room on the North Rim. Why don't you drive up and meet us?" My old childhood neighbors, Kathleen and Harlan, would be joining them.

People from the East have this problem. "You live in the same state, don't you?" they seem to think. It is 511 miles from my front door to the lodge on the North Rim. One doesn't just "run" up there. But a friend and I got the bright idea to drive to the South Rim, a mere 300 miles from Tucson, and hike the 23 miles across to the North Rim. We would save about 200 miles, and my mother and Aunt Ethel could return us to the South Rim at the end of our hike. Little did we know.

We reserved bunkbeds at Phantom Ranch in the bottom of the Canyon near Bright Angel Creek, drove to the South Rim, and headed down the South Kaibab Trail, a steep, 7-mile descent to the Colorado River. The South Kaibab follows a ridgeline into the Canyon and offers sweeping views of the Inner Gorge. We crossed the Colorado on the Silver Bridge and arrived at Phantom Ranch's small haven of stone cottages, frame bunkhouses, and assorted Park Service buildings in time for dinner. The first stirrings of the idea for this book were born when I learned that Mary Elizabeth Jane Colter designed Phantom Ranch in 1922. I thought, "A woman architect? Here?" and filed the thought away to bring out at a later date. Fifteen years later, as it turned out!

My first beer hall remains imprinted in my memory. The dining hall closes for dinner around 6:00 P.M. and reopens again at 8:00 P.M., by which time a long line curls around the cottonwood trees. We joined a table that included five math professors from Georgia Technical College in Atlanta. We had a great time and entirely too much beer the night before a 14-mile hike that would gain nearly 6,000 feet in elevation. Up at 4:30 A.M., breakfast at 5:00 A.M., and we headed up the trail.

We hiked up the North Kaibab Trail into the narrow canyon known as "the box," where seven steel footbridges cross Bright Angel Creek. Listening to the sound of rushing water between steep canyon walls, we hiked leisurely through a lush riparian habitat for several miles before reaching the open "desert bowl," where the intense July sun scorched our skin. We began a steep climb that I later learned the wranglers called Asinine Hill. The heat sapped our energy as we climbed, but we knew we could cool off in Ribbon Falls. The professors at the beer hall had extolled its beauty and told us, "Don't miss it!"

From Asinine Hill, the 100-feet-high falls glisten like a ribbon shimmering in the sun. We took the short side trip across a bridge to the falls, which cascade over a wide shelf of travertine to a shallow pool at the bottom, creating a microclimate where ferns and red monkey flowers flourish. We climbed up behind the falls to look out through the spray and to cool off in the mist.

We left reluctantly and rejoined the trail for the mile-long climb into Cottonwood Campground. There the ranger told us that we needn't have climbed Asinine Hill, as there was a shortcut at the base of the hill to Ribbon Falls! Two miles above the campground we came upon a lemonade stand operated by the Aiken children, whose father, Bruce, ran the pumphouse at Roaring Springs. We gulped and gladly donated a couple of dollars to the till.

We had 5 miles yet to go from the Aiken house to the North Rim—nearly straight up, or so it seemed when we calculated the 4,200 feet we had to gain. We left the pleasant sound of Bright Angel Creek and turned up Roaring Springs Canyon, where, less than 2 miles up the trail, water roars out the canyon wall. This is the water source for the hotels, restaurants, businesses, and housing on the south and north rims. We were tempted to take the short hike over for a closer look, but as shadows lengthened on the canyon walls, we worried about my mother. She would be sure we had met with disaster.

We came to a sign that said "North Rim 3 miles." It is the longest 3 miles in the world. My legs ached as I struggled up the switchbacks. I devised a system to keep me moving that day that has worked for me ever since. I would take twenty-five steps before allowing myself to stop for a short rest. As the shadows lengthened and the sun faded from the Canyon, I began to worry. This was new terrain. The impending darkness would make us blind to its features. Were steep cliffs ahead, like the ones we had passed earlier? Could a misstep send us tumbling to eternity?

At Supai Tunnel we rested for fifteen minutes, taking advantage of the water fountain and restroom. Our map said we had 1.8 miles to go. Could I do it? I had no choice. Above the tunnel the trail enters a deep pine forest. I counted twenty steps before each rest, then fifteen. Finally, through the trees, we saw the horizon. A

A RESIGNED GRIMACE IS ALL ONE CAN OFFER A CAMERA WITH
THREE STEEP MILES YET TO GO TO THE NORTH RIM ON THE
23-MILE CROSS-CANYON TREK. (Photo courtesy of Betty
Leavengood.)

final, long switchback and we were out of the canyon, fourteen
hours after we left Phantom Ranch.

We were there. Mother wasn't. She'd given up on us. We
had to hitchhike to the lodge. "They don't even have TV here,"
complained my Aunt Ethel. A most welcome phrase, for I knew I'd
found a home.

My prime rib dinner that night in the beautiful Grand
Canyon Lodge remains one of the most memorable meals of my life.
I basked in my accomplishment—I had hiked across the Grand
Canyon. Back in Tucson, I submitted the story of the hike to a local
publication. An account of the hike appeared in the March/April
issue of *Tucson Lifestyle Magazine*. I'd come a long way since that
first tentative foray into the Canyon in 1979. Remarried, working
at a new job, hiking across canyons, and now writing! My self-
esteem soared.

So much so that I felt qualified to show others "my" Canyon through our local community college activities program. A friend and I would each drive a van of hikers, one of us to the South Rim and the other to the North Rim, and trade keys mid-Canyon. We met some wonderful people and had some exciting times. Don and Ginny Fisher, the most totally prepared backpackers I've ever met, became entranced by the Canyon. Tom Watson, the "happy whistler," whistled off-tune the entire 23 cross-Canyon miles. Betty Carlton, a fine lady in her early seventies, hiked with us two weeks after her husband died. "He'd want me to do it," she explained. My strapping son, Rod Graham, hiked along on one trip as his college graduation gift. At the end of that trip several of us bunked in one of the Bright Angel Historic Cabins. We slept like the dead, but at 4:00 A.M. I woke to a frantic shaking. "Get up," Rod said. "We'll miss the sunrise"; so off we went in the pre-dawn light to get a good spot. Sunrise over the Grand Canyon is a time of expectation. The birds are quiet. The Canyon is shrouded in a deep gloom, waiting. Then the horizon glows, the sun hits the highest temples, and soon the entire Canyon is bathed in fiery light.

After six hikes across the Grand Canyon and three trips to the Havasupai Reservation, I decided to explore other trails within the Canyon. I'd read an article about Thunder River and suggested to my fellow hikers that this might be a good place to explore. My friend and veteran canyon hiker David Sandrock showed us slides of his Thunder River trip. "Do you think we can make it from Monument Point to Tapeats Campground in one day?" I asked, and David replied, "Easy. Piece of cake." I should have noticed then that his legs began at his neck.

That spring my friends Don and Ginny Fisher drove with me from Jacob Lake near the Utah border to Monument Point and camped at the trailhead. Ginny, ever prepared, pulled out a sun-shower and filled it with water. "When we come back," she explained, "I'll get the first shower." Sounded reasonable to me.

We started down the Bill Hall Trail looking out over Bridger's Knoll into the vast expanse of the Canyon. A group of hikers came struggling up the trail. "Stop," one warned, "before it's too late. There's rattlesnakes, scorpions, and it's hotter than hell." Another member of the group added, "Go ahead, it's worth the price of admission." It seemed unusually hot even for Arizona in late May, but going along merrily downhill, we really didn't notice.

Down, down, down we went. At one spot, we had to lower our packs with ropes. We made it to the esplanade. I had looked up the word before leaving home: "a rocky, grassy area for walking." The definition needs expanding. It is another world. Red rocks, carved by ancient waters, interpersed with gnarled trees and flowers, the esplanade is one of the most beautiful spots of the Grand Canyon.

The esplanade ended abruptly, and we were faced with the treacherous redwall formation that dropped clifflike for 500 feet into Surprise Valley. We rested at the edge of the redwall, looking at the grey expanse of Surprise Valley. Just past noon, with the sun nearly straight overhead, we descended the trail carved into the redwall and entered an oven. Don and I ran out of water. To want water and not have it is a dreadful feeling. But to want water and not have it while hiking in the Canyon's oven heat is pure torture. Your mind focuses on liquid, imagining sodas and juice. You berate yourself for not having put in that extra quart. "This is a once in a lifetime trip," Don said. "I'll never do this again." I swore off hiking too. Later we learned that all heat records had been broken on that day. Planes could not land at Sky Harbor Airport in Phoenix, and in Tucson the thermometer reached 117 degrees, an all-time record.

Then we heard it. The wonderful, welcome roar of water. Up a final knoll and below, way below, Thunder River glistened in the sun.

"Giardia," said Ginny, a nurse, "does not develop for several days," so we drank our fill without filtering before facing 2 miles of treacherous downhill to Tapeats Campground, near the Colorado River. We never made it to Tapeats on this trip. We stopped in a flat area by the bank of Thunder River, beneath several tall cottonwood trees. Don and Ginny pitched their tent. I threw my sleeping bag on the ground, ate a melted Snicker's bar, drank my eight ounces of chardonnay, and went to sleep to the wondrous roar of Thunder River.

Life looked immeasurably better the next morning as we sat in the beauty of Thunder River. When I close my eyes I can still see the red trumpet flowers and the sparkling clear water of this, the shortest river in the world. We revised our plans and, instead of staying two nights here in our makeshift campground, decided to begin the hike out that night, camping just below the redwall in Surprise Valley. At dusk, I spread my sleeping bag on a flat section of the trail and lay on my back, looking at millions of stars twinkling above.

The next morning we climbed up the redwall to the esplanade and easily made it to the trail crossroads where we'd cached water and food. As we sat, enjoying the sunset, the sky began to darken; by dusk it looked ominous. Not heeding nature's warning, I tied my hammock between two pine trees and climbed into my sleeping bag, not overly worried that a storm would hit. Around midnight, the wind whipped the trees, my hammock swayed, and the temperature plunged. Although I could not sleep, I stayed nestled within my warm sleeping bag. At daybreak, as the storm swept toward us, we ate granola bars for breakfast and hiked quickly up the Bill Hall Trail.

As the storm gathered strength, we faced strong winds and pounding rain, which quickly turned to a driving snow. Don, Ginny, and I crawled into an overhang and wrapped my sleeping bag over our legs. We could not believe our luck. Two days earlier we had nearly died in the heat, and now we were sitting in a snowstorm in an overhang on the side of a cliff wrapped up in a sleeping bag, discussing whether we had enough food to spend the night in this shelter.

Finally, as the wind died down, we decided to try to make our way back to our car. After a hard, tenuous climb through the snow and sleet, we approached the station wagon and laughed as we saw Ginny's sunshower hanging in the tree. She shook off the snow and emptied the water. My last image of that trip is of the wipers clearing the snow from the windshield. Once again, I had survived the challenge of the Canyon.

It took a while to get over the trek to Thunder River. But, like most Grand Canyon hikers, I soon forgot the bad parts and together with Don and Ginny, Nancy Thompson, Helen Murdock, Warren Jung, and Ruth Butera began planning our most elaborate Canyon hike yet. We would go down the Hermit Trail to the Boucher Trail, across the Tonto Trail to Granite Rapids, and back up Hermit. We would plan this trip carefully; there would be no surprises. We read everything we could about the trails, packed our bags with extra care, and, again in late May, headed for the South Rim. Don and I, who had both sworn off hiking in the Canyon forever, were on the trip. For me, returning to the Canyon now was never really questioned. I thrived on the adventure or misadventure.

Built in 1896 by a New York prospector and inlaid with cobblestones around 1913, the first section of the Hermit Trail is hard on the feet. We turned left on the Dripping Springs Trail and connected up with the Boucher Trail, circling Hermit Gorge along some exposed edges before reaching our night's camp on Yuma Point. Here, in one of the most spectacular parts of the Canyon, I was dismayed by the constant sound of airplanes and helicopters overhead. Only at dusk, when it became too dangerous to fly, could we enjoy the peace of the Canyon.

The next morning we dropped down to the Tonto Trail and discovered that it is anything but the flat trail it appears to be from high above. As we hiked in and out of drainages, our eyes were treated to pockets of magenta and deep yellow blossoms of the small prickly pear cacti that brightened the grey-green landscape. We camped that night at Hermit Campground, enjoying the pools and commenting on how error-free this trip was. "Good planning and experience," we told ourselves smugly. The next day we moved camp to the beach where Monument Creek enters the Colorado River at Granite Rapids.

From our perch on the beach, we watched kayakers and rafters negotiating the rapids. We were enjoying the afternoon and looking forward to a wonderful evening—and then the wind started. Within minutes we were engulfed in sand that felt like tiny pieces of glass pelting our skin. Even so, we tried to cook dinner. I can still hear the crunch of sand as I tried to eat my macaroni and cheese.

We couldn't see in front of our faces, and yet I decided to snap a few pictures of the sandstorm. "You took pictures in a sandstorm?" the camera repairman asked later in amazement, as I wrote a check for $200. At dusk we crawled in our windblown tents, hoping in vain for some respite. It was not until next morning that the sandstorm ended, as quickly as it had come, and all was calm.

We had the day to enjoy the beach. Four of us went for a walk along the river. Our throats raspy from the sand, we remarked about how good a cold beer would taste, knowing that the river excursions carried lots of beer. As we—Nancy, Ginny, Ruth, and I—sat on a log watching a large raft pull into the beach and begin to set up tables for lunch, obtaining the liquid gold became our mission.

Ruth, who wears her snow-white hair and senior citizen status proudly, said, "Watch this." Off came her hat. She fluffed up her hair and sauntered over to the scene of activity. After some preliminary chatting about the sandstorm and learning that the rafting party was a thirty-day environmental study group, she casually mentioned that she would be happy to pay for a cold beer, should they happen to have some. A six-pack of Budweisers was ours, free. "Take those over to your girls," the boatman said, and "Mama" she's been ever since.

We packed up the next morning and began the long climb out. Returning along the Hermit Trail, in typical trip fashion we hit a snowstorm below the South Rim.

I have since been on many other trips to the Canyon, some idyllic, others with an adventuresome twist. Always, I am struck by the changing beauty of the Canyon—the crisp light of a late fall sunrise, the hazy shroud of a summer sunset, and a touch of winter's snow along the rim. Always, I am drawn back.

I'm not sure I can articulate why, exactly, I am drawn to the place. Surely it is for the obvious reasons—its everchanging beauty, its immensity—but mostly, it's the satisfaction I feel as I drag my weary bones up one more switchback to the rim. The Canyon has been with me through so many changes in my life. From my first trip in 1970 when I was pregnant with my daughter Christy to my trip in August 1997, two weeks after my husband, John, died, the Canyon has remained constant.

It's not always an easy place to be. Friends said to me after my husband's death, "Why go to the Grand Canyon? Why not go to a beach resort?" My answer: On a beach I would lie in the sand and think. At the Canyon I would work.

With my three staunch Canyon friends—Ruth, procurer of beer from the rafters, and Don and Ginny, of the infamous Thunder River trip—I headed again to the North Rim of the Grand Canyon. We pitched our tents near the East Rim View, cooked our food, washed our dishes, walked a mile to the bathrooms, and gathered firewood. During those glorious late summer days we hiked and hiked—to Widforss Point, across the Kaibab Plateau on the Arizona Trail, along the Ken Patrick Trail, and to Tiyo Point to view Shiva Temple. Evenings we sat around the campfire, sipping wine and watching as lightning played in the distance and later as the full moon rose over House Rock Valley. I slept, exhausted and exhilarated. I left the Canyon ready to face life again, this time alone for the first time in my life. Would I be able to cope? I knew I would. I had learned this much, at least, from the Canyon.

Others, too, have learned from the Canyon, have grown because of their experiences there. Over the years, I began to wonder about other women and their relationship to the Canyon. In a world traditionally given over to the domain of men, women, too, have had their place and purpose amidst the Canyon's walls. The Canyon does not discriminate by gender. As with any wild place, it has practiced equality through time. It tests both men's and women's mettle against scorching heat, blinding snow, treacherous terrain, and deadly waters. Survival is often dependent merely on the level of one's own resourcefulness.

Anasazi women were probably the first to develop and survive by this brand of resourcefulness. Remnants of their adobe and masonry homes remain under cliffs in many areas of the Grand Canyon, where from ca. 700–1200 A.D. they carried out their daily tasks. No one knows precisely why the Anasazi, now more appropriately called the Ancient Puebloans, or Prehistoric Pueblo, abandoned their Canyon homes, but some theorize the area suffered from an extended drought that forced the population to move on. Many scholars and native people today believe that the Prehistoric Pueblo are the ancestors of the modern day Hopi who now live one hundred miles east of the Grand Canyon. The Hopi community of Old Oraibi, founded about 1150 A.D., is the oldest continuously inhabited site in the United States.

The people most closely associated with the Canyon today are the Havasupai. They were living in the western end of the Canyon as early as 1200 A.D. and traveled to water spots throughout the Canyon during the summer months. They spent winters hunting on the plateau. They lived undisturbed by the outside world until 1776 when the Spanish priest, Francisco Garces, descended into Havasu Canyon and remarked on the Supai's fair appearance and industry. A mere century later, Anglo ranchers coveted their plateau lands, prompting President Chester A. Arthur to establish the Havasupai Reservation that restricted the Havasupai to a narrow strip within the Grand Canyon. It was not until 1975 that the plateau lands were restored to them, mainly due to the efforts of a Havasupai woman, Ethel Jack, who lobbied in Washington for the return of the land.

The information available about the Canyon's "first" women is disappointingly limited, and this thwarted my efforts to cover some or even one of them in this book. My attempts to interview contemporary Havasupai women were equally unsuccessful. So I am able only to acknowledge here the vital place Native women have today and have had throughout the Canyon's cultural history.

The women profiled in this book are or were resourceful human beings. Most of them met the Canyon's challenge with courage, grace, and tenacity. They persevered, and most emerged from their challenges victorious. What is interesting is how differently each of them defined and met their Canyon challenge and how some succeeded where others failed. Some were content with views from the rim; others were not happy unless they were deep in the Canyon's bowels or on the mighty Colorado River. Some of the women made parts of the Grand Canyon an object of study. Some found employment there, and some found husbands. And some came and left without looking back. One thing, however, is true for all of them. Their experience at the Canyon was life-altering.

Reading about the Canyon, I came to realize that most of the available books and articles concern men—John Wesley Powell, Robert Brewster Stanton, Ellsworth and Emery Kolb, and many others. Where were the women? I remembered that a woman had designed Phantom Ranch. I set out to find the Canyon's women. I asked questions at the Grand Canyon National Park Museum Collection and library and delved through books and articles. What follows are the stories of eighteen women whose lives were entwined, some for only a brief period, with the Grand Canyon.

Ada Diefendorf first came to the Canyon in 1894. She married her tour guide, William Wallace Bass, and became a reluctant partner in his tourist business. Mary Elizabeth Jane Colter designed six structures at the Grand Canyon at a time when women were not generally accepted as architects.

By 1905, Fred Harvey had two hotels on the South Rim. His "Harvey Girls" in crisp black-and-white uniforms worked and lived at the Canyon. Among them was Elizabeth Kent Meyer, a Harvey Girl who worked at the Canyon in 1926.

I was surprised to discover from my research that the first woman to attempt a boat trip through the Canyon, Bessie Haley Hyde, graduated from my high school in Parkersburg, West Virginia. In 1930, Polly Mead Patraw convinced the Park Service that a woman could be a ranger-naturalist. In 1937 Ruth Stephens Baker became the first woman ever to set foot on Shiva Temple.

Botanists Elzada Clover and Lois Jotter collected specimens

on a river trip in 1938 and became the first women to successfully complete a boat trip through the Canyon. Doris Nevills ran the river in 1940, becoming the first woman to follow the route of John Wesley Powell by traveling from Green River, Wyoming, to Lake Mead. Gale Burak began hiking the Canyon in 1942 and finished her last stint as ranger in 1991. Georgie White Clark ran "Share the Expense" river trips for forty years and introduced thousands of people to the Colorado River.

Louise Hinchliffe left Massachusetts in 1951 to work for the Park Service at the Grand Canyon and stayed for nearly thirty-four years. Today the Grand Canyon library is named in her honor. Katie Lee's songs of protest challenged the building of the Glen Canyon Dam in the 1950s and continue to provide a voice for the growing movement to drain Lake Powell. Kitty Marr and Bernice Reeves have wrangled mules off the North Rim for nearly ten years. Polly Knox has been wrangling mules off the South Rim for almost as long. Louise Teal in 1972 became one of the first women to work as a boatwoman on the Colorado River through the Grand Canyon. She's been on the river ever since. Denise Traver leads backpacking trips for women into the Grand Canyon.

These women are representative of countless others whose lives have been deeply touched by the Grand Canyon. They are exemplary Canyon women who have carved the path and made it easier for other women to follow in their footsteps. If you embark on a mule ride, raft the Colorado River, take a nature walk along the rim, or participate in a ranger program, a woman is as likely to be in charge as a man. As for me, I return again and again, each time with renewed humility, ready to meet my next challenge.

A Lady's Rough and Tumble Life

ADA DIEFENDORF BASS

(1867–1951)

PORTRAIT OF ADA BASS, CA. 1908. (Photo courtesy of the Arizona Historical Society, Tucson, Arizona, Bass Collection.)

*A*DA *DIEFENDORF HELD* on to her seat as the stagecoach carrying a group of six tourists bounced along the rough road from Williams, Arizona Territory, to the Grand Canyon. She wondered how she would manage the 70-mile ride to Bass Camp, where their guide, William Wallace Bass, promised grandeur such as they had never seen. This vast, unsettled land contrasted sharply to the neat, rolling farmland surrounding her home in East Worcester, New York. The year was 1894.

Born August 29, 1867, in Charlotteville, New York, Ada grew up in East Worcester, where her father ran an undertaking and wagon business. As a child, she would rather practice her piano and organ, teach herself to play the violin, or read books than play with other children. In 1883, at age sixteen, she passed the teachers' exam and spent the next several years either teaching or studying music at the seminary in Stamford, New York, and the Boston Conservatory of Music. She was a tall, serious young woman with a stern countenance and a dry sense of humor.

When Ada traveled cross-country by train late in 1893 to visit an aunt, manager of the Commercial Hotel in Prescott, Arizona Territory, she would have been, at twenty-six, considered a spinster. In that era society measured a woman's worth by her husband and children: to be unmarried was a disgrace. But the odds of marriage were stacked against her. In New York in 1894 women outnumbered men by a ratio of two to one. Perhaps Ada hoped to meet an eligible man in the West, where the ratio was switched, two men to every woman! She stayed in Prescott for several months, giving music lessons during the spring and summer of 1894. While in Prescott, Ada learned of Bass's excursions to the Grand Canyon and decided to join an August trip.

William Wallace Bass had been a dispatcher for the elevated railroad in New York City. After he suffered a nervous breakdown, his doctor recommended that he go west to live a more physical, less stressful life. Bass established a camp on the South Rim of the Canyon in 1884 and took up the life of a miner, locating several mining claims—including ones for zinc, lead, and silver—in the Canyon. Although he continued to prospect and mine, Bass soon realized that people would pay to see the Grand Canyon; in 1885 he organized the Canyon's first tourist excursion from the town of Williams to his camp, which became known as Bass Camp. The camp consisted of a small cabin that served as a kitchen and a large white canvas tent where guests slept and ate. Assorted sheds, outbuildings, and corrals completed the compound.

So that his customers could arrive in relative comfort, Bass built a road from Williams and one from Ashfork to his camp. Once there, tourists would accompany him on horseback down the Mystic Springs Trail to see the Canyon and occasionally venture along the Tocopoba Trail to the Havasupai village of Supai. Guests came to Bass Camp as much for the charms of their host as they did for the scenery, for Bass was charming, a visionary, and able to keep tourists in stitches with his stories. He liked to have fun and thrived on adventure. He played the violin and wrote poetry, which impressed Ada.

The night before embarking on her stagecoach ride to the South Rim, Ada went by train from Prescott to Williams and spent the night at the Hayward Hotel. She and her companion travelers left early the next morning; by evening, after 32 miles of jostling in the stagecoach, they faced a flooded Cataract Creek. Ada wrote, "Twilight was just deepening with the gloom of night, and the murky waters as they rolled by with a rush and roar had an ominous look. The driver of the stage load of provisions had reached there before the flood came and succeeded in crossing the stream."[1]

Bass drove the stage downstream to a better place to cross. Everyone walked down to the banks of the stream to look through the darkness at the raging water. Bass next built a large bonfire on the bank, and despite the protests of one man, who was certain his bones would be washed up on a beach in California, crossed the creek by the light of the fire. Relieved and safe, the party camped there for the night.

They traveled by stage all the next day, arriving at Bass Camp just as the sun was setting. Traveling was hard work in those days, which perhaps made the tourist experience all the more rewarding. Ada marveled at the Canyon, writing in her diary, "Our party got its first view of this great panorama just as the light of day was being shaded by the curtain of night. Bright and early, before the sun was out the next morning, the entire party was out again to feast their eyes on what we had briefly looked upon the night before."[2]

The Canyon fascinated Ada, but not as much as the man who was already known as the "Grand Canyon guide." Bass apparently reciprocated, for following her visit, Ada traveled back to East

Worcester to collect her personal possessions and returned to marry him. She was leaving the East's civility for the wilds of the Arizona Territory. Though she planned to marry a man her parents had never met, they were no doubt relieved that she would not end up an "old maid."

Only five months after they met, Ada became Mrs. William Wallace Bass at the Methodist Parsonage in Williams on January 6, 1895. That evening Bass's friends threw a "shivaree," a frontier custom where friends gathered outside the couple's nuptial quarters and made noises with bells, tin pie plates, and shotguns until the couple came out and acknowledged their presence. Ada, unaccustomed to such affairs, noted that they "were serenaded by a band and nearly drove crazy."[3]

The man she married, almost twenty years her senior, had no permanent home and little money, but he was intelligent, ambitious, and determined to succeed with his plans to make money showing people the Grand Canyon. Ada may have shared that plan initially, but the harsh realities of frontier tourism soon cast shadows on her dreams.

Within a week of their marriage, the couple left Williams for Bass Camp, accompanied by a paying customer—a photographer who hoped to sell his pictures of the Grand Canyon—and a man they hired to look after the horses. Ada looked forward to her "honeymoon," writing in her diary, "I thought it would be fine to go along with them and get a taste of camping outside."[4]

Bass drove a four-horse stage heavily loaded with a month's supplies and pulled by two mules and two horses. Not long after they started out, black thunderheads appeared on the horizon and the wind changed directions and came roaring out of the southwest. Bass urged the animals forward, hoping to cross Cataract Creek before the storm sent water rushing down the normally dry creekbed. They were too late. The creek churned with muddy, swirling water.

Ada watched as the horses and mules were unharnessed and taken to the bank to drink. Bass explained that this would prevent them from stopping to drink in midstream and allowing the wagon

WILLIAM WALLACE BASS AND ADA BASS AT BASS CAMP. AS EVER, ADA STAYS WITHIN LIMITS OF PROPRIETY BY RIDING SIDESADDLE. (Photo courtesy of the Arizona Historical Society, Tucson, Arizona, Bass Collection.)

to settle and become mired in mud. The tactic didn't work, as Ada wrote: "Old Jerry, one of the mules, refused to drink when he had a chance, but, when the outfit reached midstream he suddenly became thirsty and halted, stopping the rest of the animals and we were stuck in the deep mire in the stream which was gradually rising and nearly reaching the box of the wagon."[5]

The men jumped into the stream, urging the mules to move; the mules remained steadfast, and so they were loosened and led to the bank. Ada struggled to save the flour, sugar, and other perishable supplies from the water seeping into the box of the wagon. One of the men propped a piece of lumber under the wagon tongue, and Ada walked to the opposite bank.

The men finally coaxed the horses across the stream, and the party was able to make it to the camp Bass called the Caves. They built a fire, dried their bedding, and made some coffee before turning in for the night. The storm's persistence the following morning meant that they'd be stranded at the Caves for at least a few days. The men shot several rabbits for breakfast. Ada fried the rabbits and made some biscuits and black coffee; the food, she noted, "made us feel like a million, after the incidents of the day before."[6]

The start of Ada and Will's life together was humble enough. Ada described her temporary home: "A tent erected over a wood floor was used for sleeping and warmed by a sheet iron stove when fuel was available. The kitchen and dining room combined was reached by going down a ladder into the cave. An old cookstove had been installed and the stove pipe emerged through a natural opening in the roof of the cave. A rough table of boards and dry goods boxes for seats and also for cupboards were the main furnishings of the underground kitchen." This set-up was adequate during dry weather, but, wrote Ada, "when it rained, streams of water trickled down the crevices of the rocks, and on down to the next cave below."[7]

Those few days at the Caves turned into weeks as the rain persisted, keeping roads soft and impassable. Late in January Ada became ill. "I was sick two days in this godforsaken place," she wrote in her diary, and she was more than ready to leave. The civility of the East was far away indeed. It was nearly a month before conditions permitted them to leave for Bass Camp. "What a honeymoon," she wrote.[8]

Had Ada known this trip foreshadowed times to come, she might have opted to stay single, old maid status and all. Ada's diary that first year records a rather gypsylike existence: to the Caves, to Bass Camp, to Ashfork, to Williams, back to the Caves to start again. She would later write that she had either cooked a meal or slept under every tree and beside every bush between Bass Camp and Ashfork. No sooner would she get settled than her husband would say it was time to move again. Time for a new group of tourists. Time for Ada to cook their meals, make their beds, and do their laundry.

Six months into their marriage, Ada began using the abbreviation S.O.S. in her diary. It most likely means "Same Old Stuff," a phrase she used in later years to comment on the drudgery of her life and perhaps a not so ironic plea for help. On August 11, she commented, "S.O.S. hunting horses and cleaning up dirt." Her September 6 entry is simply, "S.O.S. S.O.S."[9]

Exacerbating the constant moves and work was the lack of financial resources. When Will did make money, he often celebrated with a drinking binge in town. Because the couple had no permanent home, they relied on boarding houses or friends when they were in Williams or Ashfork. Will often left Ada to fend for herself for extended periods while he worked in his mines or explored new routes for trails into the Canyon or just "disappeared." When she ran out of money to pay for her board, she slept in the stage and washed dishes for meals. "I am putting in a wretched existence," the new bride wrote, and by November she was forced to sell personal items to make ends meet. On Thanksgiving Day Ada even played for a dance to earn a few extra dollars. Just a week shy of her first wedding anniversary, Ada wrote, "Thus endth this horrible year, can the next be worse?"[10]

The answer? Yes. Ada, now pregnant, spent most of January and February in Williams alone, struggling to make ends meet. When Will finally returned in late February, she accompanied him to Bass Camp to check on the water supply and help get the camp in order for a small group of tourists due to arrive within the week. Enough water was in the rock cisterns near the trail into the Canyon for the animals and house use. Will decided that with an extra barrel of water for drinking and cooking, the supply would be sufficient for the group. What luck! They would not have to haul water.

But while they slept, a group of Havasupai came to their camp with several horses, whose thirst emptied the cisterns. Bass awakened, lectured the group, and ordered them off his property.

Ada and Will now had to return to the Caves and haul water back to Bass Camp. They arrived at the Caves after 10:00 P.M., watered their horses, and turned them out to graze before going to bed.

By morning a strong wind whipped snow flurries through the camp as Will searched for the horses. Ada grew apprehensive with the memory of her stay at the Caves just a year before. Unable to find the horses, Will returned, exhausted and feeling ill. Ada, now four months pregnant, watched as Will grew progressively weaker and had chills. Ashfork was 35 miles away, and she began to panic. "The days passed and no one came our way," she wrote. "There was a cold wind blowing and no wood for fuel to keep him warm. I had to saw down the logs of the corral and cut them up. The water in the cistern was getting very low. In fact, it was not fit to use. Our food supply was dwindling and the situation growing very serious. I walked, in different directions from the camp each day, hoping to find a horse I could use to ride for help. I wrote notes and fastened them on bushes along the road telling of our plight and I hoped someone passing would find them."[11] They had been stranded at the Caves for nearly eight weeks. Not a living soul had passed by. Ada's imagination ran wild. Would they starve to death? Freeze to death?

Will's condition worsened with each day, and Ada grew desperate. "One day I walked to the old dam, about three miles down the Cataract. Here, I found an old grey horse blind in one eye. I herded him back to Camp and began to plan for the trip to Ashfork for help. Mr. Bass was too sick to get out of the bed and I knew we could not subsist very long on what food we had."[12]

Ada put all available food and water within Will's reach in preparation for her departure. She packed her blankets on the horse and was getting ready to leave when their dog began barking and leaping at the door. "I stepped quickly to the door. I looked in the direction of the dog's bark, and, behold a man coming on horseback, leading a pack horse. I waved him to come our way and told him of our terrible plight." The man rode into Ashfork to seek help. Ada waited two more days. "The second night I heard the rattle of the wagon and horses' hooves. He brought us food. The next morning we left early for Ashfork, stopping once for lunch."[13]

Safe, warm, and comfortable at last, Will began to recover, but the ordeal left him and Ada without any financial resources. "Our money is all gone and old Cervis, the only store in town, don't like to trust us for groceries. God Help Us," she wrote.[14] In early April, Ada sold her embroidered bedspread, a fine pieced quilt, and pillow slips with lace to pay their rent. Two days later, she sold her silverware and music book to buy something to eat.

By May of 1896, Ada had had it. "Began packing my trunk to beat it, back to home and mother," she wrote, and in mid-May she arrived by train in East Worcester. Surrounded once again by the comforts of a civilized home, Ada showed little interest in returning to the Canyon or Will. Her first child, Edith Jane, was born that August 20. "Dr. Smith and Mrs. Leape attended," Ada wrote. "It's a wonder I'm alive to copy this. Such help."[15]

Will wrote occasionally, keeping her informed of events "at home." Meanwhile, she renewed her teaching certificate and taught school in West Richmondville for the 1898–1899 school year. Then, whether absence made the heart grow fonder or time eased the wretchedness of hardship, somehow Will persuaded Ada to return to him after three years' separation. By fall of 1899, she and Edith were living at Bass Camp. Will was in the process of adding a kitchen to the one-room building at Bass Camp.

Just why she returned to this "godforsaken place" is unclear. Did her life at the Canyon look better from afar? Did the social mores of the day require that she stay by her husband's side? Did she feel an attraction to the place called Grand Canyon? Or, did she once again succumb to the charms of William Wallace Bass? Whatever the reason, her nomadic existence resumed, this time with the added responsibility of little Edith.

The winter of her return was harsh and unrelenting. Will decided to move the family to his newly built camp on Shinumo Creek down in the Canyon. On January 9, 1900, the Basses opened the new century with a ride into the Canyon down the Mystic

Springs Trail. Ada, now pregnant again, proudly wrote that three-and-one-half-year-old Edith was "probably the first child to ride a horse to the River alone."[16]

With warmer temperatures, protection from the wind, and ample water, Shinumo Camp was a refuge from winter. Bass had a vegetable garden and an orchard along the creek. He repaired prehistoric irrigation ditches (Shinumo is a Paiute Indian word for "old people") to water his trees and crops. Ada happily took care of the tent house and little Edith, who loved playing on the sandy beach near the river. It was late March before the weather had warmed enough for the family to return to Bass Camp and the drudgery of a tourist leader's wife.

Ada found that the kitchen roof had been damaged by the hard winter. Before Will had time to make repairs, he escorted a tourist party, the Winegards, around the Canyon. As Ada prepared their food, it began to rain. "I had to hold an umbrella over my head to cook meals," she wrote, and when the Winegard party left, Ada wrote, "I was happy to get rid of the cussed outfit."[17] By now any enthusiasm Ada had for the tourist business had disappeared. The reality of Will's enterprise meant hours of extra cooking and cleaning for Ada—and little else.

Ada had planned to return to East Worcester for the birth of their second child, and her father sent her money for the trip. But the baby, William Guy, arrived early, on July 26, 1900, in Williams. To celebrate the birth of his son properly, Will used Ada's travel money to get roaring drunk.

As soon as she was able, Ada borrowed money and left on the midnight train for East Worcester with Edith by her side and little Willie in her arms. Although it is clear what Ada's life with William Wallace Bass entailed, her diaries reveal nothing to explain why she chose *again* to return. The following summer, after nearly a year in East Worcester, she journeyed back to Bass Camp to take up what she surely knew was a difficult life. On top of caring for two young children, cooking and cleaning for tourists, and living in a harsh land, she also had to endure the whims and peccadilloes of her charismatic husband. By early 1903, Ada was once again pregnant.

To be near the doctor for the birth of their third child, Ada left the Canyon that July and rented a cottage in Williams. Hazel Canyonita arrived on October 5, 1903, weighing barely five pounds fully clothed. Will came to meet his new daughter a few days later, "half drunk as usual," as Ada remarked in her journal.[18]

Ada's brief "maternity leave" ended in early November, when Will picked her up in a four-horse stage so as to have room not only for Ada and little Hazel, but for the latest group of tourists bound for Bass Camp. That year ended with Will absent again, this time off to give lectures about the Canyon in Chicago, Washington, and New York, leaving Ada alone to care for the children and an occasional tourist. Christmas passed without celebration. On the last day of the year she wrote, "This sure is a fine place to be marooned in for the winter. God help us all, this next year."[19]

Nearly five months would pass before Will returned from the East. When she unpacked his suitcase she "found all his ladies letters which he forgot to destroy and other interesting information."[20] Now added to the strain of hard work, the harsh land, and the care of the children was the humiliation of Will's infidelities. What did Victorian women do in the face of such realities? To whom could they turn with the shame or guilt? Ada did what women of her age were compelled to do. She swallowed rage, bit back tears, harbored bitter resentment, and stayed with her husband. And she became pregnant again in the summer.

To make room for his growing family—and perhaps to assuage his guilt—Will enlarged the house at Bass Camp. It now had three bedrooms, a living room, dining room, kitchen, pantry, and storage room. Porches were added on the west and east sides. Guests still stayed mostly in tents, but occasionally, despite Ada's objections, they were allowed to sleep in the main house. Ada rarely had time to enjoy the new addition or to play the piano, her one tie to her former life. Business was improving, and Ada was kept busy helping with tourists. She wrote on July 18, "All this gang on my hands to cook and fix beds for and all the children to wash for. I'm tired enough to die and can't stand this much longer and no one to help me."[21]

With the end of the summer tourist season, Ada once again escaped to East Worcester in September to await the birth of her fourth and last child. Mabella Melba arrived on April 25, 1905, weighing in at seven and one-half pounds. It was, according to Ada, "a cold, windy disagreeable day for the event."[22]

Ada remained in the East for the summer helping her mother who had had a stroke. She did not return to the Canyon until August 20. She came back to a new stop for the train, which became known as Bass Siding, and a nearly completed new house. Bass had built the siding and the house in response to changes at the Canyon. Most people now came to the Grand Canyon by train, which the Santa Fe Railroad extended to the Canyon in 1904, and were more likely to stay at the newly opened El Tovar Hotel, just across from the railroad tracks, than at Bass Camp, a 25-mile stage ride away. Plus, they were increasingly more interested in short tours around the rim of the Canyon than long treks into the Canyon.

The new house, which because it was painted white they called the White House, suited Ada well, and she spent much time papering the walls and getting it in order. She still faced moves to Bass Camp and even to Shinumo Camp as Will's clients demanded, yet life at the White House was better than before.

Ada became concerned about the children's education and, using her experience as a teacher, gave them lessons at home. For several winters Ada took the children to Phoenix to attend school, but they usually remained only a couple of months, either running out of rent money or responding to Will's requests that she come home. Finally, when enough people were living at the Canyon to start a school, Bass donated lumber for a school building, and Ada boarded the teacher part of the time. The Bass children made up half of the first class.

By 1911, Will decided that he needed to be even closer to Grand Canyon village—the tourist complex that was home to

EDITH JANE, HAZEL CANYONITA, WILLIAM GUY, AND MABELLA MELBA BASS.
(Photo courtesy of the Arizona Historical Society, Tucson, Arizona, Bass
Collection.)

employees of the Santa Fe Railroad and Fred Harvey Company—to
capitalize on the increased demands for short tours by tourists coming in on the train and remaining just for the day. He built a house
on land leased from the Forest Service. As the sides were covered
with pressed tin, they called it the Tin House. Ada's piano, always
her most prized possession, was moved once again. This two-story
house was much to Ada's liking. She was able to socialize with
friends in the village and had less work now that most tourists came
just for day trips.

By the outbreak of World War I in Europe, tourism was
flourishing at the Canyon. Will now had four surreys and two
larger wagons. Edith, now nineteen, was a natural with tourists,
having inherited her father's gift of gab and love of the Canyon. She

was a skilled horsewoman and often took people into the Canyon by herself. Willie, now called Bill, also helped, as did a couple of hired hands. One, Bert Lauzon, had an eye for Edith. Already a Canyon legend for having accompanied the Kolb brothers on their 1911 trip on the Colorado River, Bert was a great asset to Will, although Will disapproved of his interest in Edith.

Bass was finally prospering after years of hard work. There was money for a new piano for Ada and a Studebaker car for Will, and Ada traveled to Coronado Island and San Diego to visit relatives. In 1915 the income from Will's tourist business was $20,000, a tidy sum in those days. The next year, Will purchased property in Wickenburg, Arizona, looking toward a possible retirement.

But the good times at the Canyon did not last. Despite Will's disapproval, Edith married Bert Lauzon in 1917, the same year that Bill went to work as a driver for Fred Harvey, owner of the Harvey tourism empire. That year, also, the National Park Service was established, and in 1919 the Grand Canyon became a national park. In 1920, Fred Harvey became the park's main concessionaire. This action signaled the beginning of the end of the Bass tourist business. William Bass couldn't compete with Fred Harvey's Pierce Arrows and uniformed drivers. In 1923, the Basses entertained their last guest.

Perhaps it was time. Tragedy struck when, on September 21, 1924, Edith, so vibrant and so suited for life at the Canyon, died unexpectedly of complications following surgery for removal of her appendix. That same year, when William Bass was seventy-five, he did not renew his lease on the Tin House and agreed to let the Forest Service tear it down. Ada and Will moved back to the White House. Three years later they sold their holdings to the Santa Fe Railroad Company, with Ada insisting that half of the $20,000 selling price be in her name. She knew her husband too well to trust him with the entire amount.

Ada and Will "retired" to Wickenburg, a small town northwest of Phoenix, in 1927. Will, ever restless, staked a gold-mining claim in the nearby hills and opened what was probably the first motel in Arizona. Under a grove of mesquite trees, Will had cots and wash basins for motorists, later adding a gasoline station and a swimming pool. Son Bill moved down from the Canyon to help with this new business and later built the modern La Siesta Motel that remains in business in Wickenburg to this day.

Will died in 1933 at the age of eighty-five. At his request, his ashes were scattered on the 6,703-foot-high Holy Grail Temple, known for many years as Bass Tomb, high above Shinumo Creek. Ada spent her remaining years in Wickenburg, often visiting her daughters in Phoenix and her grandchildren at the Canyon. Little remains of the Bass complex: Bass Camp, the White House, and the Tin House live only in memory, but Bass Trail, which so long ago carried the footsteps of the young Ada Bass, remains. Hikers today can follow the steps of Ada Bass to the river she first descended a hundred years ago. It is still an amazing trail.

When Ada was in her early eighties, her son Bill took her to the North Rim of the Grand Canyon. Bill had always wondered why Ada stayed so long at the Canyon and endured so much. As they sat on the veranda of the North Rim Lodge looking across the Canyon, Ada sat silently for a long time; then, as if to answer all his questions, she said, "You know, I love the Canyon too."[23]

Ada died in 1951 at the age of eighty-four. She lived long enough to realize her place in the history of the Grand Canyon. She was the first non-Indian woman to raise a family at the Canyon. She was, albeit reluctantly, a partner in the beginnings of tourism that today has reached numbers she could not have imagined. Today Ada Bass lies finally at rest in the Grand Canyon Pioneers Cemetery on the South Rim.

Building A Legacy

MARY ELIZABETH JANE COLTER

(1869–1958)

MRS. HAROLD ICKES (LEFT), WIFE OF PRESIDENT FRANKLIN ROO-
SEVELT'S SECRETARY OF INTERIOR, LOOKS OVER COLTER'S PLANS
FOR THE BRIGHT ANGEL LODGE, 1935. (Photo courtesy of Grand
Canyon National Park Museum Collection.)

*M*ARY *ELIZABETH JANE COLTER* designed and supervised
the construction of six structures in the Grand Canyon National
Park. As architect for the Fred Harvey Company and the Santa
Fe Railroad, she utilized native materials from the Canyon to blend
with the natural surroundings. People who worked with Miss Colter,

as she was generally addressed, remember her as a perfectionist and a stern taskmaster. We're lucky she was, for her buildings have proven timeless and inviting. They continue to delight park visitors, making their stay pleasant, comfortable, and meaningful.

Colter's Hopi House, which opened in 1905, resembles a traditional Hopi dwelling and is today a gift shop featuring Native American handicrafts. Hermit's Rest and Lookout Studio, both built in 1914, blend so well into their surroundings that from a distance, each appears to be part of the Canyon rim. Both serve today as pleasant places to relax and enjoy views of the Canyon. Hermit's Rest still offers tourists a cold drink and a snack, although not for the original charge of fifty cents.

Phantom Ranch, a series of stone cabins along Bright Angel Creek on the Canyon floor, opened in 1922 and continues to welcome weary hikers with rustic accommodations and a hearty meal. In 1933 Colter completed the Watchtower, a tour-de-force modeled after similar, though smaller, Indian towers. Tourists today clamour up the spiraling stairs for views of the Grand Canyon. Bright Angel Lodge, which opened in the summer of 1935, still provides moderately priced housing for guests, serves as headquarters for the Grand Canyon mule rides, and includes a restaurant, saloon, and gift shop.

Mary Elizabeth Jane Colter was born April 4, 1869, in Pittsburgh, Pennsylvania, the daughter of William and Rebecca Colter. In 1880 the family moved to St. Paul, Minnesota. Mary became fascinated by the Sioux, the first American Indians she had ever seen. A friend gave her some Sioux drawings, and so dear were they to her that when a smallpox epidemic swept the Sioux population and Mary's mother burned all of the Indian articles in the house, Mary hid them. Collecting Native American art became a lifelong passion.

When Mary's father died suddenly in October 1886, leaving the family to survive on a small inheritance, Mary persuaded her mother to use some of the money to send her to the California School of Design, where she could get teaching credentials to support the family.

A mature seventeen years old, Mary traveled alone to San Francisco, determined to succeed. As she told her mother, her dream was not to teach but to design and decorate buildings. While in school, she worked as an apprentice in a San Francisco architect's office. Local architects then were developing a new building style more suited to California's landscape and heritage than copies of the latest European styles. By the time Colter graduated in 1890, many California architects were patterning their designs after the early Spanish missions, a trend that deeply influenced her work.

Colter returned to St. Paul and taught freehand and mechanical drawing over the next fifteen years. During this time, she also gave lectures on world history and architecture at the University of Michigan, reviewed books as literary editor of the *St. Paul Globe,* took courses in archaeology, and traveled. On a trip to San Francisco, Mary visited a friend who worked in a Fred Harvey gift shop. Recognizing opportunity, she indicated to the manager of the shop that she would be interested in working for Fred Harvey, perhaps as an interior decorator or designer.

The Fred Harvey Company, already well known for excellent hotels and food service at railroad stations, was considering featuring Native American crafts in their gift shops. The company noted the way train passengers would crowd around the Indians selling their crafts at the stations. Herman Schweizer, a buyer for Fred Harvey, urged the company to merchandise Native American jewelry and crafts in its gift shops and hotels.

In the summer of 1902, Mary looked down from the roof of her cabin in the Minnesota backcountry, where she was making repairs, to see a Western Union boy waving a telegram. The Fred Harvey Company wanted Mary to decorate an Indian museum and salesroom for Native American handicrafts adjacent to its new Alvarado Hotel in Albuquerque, New Mexico. Mary accepted immediately. She traveled to Albuquerque and began working long days painting, building display tables and shelves, and arranging then rearranging merchandise until she was satisfied with the results.

Navajo rugs covered the floors, baskets hung on the walls, and pots of all sizes filled tables and shelves. A log burned in the fireplace, adding atmosphere and the aroma of a wood fire to the rooms. Native American craftspeople worked in the shop during business hours, weaving, making baskets and jewelry, and attracting buyers. The shop was the first of its kind, and judging from the preponderance of such shops today, it's safe to say Colter's project was a tremendous success. But, once the job was complete, there was no more work for her. She returned to St. Paul and her teaching job.

Mary did not hear from Fred Harvey again until 1904, when the Santa Fe Railroad extended the line north from Williams, Arizona, to the South Rim of the Grand Canyon and commissioned Charles F. Whittlesey, the architect responsible for the Alvarado Hotel in Albuquerque, to design a new hotel at the South Rim. As the Harvey Company had specified at the Alvarado, plans called for an "Indian building" near the new hotel. The Santa Fe Railroad Company hired Mary to design the entire building, exterior and interior.

Drawing on her training and instincts, Colter designed a building that belonged to the area. Hopi House, as it came to be called, was built of wood and stone native to the area and constructed primarily by Hopi workers.

Just as the Hopi had done for centuries, Mary built a solid square building on several levels, with stone steps and ladders connecting one rooftop to the other. Massive interior rooms were covered with a light brown adobelike plaster, and strong ceiling log beams supported smaller branches lying across them. The mudlike floors were actually cement. Hand-hewn tables laden with Indian baskets, pots, and other crafts filled the rooms. Brightly colored Navajo rugs dressed the floors, and a Totem Room displayed carved masks and bowls made by Indians from the Pacific Northwest. A special exhibit featured the Harvey collection of old Navajo blankets, winner of the grand prize at the 1904 St. Louis Exposition.

Hopi House opened on January 1, 1905. As she had done at the Alvarado, Colter hired Native American artisans to work daily in the shop, making pottery, blankets, jewelry, and baskets. Every evening at five o'clock, Hopi dancers entertained on the patio.

Although Hopi House was a tremendous success, the Harvey Company once again took its time before offering Colter another project. In 1910, the Fred Harvey Company and the Santa Fe Railroad jointly offered Mary, now forty-one, a permanent position as company architect and designer. Impressed with her work at the Alvarado Indian Building and Hopi House, the companies believed Colter had the style, imagination, and strength of personality to see her ideas through to actual construction.

Colter's position was really quite remarkable, for at the time it was unheard of for a woman to excel professionally with such a large company, let alone be successful in a field almost exclusively male. The job required serving two masters. The Fred Harvey Company operated the restaurants and hotels of the railroad, but it owned only the furnishings; the buildings and land were owned by the railroad. Often her plans would be approved by the Harvey Company only to be altered by the railway engineers. Colter's will and strong personality helped her navigate the waters between these two powers. Admirers recall her as a "determined, positive person" who knew how to get her way. Critics remember her as "outspoken and sometimes even cruel."[1]

Colter moved to the Harvey Company headquarters in Kansas City, Kansas, and began work on various projects unrelated to the Canyon. In 1914 she was sent back to the Grand Canyon on orders from the company, which had recently completed the building of the Hermit Rim Road along the edge of the Canyon. The 8-mile roadway was designed to accommodate horse-drawn touring stages; Fred Harvey wanted a building at the end of the road where tourists could have refreshments and enjoy the views.

Colter considered various designs, including the then-popular Swiss chalet style with gingerbread trim, but she decided to continue the indigenous style she'd used with Hopi House. When completed, Hermit's Rest looked as if it had been haphazardly designed by someone hurriedly piling rocks for shelter. Railroad men teased Colter about the structure's appearance, saying, "Why don't you clean up this place?" to which Colter replied, "You can't imagine what it cost to make it look this old."[2] An arch of uneven stones formed the entrance, a broken mission bell Colter found in New Mexico swung under the arch, and a lantern hung from one of the projecting stones.

Tourists sat on chairs made from twisted tree stumps and sipped coffee and lemonade on a porch extending to the edge of the Canyon. Crude handhewn wooden posts supported the log beams of the porch. On cold days a fire burned in the massive fireplace, warming the interior. Tour participants relaxed by the fire, their feet on a bearskin rug, enjoying free tea and cookies as they viewed the Canyon through a row of large glass windows. Visitors not on a Harvey tour had to pay 50 cents for the refreshments and view.

Later in 1914 Colter designed Lookout Studio in similar fashion. Built on a point west of El Tovar, the Lookout provided outstanding views of the Canyon. Stairs descended to the very brink of the Canyon, and high-powered telescopes on the porch gave visitors a close-up glimpse of the Inner Canyon. Viewed from a distance, Lookout Studio seemed to be part of the Canyon itself. Built of native stone with an uneven, ragged construction, Lookout Studio could be mistaken for an ancient Indian ruin.

The Grand Canyon became a national park in 1919, and with World War I over and tourism on the rise, the Fred Harvey Company and the Santa Fe Railroad received permission from the Park Service to build tourist lodging at the bottom of the canyon along Bright Angel Creek. This facility, to be named Roosevelt Chalet, would permit mule riders to spend a night in the Canyon. A swinging bridge across the Colorado River was completed in 1921, allowing easier access to the Inner Canyon.

Mary, now fifty-two, rode a mule into the depths of the Canyon to work on the design. Building the facility proved an onerous task. Although builders were able to use native stone, all other materials had to be hauled in by mule. Mules carried wooden crossbeams down the Bright Angel Trail and across the swinging bridge. No piece could be longer than six feet, and construction of longer

THE IMPRESSIVE LOOKOUT STUDIO. (Photo by Betty Leavengood.)

beams to hold up the roofs took some careful calculations. When all was completed, the small lodge—containing a kitchen, dining room, and a storage area—and four individual cabins stood solidly along Bright Angel Creek.

Colter called the complex Phantom Ranch, naming it after nearby Phantom Creek, a far more intriguing moniker than Roosevelt Chalet. Gale Burak, who began hiking in the Canyon in 1942 (see chapter 9), remembers Colter as "a very imaginative and intelligent person who was quick to get the romanticism and impact of a name that would lend intrigue to somebody. Certainly they wanted people to come down, and Phantom would be a very nice name for something down in the deep recesses, out of general sight on the rim of the Canyon."[3]

PHANTOM RANCH, GRAND CANYON, WHEN FIRST COMPLETED IN 1922. (Photo courtesy of University of Arizona Library Special Collections, Fred Harvey Collection.)

The origin of the creek's name remains a mystery, giving rise to some good stories. Some say the cliffs near the creek look like a phantom in the moonlight, and others contend that the ghost of John Wesley Powell wanders the Canyon at night. It could be because cartographers in 1902 found this part of the Canyon so narrow that its convolutions would appear and disappear on their topographic maps like a phantom. Whatever the origin of the name, Mary Colter liked it, and Phantom Ranch it remains.

On opening day, November 9, 1922, Colter rode a mule to Phantom Ranch and signed the register with a firm hand. Phantom Ranch today remains much as Colter designed it. The cottonwood trees have matured, the dining hall has been expanded, and more cabins and bunkhouses have been added, but the atmosphere remains. On a quiet evening, sitting on the porch of one of the cabins, one still hears the sound of Bright Angel Creek rushing to the Colorado. Too, the happy sound of laughter drifts from the beer hall each night, as people from around the world gather to celebrate their journey into the Canyon.

Other projects kept Colter away from the Grand Canyon until 1931, when she returned to design a rest station, gift shop, and lookout at the eastern end of Fred Harvey's sightseeing tours. Colter envisioned a structure that would provide dramatic views of the Canyon. In her study of archaeology, she learned about prehistoric Indian towers, particularly those at Mesa Verde Cliff Dwellings and in Canyon de Chelley.

Colter chartered a small plane to locate and study tower ruins. She then went overland to photograph and sketch the towers. Before finalizing her plans, she had a 70-foot wooden platform built on the site. She climbed the platform to see if the height provided the view she wanted. She then made a clay table-sized model that included the proposed tower and an exact replica of the terrain.

"She was brilliant and a perfectionist," recalls Elizabeth Kent Meyer (profiled in the next chapter), who lived at the Canyon while the Watchtower was being built. "When that tower was halfway up, there was one rock in she didn't like. She made them take it out and replace it!"[4]

The finished tower was not a replica but rather what Colter called a "re-creation" of an Indian watch tower. It was, at 70 feet tall and 30 feet in diameter, much larger than any known Indian tower. It was built of carefully selected native stones with an internal frame of steel made by the bridge department of the Santa Fe Railroad.

The first floor of the tower, reached by climbing the stairs out of the sunken kiva, is called the Hopi Room. Mary chose Fred Kabotie, a Hopi artist, to decorate this room because "the Hopi people are the most closely associated with the Grand Canyon of any Pueblo Indians." Years later, in his book *Fred Kabotie: Hopi Indian Artist*, Kabotie tells what it was like to work with Colter:

MARY ELIZABETH JANE COLTER AND UNIDENTIFIED MAN EXAMINE
AN OVAL TWIN TOWER RUIN IN HOVENWEEP, UTAH, IN PREPARATION
FOR DESIGNING THE WATCHTOWER, 1931. (Photo courtesy of Grand
Canyon National Park Museum Collection.)

Miss Colter was a very talented decorator with strong opin-
ions, and quite elderly. I admired her work, and we got along
well . . . most of the time. But once and awhile she would be
difficult, especially when it came to matching colors. I remember one day she kept sending me up in the tower with
little dabs of oil colors, too small to match. I don't know
whether you'd call her thrifty or stingy, but I finally lost my

patience. "Let me have that tube," I said, and slashed it open. I squeezed everything out, and stirred in the color I felt was right. "We're through—you've ruined everything," she gasped. "And you've used up all the paint!" "But Miss Colter, we haven't tried it yet," I said. I took a little dab and ran back up in the tower. Fortunately it matched, the very color we'd been seeking. So that saved my life—and hers.[5]

Kabotie was not alone in his assessment of Colter. Others remarked about difficulties getting along with "Old Lady Colter."[6] One employee recalled, "Everyone hated to see her come on the job." A coworker, Harold Belt, said, "Like most creative people and people of large accomplishment, she was very demanding of those over whom she had authority."[7] Her habit of calling the draftsmen and engineers who worked for her "boys" irritated workers. Yet, over the years, those who clashed with her came to respect her tremendous talent and determination.

The dedication of the Watchtower on May 13, 1933, was done with typical Harvey flourish. The kiva and tower were blessed by Hopi dancers. The strange staccato chant of the "Keeper of the Kiva" could be heard above the rattle of gourds, the clatter of tortoise shells, and the rhythmic thuds of the tom-toms as he thanked the spirits for their presence. This was the first time this blessing had been done away from the Hopi villages. Paramount News filmed the dedication and showed it in theaters across the nation. Radio networks broadcast live reports, and more than six hundred newspapers in forty-five states detailed the festivities. The Watchtower remains today as the most striking example of the genius of Mary Elizabeth Jane Colter.

The design and construction of Bright Angel Lodge on the South Rim was Colter's final major Grand Canyon project. When the Santa Fe Railroad completed its line to the Grand Canyon, it had acquired the old Bright Angel Hotel, built in the 1890s by John Hance. In 1934 the Fred Harvey Company decided to replace most

THE WATCHTOWER, COMPLETED IN 1933. (Photo by Betty Leavengood.)

of the old structure. Colter first made models of stone buildings close to the rim, but the Park Service did not approve of a building that blocked views of the Canyon. She then designed a pioneer-style building in natural wood set back from the rim that met with Park Service approval.

A distinctive feature of Bright Angel Lodge is Colter's "geological" fireplace, designed to represent the geological layers of the canyon, from the water-smoothed stones of the Colorado River to the Kaibab limestone that forms the top rim of the Canyon. In typical Colter perfectionism, Mary was determined to have each stone personally selected by an expert on the canyon's geology, then packed up by mule and reassembled. Edwin D. McKee, park naturalist and expert on geology, agreed to help her. When he had to unexpectedly leave the Canyon for several weeks, he turned the job over to a younger associate. Colter was furious. She excoriated McKee in an April 1, 1935, letter and informed him that she had to halt all construction until his return.[8] McKee came back to help finish the fireplace. Today the geological fireplace is in the "history room" of Bright Angel Lodge.

Sharing the grounds with the lodge is a small village of individual cabins and several historically significant buildings, including the first post office at the Grand Canyon, a two-story log building of hand-squared log construction, and a cabin that belonged to Bucky O'Neill, a colorful, early-day sheriff who died fighting with Teddy Roosevelt's Rough Riders in the Spanish American War. Colter's plan protected both structures. On June 22, 1935, two thousand people attended the barbeque celebrating the opening of Bright Angel Lodge.

Colter returned to the Canyon that year for Christmas. Ruth Stephens Baker, who grew up at the Canyon (see her profile in this book), remembers the first Christmas after Bright Angel Lodge opened. "I was home from college, and they had the most beautiful Christmas tree in the lobby. Mary [Colter] was there, and she wanted to have it look like an old-fashioned Christmas. We spent the afternoon with the snow gently falling outdoors, stringing popcorn and cranberries. The big fireplace was going, and we were singing Christmas carols, and guests would come in and sing with us. It was one of the most beautiful things you can imagine."[9]

Colter retired from the Santa Fe Railroad Company on January 1, 1944, at the age of seventy-five. She stayed on with the Fred Harvey Company a few more years and, in 1946, when tourism surged at the Grand Canyon, rode a mule into the Canyon at age seventy-seven to make some alterations to Phantom Ranch. Two years later, Colter officially retired from the Fred Harvey Company.

Colter traveled extensively in her later years, thanks to pensions from the Fred Harvey Company and the Santa Fe Railroad, and a lifetime pass on the Santa Fe Railroad system. She wore false teeth that didn't fit properly, and comments about her in her later years invariably refer to her clicking teeth. One day Earl Shirley, the manager of Fred Harvey Transportation, was driving Colter from the Grand Canyon to the Del Rio Ranch in Chino Valley. At one point, unable to bear the clicking of her teeth further, he stopped the car and said, "Miss Colter, you are just going to have to remove your teeth or else you will have to walk the rest of the way."[10]

Before her death in 1958 at age eighty-eight, Mary donated her magnificent collection of Indian jewelry to Mesa Verde National Park, in addition to $2,000 to buy glass cases for the collection. She bequeathed her large estate, $150,000, to over fifty persons and organizations.

Today, when women enter most professions with relative ease, it is hard to appreciate the difficulties Mary Elizabeth Jane Colter faced. To be on a construction site, ordering male workers to redo their work and to get it right, required strength of character and belief in herself. Colter left no diaries and gave no interviews, leaving us to speculate on just how deeply the Canyon affected and influenced her. We do know she was somewhat ahead of her time in her recognition of the beauty and talent of indigenous peoples' craftwork. How lucky we are that her genius remains a part of the Grand Canyon and that she had the foresight to procure and maintain the Canyon's natural elegance through her work.

A Harvey Girl

ELIZABETH KENT MEYER

(1907–)

BETTY KENT IN HER HARVEY GIRL UNIFORM. (Photo courtesy of Elizabeth Kent Meyer.)

*C*RISP. *CLEAN.* *STARCHED.* Pressed. And pretty, very pretty. Those were the first impressions anyone had on seeing a Harvey Girl for the first time. Their long black skirts, smartly hemmed 8 inches from the floor, were met at the waist with crisp white blouses that were buttoned tight to the neck. Topping off the uniform was the attractive Harvey Girl smile, worn on a face where, by contract, makeup was prohibited. Harvey Girls were the very picture of cleanliness, their inviting demeanor the very essence of hospitality. By delivering such sharp and friendly service, these exuberant hard-working young women helped Fred Harvey build his tourism empire.

Harvey, an ambitious English immigrant whose early work on the railroad helped him develop his reputable services for railroad customers, did not originally hire women as waitresses. The idea surfaced after a group of male waiters at the Harvey House in Raton, New Mexico, got into a drunken midnight brawl and were too battered up to report to work the next morning. A furious Fred Harvey fired all the waiters and the manager. The new manager, Tom Gable, suggested to Harvey that he hire women because they were less likely "to get likkered up and go on tears."[1] Harvey agreed.

Critics of Harvey's plan thought the idea laughable. For one thing, female waitresses at the time were better known as "saloon girls," and they typically delivered more than a steak and a beer to those they waited on. It would be difficult to replace the "saloon girl" reputation with the wholesome, clean image Harvey wanted. For another thing, critics could not imagine how Harvey would entice women to come to the West, where they'd have to abandon city civility and endure the wild world of the new frontier. The men who populated the West and frequented its saloons were miners, ranchers, gamblers, cowboys, and other rough and ready types. No civilized woman, critics thought, would willingly subject herself to the likes of them or to a society that permitted such behavior.

The critics were wrong. Thousands applied. Why? The prospect of finding a husband was certainly one reason. The 1870 census listed 172,000 women and 385,000 men from the Mississippi River to the Pacific Ocean. The men of the West may have been roughly hewn, but there were lots of them, and a few good ones were likely to be found in the bunch. With women outnumbering men in the East two to one, many women found their prospects of marriage slim to none and so went west eagerly, bringing with them visions of romance and the opportunity for marriage to willing frontiersmen. Women from lower-income families especially viewed this as an opportunity to improve their lives.

Harvey advertised in midwestern and eastern newspapers and in women's magazines for "young women 18 to 30 years of age, of good character, attractive and intelligent"[2] to come to the West to work. The requirements were strict. A Harvey Girl had to be educated, which at that time meant finishing high school or eighth grade. She had to speak clearly, have good manners, and be neat in appearance. Typical contracts required six, nine, or twelve months commitment; when a young woman signed a contract she agreed to learn the Harvey system, follow instructions to the letter, obey employee rules, accept whatever location she was assigned, and abstain from marriage for the duration of her initial contract. If she broke the marriage contract, she forfeited her pay and railroad pass home.

Successfully beating the odds critics set before him, Harvey hired his famous "girls," and soon they were a key part of his business. Harvey's restaurants and hotels became increasingly popular among late nineteenth and early twentieth century tourists, and Harvey Girls became the emblem of superior service. They wore the Harvey Girl uniform proudly, and they stood out among women.

Girls typically lived upstairs in the facility they worked in or in a nearby dormitory. Housemothers enacted a strict curfew, and when girls did go out, they were closely chaperoned. Although men were allowed to meet with the girls in the parlor, they were not allowed in the bedrooms. The rigors of such strict rules were bound to try the will of even the best-intentioned Harvey Girl. Add to this that most Harvey Girls were independent, adventurous, and resourceful, and you had a recipe for mischief. Many a Harvey Girl had stories to tell about climbing the trellis or bribing the cook to let them in.

Elizabeth ("Betty") Priest was in many ways a typical Harvey Girl. She was fun-loving, hard-working, and above all, independent. Having been abandoned by her father at the age of fifteen, Betty was shuffled from household to household. She became self-reliant, a trait that helped make her a capable Harvey Girl.

"My mother and father separated when I was only three and a half," Betty explained, "and mother had other kids after me. My father got custody of me, then left me with a cousin. He never came back after me until I was ready for high school." Betty moved with her father and his second wife to Prescott, Arizona, where she attended school and worked part-time in a hotel. "One day before I went to school, my father asked me for my check, which I had just gotten," Betty said, "and when I came home, he and his wife were gone."[3]

Betty was fortunate to find a job caring for the daughter of the school orchestra leader. She lived with them and finished high school. "The State of Arizona located my father, and he sent me a pass to go to Albuquerque, where he had relocated, but I was afraid to go. I told the officer about a relative, Mother Holladay, in Kansas City, so the Santa Fe Railroad gave me a charity pass to go to Kansas City."

It was while she was in Kansas City that Betty took a dare from a friend to apply at the Fred Harvey Company office at the Union Station. She was just seventeen. Betty was accepted into the Harvey Girl program and passed her training with flying colors.

Early on, she learned to listen for the sound of the train whistle—a sound that energized the Harvey staff into frantic activity. "The porters took orders from people on the train and radioed them ahead, so we'd know to set up the dining room. Customers could have a full meal—salad or soup, and a full dinner, and a dessert, and coffee—for one dollar. A mile or so out, the train blew the whistle. The manager met the customers at the door and told them which way to go and where to be seated. We did all of our own set-ups. We didn't have busboys in the dining room."

Betty loved the work—especially the money, which meant freedom and independence. "I was able to pay back all Mother Holladay's charge accounts that I had charged clothes on and still was able to buy a beautiful blue coat with a genuine squirrel collar." Part of that coat money was earned in Kansas City, where she had been sent on a temporary assignment to work at the Republican Convention.

"I will never forget the biggest tip I ever got was in Kansas City at Union Station," Betty explained. "There were four men

A GROUP OF TYPICAL HARVEY GIRLS, CA. 1895. (Photo courtesy of the Kansas State Historical Society, Topeka, Kansas.)

playing poker at the table. They had all ordered special steaks, so I came out with the steaks and they were piping hot. I said, 'You have to eat your steaks now.' One replied, 'We're not through here. This is a big pot,' and another one said, 'Now what'll we do with the pot? Who's going to win this pot? We're not going to divide it.' Then someone said, 'I guess the waitress wins it!' and they scraped the money into my apron pocket. I had $67! I've never forgotten that $67."

Betty jumped at an opportunity to work at the Alvarado Hotel in Albuquerque, New Mexico. "I wanted to go west because I knew that my father was the freight man on the run out of Albuquerque, and I thought I might find him." She had not seen her father since he had abandoned her two years earlier in Arizona.

She did find her father in Albuquerque. She also found a

man whom she thought was her true love, becoming engaged to a barber who worked on the Santa Fe train that ran between Albuquerque and San Francisco. "We made arrangements that I would come to San Francisco and get married, and then we would travel back to Albuquerque together," Betty explained. "My father was driving to San Francisco to get his wife, so I rode along with him." By this time, Betty had completed her initial contract with the Fred Harvey Company and was free to get married.

As fate would have it, Betty and her father decided to stop at the Grand Canyon on the way. "I walked into the dining room at Bright Angel Lodge, and there was the head waitress I had worked for at the Alvarado. She'd been transferred to the Canyon. 'You're an answer to my prayers,' she said when she saw me. 'Can you go to work?' Sure," Betty replied, "and the next morning I was on the floor!"

That evening, unknown to her, Betty was being "checked out." Two Santa Fe Railroad workers sat on the railing outside the lodge watching the new Harvey Girl through the windows of the dining room. Bill Kent and John Cunningham considered it their duty to check out anyone new to the Grand Canyon, especially a Harvey Girl.

"Who's the new girl?" asked Bill.

"That's my girlfriend Alice's new roommate," John replied. "Stick around and when they get off work, I'll introduce you."

The two young men sat awhile longer, their backs to the Grand Canyon, watching as the attractive young woman in the spotless white and black uniform hurried about inside. Finally, Bill turned to John and said, "I'm going to marry that girl!"

"That's the silliest thing I ever heard. You haven't even met her yet," Johnny laughed.

"I don't care," Bill retorted, "I'm going to marry her."

Betty met Bill at the Saturday night dance. "I forgot all about the barber!" Betty laughed. Harvey regulations normally forbade dating among employees, but the Grand Canyon, a world unto itself, rendered such regulations unenforceable.

Despite the romantic diversions, Betty put in long, hard days at Bright Angel Lodge, which was at that time a collection of cabins with a cafe–dining hall. "We worked according to how the buses and the trail trips went," Betty explained. Her day began at 6:30 A.M., when the mule riders came in for breakfast, followed at 7:30 A.M. by people taking bus tours. Once they left for the Canyon she'd have a short break until lunch, when the bus tours returned. Afternoons were free until dinnertime, when the mule riders and afternoon tours returned.

Betty enjoyed her afternoons. She liked to walk along the rim of the Canyon, looking out over the edge. Its vast expanse made life seem full of promise and possibilities, and Betty was glad to be right where she was. Some afternoons she'd take a nap or walk along the rim of the Canyon. Other days she'd sit in the sun and chat with fellow Harvey Girls about their dates and the customers.

One of Betty's favorite customers was none other than the governor of Arizona, W.H.P. Hunt. "Governor Hunt came to the Canyon several times when the union was trying to organize us," she explained, "and he had a colored chauffeur that drove with him everywhere." On Governor Hunt's first trip, he got a table for lunch at El Tovar while his chauffeur parked the car. "When the chauffeur came into the dining room and sat down with the governor, the waiter said, 'No, you go in with the colored fellows where the train porters are. You have to eat in there—you can't eat in the dining room,'" Betty said. "Governor Hunt was furious. He went down to Bright Angel, and he asked the manager, 'Can my chauffeur eat with me?' The manager said, 'Yes, you both can eat any place you want to in here.' And so, he and his chauffeur always had a table at Bright Angel. He was very nice and easy to wait on."

Aside from the excitement of waiting on Governor Hunt, it was the "after hours" life that Betty relished and remembers best today. After the tours ended, the restaurants closed, and the tourists had gone for the day, the rising moon brought more than light to the Canyon. Harvey employees played as hard as they worked. They went on hay rides, held dances, played cards, and brought in

THE BRIGHT ANGEL "GANG." (Photo courtesy of Elizabeth Kent Meyer.)

movies. Couples would steal away under the cover of night to take long walks (with some long pauses!) along the rim of the Canyon. They'd frequent their favorite nooks tucked under the rim to look at the stars or watch a storm sweep across the horizon. This is how dating at the Canyon came to be called "rimming," and between the continual arrival of Harvey Girls and the steady supply of working men, there was a whole lot of rimming going on.

Before long, Betty and Bill began "rimming" in earnest. "There are so many wonderful shelves or cavelike spots where you can sit and hang your feet over the edge," Betty remembers. "With a 3,000-foot drop below you, it really was an exciting place for spooning. One of our favorite places was under the Lookout Studio, where one could look at the peaceful moonlight in the big Canyon."

Just six weeks after he set eyes on her, Bill offered Betty a

BETTY KENT IN HER WEDDING DRESS, GRAND CANYON, ARIZONA, 1926. (Photo courtesy of Elizabeth Kent Meyer.)

diamond ring. She promptly rejected it. "The fourteenth of August!" she exclaimed. "That's too soon! I don't know you that well." But Bill persisted, and ten days later Betty accepted the ring. Betty admits that Bill had his own version of the engagement. "Bill loved to tell the story that I proposed while he had his back against the railing under the Lookout Studio. He'd say he had to say 'yes' or I would have pushed him 3,000 feet into the Canyon!"

Betty and Bill married at Rowe's Well, a small tourist camp on the South Rim, on October 6, 1926. Soon after marrying, Betty resigned from her job at the lodge, and the couple moved to a rented room in Grand Canyon Village. Their rented room had an oil stove, a table, chairs, bed, and a dresser. Modest beginnings, but serviceable for life together at the Canyon. Making herself a proper housewife, however, proved more challenging for Betty, who was better at serving food than cooking it. "At the time I was a teenager who didn't know how to boil water, and at 7,000 feet most real cooks didn't know either," Betty laughed.

Betty rode the train into Williams twice a month for provisions. "All Santa Fe Railroad wives met their husbands at the depot on paydays—the sixth and twenty-first of each month. Our husbands cashed their checks, and we got our $20 and left on the 10:00 A.M. train to buy our groceries," Betty explained. "I only spent $10 at the 'Pay and Take It' and saved the rest for emergencies. We arrived home at 3:00 P.M. Our husbands would meet us at the 'Y' where the train backed in so they'd be headed out the next morning."

Money went a long way in those days. "For $10 we bought flour in 25-pound sacks, coffee, lard, and canned goods. It was all the boys could do to carry the big boxes home. We didn't know what fresh vegetables were, being so far from Phoenix and Los Angeles. I still like canned peas," she admitted. Betty purchased butter and eggs by the case from a farmer in Utah. A dairy in Phoenix delivered milk and cream once a week. The men hunted for venison and antelope on their days off.

To this day, Betty won't eat rabbit because of all the rabbit she had in the early days of her marriage. "On Sundays, the men would have a rabbit hunt. They'd catch the little train that goes into Anita and they would divide into two teams, about fifteen men on each team. They'd have shotguns and gunny sacks and hunt for about three hours. The losing team had to clean and cook all of the rabbits and serve a big meal at the Fred Harvey Mess Hall. I never knew there were so many ways to cook rabbit—stewed, fried, baked, à la king!"

As was true for most of the American Southwest, the scarcest item at the Canyon was—and still is—water. All water had to be brought in by train from the Harvey Company ranch at Del Rio, Arizona, where the company pastured the mules in the winter. The train came in twice a week in the winter and every day during the summer. "We had to be careful about water," Betty explained, "because we were charged fifteen cents a hundred gallons. We put bricks in the toilet and saved the bath water to fill the tank. Bill took his showers at the Power House, and I took spit baths, only taking a tub bath once a week."

Betty and Bill spent the first years of their marriage happily, living amidst the Canyon that had brought the Harvey Girl and railroad worker together. But 1929 was an unlucky year for most Americans, and those at the Canyon were not spared the effects of the stock market crash. Bill's hours were cut, and to make ends meet, Betty donned her Harvey Girl uniform and went back to work as a waitress at the Bright Angel lunch counter for $35 a month plus meals and tips.

Tourism at the Canyon dwindled as the Depression deepened, and Betty eventually lost her job at the lodge. Bill's hours were cut yet again, and he tried to offset the loss by working as a Harvey tour driver. Betty worked part-time at Babbit's General Store near Grand Canyon village and at the telephone company as a relief operator. The telephone office was the hub of the town as well as the source for one of Betty's more amusing stories. "The telephone office was next door to the naturalist's office," she explained. "One evening I was working relief when to my amazement the door of the naturalist office cracked open and a big six-foot snake crawled out and into the phone office. I climbed on top of the switchboard and called the ranger!"

Although money was tight in the mid-1930s, Betty and Bill jumped at the opportunity to move into one of the new village houses built by the Santa Fe Railroad. "We couldn't afford to buy much furniture. We sent to Montgomery Ward for a pretty gray enamel cookstove and a linoleum rug for the floor and found a discarded Fred Harvey table and old chairs. Then we bought a bed and dresser from Babbits. The rest of the house we left empty."

The Great Depression was hard on all Americans, and the stories of how people retained a positive outlook throughout its long term are remarkable. Despite Betty and Bill's financial difficulties, Betty remembers mostly good times at the Canyon during the Depression. "There was no entertainment in the village," Betty explained, so, typical of Harvey employees past and present, "we had to make our own. The Park Service built a community building behind the Fred Harvey garage, so all social activities were held there, including Saturday night dances, Sunday morning services, and Sunday night movies. The Fred Harvey Company rented the movies, and one of the chauffeurs ran the projector. A group of guides and chauffeurs organized an orchestra."

Hard times seemingly made for the best times at the Canyon. "If only that hall could have told stories about the parties we held there," Betty laughed. Prohibition was in full swing at the time, but some bootleg whiskey always seemed to be around. "When Millie and Johnny Schmidtkie were married, we had a big punch bowl by the window, and everyone that came in added some whiskey. By 10:30 P.M. the punch was pure moonshine and bootleg whiskey. Bill was dancing with Millie, and they fell down. Everyone kept on dancing over them. I had to clean his suit, and there were footprints all over it!"

One of the most memorable Depression parties Betty remembers was the unofficial dedication of the Watchtower (see previous chapter) on New Year's Eve, 1934. The tower had been completed in May 1933 and officially dedicated then, but, Betty said, "Our gang decided it needed a real dedication. The evening girl stationed at the tower was one of us, so we had quite a party." "One of us" meant the girl stationed at the tower had the spirit of a true Harvey Girl, only they weren't climbing trellises this time. "We sneaked in food and liquor. By midnight, all the men that could make it up the stairs took their shotguns to the top and shot into the air." Happy New Year.

Betty remembered Christmas as being especially wonderful at the Canyon. "We always had Christmas caroling throughout the

ELIZABETH KENT MEYER, PHOENIX, ARIZONA, 1996. (Photo by Betty
Leavengood.)

town, and then we went to the community hall for Santa Claus. The
Indians came in from the reservation in wagons, camping out for
three days so that the youngsters could see Santa Claus and get an
apple and orange and a sack of hard candy. It was such a wonderful
treat, and they came every year."

The advent of World War II brought a close to Bill and
Betty's Canyon life. Tourism slowed to a trickle. "Anyone that didn't
have children was asked to go work in the war plants," Betty said,
and so she and Bill went to California, where she found a job with
Douglas Aircraft. Although he was forty-five years old, Bill enlisted
in the army; he was sent to Alaska as a mechanic. "When he left, he
took a front door key. He said he wanted to know he had a place to
come home to. I'll never forget the day he came home," Betty said.

"He caught a plane out of Fairbanks headed for the United States, then caught a bus from the airport. I didn't know he was coming, and I worked nights—so I was asleep when he came in the door and yelled, 'Throw the sailors out, I'm home!'"

The former Harvey Girl and Santa Fe Railroad worker remained in Los Angeles. They missed their beloved Canyon, but as Betty pointed out, "most of our friends had left, too." Many of their friends also had relocated to Los Angeles, so it was not too difficult a choice to stay. And though the Canyon was a thousand miles away, its grandeur and memories of good times dwelled in their hearts. "To go back would not have been the same," Betty added. "We were at the Grand Canyon at the good time. Everything has changed now."

And it has. The little village once home to Harvey Girls and railroad workers is now a city of approximately 1,600 people, no longer isolated from the world. Getting milk, butter, and eggs requires a simple trip to the grocery, and water, though still scarce, is a simple matter of turning a faucet. The lodges and shops serve over five million visitors a year. Although the lodges now are operated by AmFac Corporation, they still use the Fred Harvey name. As for the Harvey Girls, they have long vanished from the Canyon, along with their "frontier" smiles and starched uniforms. Still, their spirit is present in the eyes and exuberance of present-day employees who are just as excited to be where they are as any Harvey Girl ever was.

4

A Face in the Rain

THE FATE OF BESSIE HALEY HYDE

(1905–1928)

GLEN AND BESSIE HYDE, GRAND CANYON, ARIZONA, NOVEMBER
1928. (Photo by Emery Kolb; courtesy of Emery Kolb Collection,
Cline Library, Northern Arizona University, no. NAU.PH.568-
4035.)

N<small>O ONE WOULD</small> have imagined the turn Bessie Haley's life
would take after her successful high school years in Parkersburg,
West Virginia. A model student, the diminutive Bessie—just 5 feet
tall and 90 pounds in weight—participated in the Debating Club,
wrote for the school newspaper, acted in plays, drew sketches for ad-
vertisements in the school yearbook, and showed promise as an artist
and writer. Indeed, that was her ambition. When Bessie graduated

second out of seventy-eight students in the 1924 class, her school yearbook predicted "a great future" for her, a future that would include glamourous travel "accompanied by a dark-haired man."[1] Neither Bessie nor her classmates knew then that she would one day set out to be the first woman to travel the length of the Colorado River through the Grand Canyon.

In 1926 she and her high school sweetheart, the "dark-haired" Earle Helmick, married secretly while attending Marshall College in Huntington, West Virginia. Just why they kept their marriage a secret and never lived together is not known. Whatever the reason, the youthful romance would not survive the pressures of adulthood. Only a few months after their clandestine marriage, Bessie left alone for San Francisco to study at the California School of Fine Arts. In a collection of unpublished poems she titled *Wandering Leaves*, Bessie alludes to a possible reason for her leaving. In "A Visitor" she wrote:

> *This soft bundle*
> *so close to me,*
> *Is yours and mine*
> *Come, love, and see.*
> *I'm glad the stork,*
> *In hurried flight,*
> *Took time to stop*
> *In here tonight.*

If Bessie had a child, what happened? "Mermaid Doll" may reveal a startling, possible reality:

> *Oh! mamma dear, please come!*
> *My dolly must be drowned,*
> *When I put her on the creek,*
> *She sank without a sound.*
> *Wee Betty's eyes filled with tears.*
> *Where could poor dolly be?*
> *Perhaps she's turned into a mermaid,*
> *And drifted out to sea.*[2]

Whatever purpose compelled her, Bessie fled marriage and the responsibilities that accompanied it—though if her poetry is any indication, she apparently did so reluctantly and with great sadness. Whether it was marriage, motherhood, or "the dark-haired man" that caused her to flee remains as mysterious as the unfolding of her fate.

She met her fate when she met Glen Hyde in San Francisco that same year. He was an intense, driven man—also dark-haired—whose charismatic charm attracted Bessie like a magnet, helping her to abandon whatever feelings she may have had for Earle.

Glen was a tall, muscular man who helped his widowed father, R. C. Hyde, run their ranch southeast of Twin Falls, Idaho, but craved a level of adventure and danger that living on a ranch did not provide. Glen escaped the humdrum of the ranch whenever he could to run rivers. He'd rafted the Peace and Fraser Rivers in British Columbia when the family lived in Canada, and after moving to Idaho, he and his sister Jeanne spent ten days in the fall of 1926 traveling down the Salmon and Snake Rivers. By the time he and Bessie met, Glen was talking about running the Colorado River.

Glen looked older and seemed wiser than his twenty-eight years. He was poised, opinionated, and astonishingly self-assured. His six-foot stance all but consumed Bessie's petite frame, and the two undoubtedly made a striking pair. Glen knew he wanted tiny Bessie to run the Colorado with him as his wife. After an embattled, drawn-out fight with Earle, Bessie and Glen finally married on April 12, 1928, the day after her divorce was final.

Glen persuaded Bessie to accompany him on a honeymoon trip down the Colorado, and they spent their first summer together, in between chores at the Idaho ranch, planning and preparing for it. He hoped the trip would ensure their fame as the first couple to run the Colorado River through the Grand Canyon. Bessie would be the prime attraction in a lecture tour as the first woman to make the trip. Rekindling interests in her earlier ambitions, Bessie planned to write and illustrate a book about the trip. Their future together did indeed look "great."

That October, with fall chores finished on the ranch, Bessie and Glen traveled to Green River, Utah, where Glen built their on-river home, a flat-bottomed scow 20 feet long, 5 feet wide, and 3 feet deep with long sweep oars at the bow and stern that Glen controlled from the middle of the boat.

Harry Howland, an experienced riverman, watched Glen building the scow at Green River. He told his friend Bill Reeder, who had rafted through Cataract Canyon in 1914, "Looks like he's building himself a coffin. Maybe you can tell the kid something."[3] Reeder tried to convince Hyde to take life preservers, but he shrugged off the idea. Glen's sister Jeanne later recalled that Glen considered life preservers "sissy."[4]

Glen finished the craft in good time, and together he and Bessie loaded the scow with food, tools, utensils, a set of bed springs, a mattress, and a small stove. They would take as their only guide a copy of *Through the Grand Canyon from Wyoming to Mexico,* Ellsworth Kolb's account of he and his brother Emery's 1911 trip.

October 20, 1928, was a crisp autumn day in Green River, Utah. With puffy white clouds billowing into the blue sky, Bessie and Glen launched their scow onto the Green River and began the journey of their lives. From here, the two would join the Colorado and "float" 660 miles over some forty-nine days, with plans to reach Needles, California, on December 9. Glen's father would be waiting for them.

But did the couple realize what lay ahead of them? In those 660 miles, the Colorado ran across perilous rapids and through an unforgiving Canyon whose waters did not differentiate between a tree pulled violently from its roots or a body jostled over the safe edge of its craft. A few people among the small crowd that had gathered to see the couple off might have suspected they were ill-prepared for the waters they would meet.

The Hydes' trip began peacefully enough. The Green is a patient and kind river, and it carried them through Labyrinth and Stillwater Canyons without incident. Past the confluence with the

PETITE BESSIE HYDE SHOWING OFF THE SCOW. (Photo by Emery Kolb; courtesy of Emery Kolb collection, Cline Library, Northern Arizona University, no. N.A.U.PH. 568-4027.)

Colorado, however, lay their first real challenge: Cataract Canyon, curling 40 long miles through narrow walls and across twenty-seven furious rapids.

At that time—the late 1920s—the section of the Colorado that ran through Cataract Canyon was one of its fiercest and wildest. It harbored treacherous whirlpools, deep holes, and huge, obtrusive rocks that could wrap a boat like a sheet of paper; its waves could reach as high as 15 feet. Working a scow through such water was an enormous challenge and required a vast reservoir of strength. The canyon's rapids are as relentless as they are unpredictable, and the river afforded no one time to study its water or line a boat through an especially treacherous section. Once you began the run, there was no turning back.

With the raging water roaring in their ears, Glen shouted orders at Bessie that she could barely hear. The flat-bottomed scow rocked and jerked across the rapids as red canyon walls rose to dizzying heights above them, denying any means for an alternative passage. The sky narrowed to a blue strip high above, and trees clung precariously to the banks. Rocks and shrubs along the water's edge seemed to dip and bob with the churning of the boat. Whirling, turning, lunging, twisting—a roller-coaster ride running the motions of an egg beater would produce a more pleasant ride than did Cataract Canyon! Glen maneuvered the oars in frantic sweeps to avoid crashing into boulders. Bessie held tight, helping to push or pull the oars when she could, checking often to see that their gear was secure. Each rapid sucked them into a headlong dip and sent them plunging, blue sky disappearing above and muddy water opening up below, a gaping mouth ready to swallow them whole. Water washed across the bow in torrents, leaving them fully soaked. Then, just as suddenly as they were sucked in, the rapid spit them out like a wad of tired gum, advancing them toward the next raging dip. After each rapid, they were allowed only a few moments' rest before the next one was upon them.

For 40 grueling miles, the spray lashing them in the face like a driving rain, their muscles aching with fatigue, the Hydes fought the river—and conquered it. Exhausted, cold, and soaked to the bone, the two exited the canyon as victors. Bessie was the first woman to run Cataract Canyon. Exhilarated by their tremendous feat, the Hydes pushed on toward fame.

The next several days brought a welcome respite from Cataract as the two floated peacefully through beautiful Glen Canyon. The couple then stopped at Lees Ferry, Arizona. Owen Clark, the man in charge of keeping flow records at the Lees Ferry river-gauging station, advised Glen not to "put all his eggs in one basket"[5] and suggested he take a second boat along for safety. But with the victory of Cataract Canyon fresh under their belts, Glen said they could conquer anything now. It seemed to Clark that Bessie also was enthusiastic about the trip.

Sockdolager, the first rapid in Upper Granite Gorge, lived up to its reputation. The men of John Wesley Powell's second expedition (1871–1872) had called this furious rapid a "sockdolager," a nineteenth-century slang term meaning "knockout blow." As Glen tried to hold the boat in the middle of the channel, the handle of a sweep hit him under the chin, knocking him overboard. Tiny Bessie grabbed both sweeps, threw Glen a rope, and managed to keep the scow going straight ahead. Glen caught the rope and made it back to the craft. It was a close call.

On November 15, twenty-six days and 424 miles past their put-in on the Green River, they stopped where Bright Angel Creek empties into the Colorado River. Here they planned to order additional supplies, traveling on foot up to the Grand Canyon's South Rim. They spent the night at Phantom Ranch, the tourist camp one mile up Bright Angel Creek, signing the register "going down the Colorado in a flat-bottomed boat."[6] There they met Adolph G. Sutro, a San Francisco businessman and adventurer, also staying at the ranch. He arranged to accompany them downstream to Hermit Camp when they returned from the South Rim.

The next morning, Glen and Bessie hiked up the steep 9-mile Bright Angel Trail to the South Rim. A tired Bessie, happy to be sleeping in a real bed, wrote to her parents, "I just had a nice hot bath and am pretty sleepy 'cause this has been a long day."[7] The next morning she talked to a reporter from the *Denver Post*, saying, "Our main object in this trip was to give me a thrill. It's surely been successful so far. I have been thoroughly drenched a dozen times and I'm enjoying every minute."[8]

Glen spent most of his time at the Kolb studio on the South Rim, talking with Emery Kolb, noted photographer and river runner. Impressed with their success but concerned that they had no life preservers, Kolb urged Glen to take a life jacket or to at least

THE HYDES' FATEFUL TRIP DOWN THE COLORADO.

A LONELY LOOKING BESSIE HYDE ON A DEBRIS-STREWN SHORE OF THE COLO-
RADO. (Photo by Emery Kolb; courtesy of Emery Kolb Collection, Cline
Library, Northern Arizona University, no. NAU.PH.568-4035.)

buy inner tubes from the Fred Harvey garage to use for flotation.
Glen pshawed the advice as he had the first time it was offered, jus-
tifying his decision by telling Kolb he and Bessie were good swimmers, then quickly changing the subject. He ordered two mule loads
of supplies to meet them at the foot of Hermit Trail.

As they left, Emery, with his wife Blanche and daughter
Edith, accompanied them to the head of Bright Angel Trail. Bessie
looked at Edith's new dress shoes and remarked, "I wonder if I
shall ever wear pretty shoes again."[9] Despite all her outward enthusiasm and comments to the press, Kolb sensed that Bessie was ready
to quit.

The Hydes hiked back down the Bright Angel Trail and met
up with Adolph Sutro as planned; he joined them for the overnight
ride to Hermit Trail, where supplies would be waiting. The trip had
barely gotten underway when Sutro fully realized Bessie's fears as
she hung onto the side of the scow. Amazed at Glen's carelessness
and lack of precaution, Sutro couldn't understand how they had
come that far. "It was the most inadequately equipped outfit I'd
ever seen," he said later.[10]

Although Glen talked excitedly of vaudeville lecture tours around the campfire that evening, Sutro noted Bessie's lack of enthusiasm. The next day they met the supply mules at the foot of Hermit Trail, and Sutro was glad he'd completed his journey safely. As he climbed on one of the mules for the ride out, he waved goodbye and wondered if anyone would ever see the Hydes again. The day was November 18.

On December 9, 240 miles below Hermit Trail, Glen's father waited for the couple at Needles, California. The day came and went, and the couple did not show. They had sent no word ahead, and no one had seen them since they pushed off from Hermit Trail. The senior Hyde naturally grew concerned as the next few days passed, fearing that his only son and Bessie were in trouble. He envisioned them trapped on a sandbar or hanging on the side of a cliff, waiting for help. Convinced they'd met trouble, Hyde took action. He telephoned the governor of Idaho, urging him to call army headquarters in Washington and ask for search planes to be dispatched from the nearest base in California or Arizona. He then boarded a train for the Grand Canyon.

The army's response was immediate as they launched the first air search in Grand Canyon history. Two Douglas O-2 airplanes from March Field, California, landed at Red Butte Airport on the South Rim of the Canyon on December 18.[11] That day's *Prescott Evening Courier* announced, "Army plane is ordered to scan Grand Canyon for two lost thrill seekers."[12] The story also reported that R. C. Hyde was offering a $1,000 reward for locating the missing couple.

Preston P. Patraw, assistant superintendent of the Grand Canyon National Park, and Bob Francy, supervisor of trail rides for the Fred Harvey Company, accompanied the army pilots, Lieutenants L. G. Plummer and H. G. Adams, for an early morning search. In a hair-raising flight between narrow canyon walls scarcely 75 feet above the river, they spotted the empty scow floating in a quiet pool 11 miles below the mouth of Diamond Creek, 138 miles from Bright Angel Creek. There was no sign of Glen or Bessie.

Glen's father believed that Glen and Bessie were alive in the Canyon. Diamond Creek offered one of the few points by which the river could be reached. A drilling crew testing the rock foundations for a possible dam had established a temporary camp there a few years before. Hyde planned to use the abandoned camp as a base for a ground search.

He asked Emery Kolb for help. Kolb flew above the site and returned to suggest that a small party take oars and camping equipment to the old drilling campsite. There they would build a boat and float down to the scow. Kolb telegraphed his brother Ellsworth, then living in Los Angeles, to join them for the search.

Hyde agreed with this plan but also wanted someone searching above Diamond Creek. He offered Bob Francy and Jack Harbin, owner of Rowe's Well, a tourist camp on the South Rim, $1,000 to conduct the search. The men hiked down Bright Angel Trail to the river, and using an old boat left by the trail, floated downstream. Temperatures plunged as a cold front moved across the Canyon, and the searchers donned several layers of clothing and sheepskin coats to stay warm. Unless Bessie and Glen had thought to bring warm clothes, the possibility of their survival looked grim.

The search caught the attention of the media, which was, then as now, eager for any gory details that might surface. On December 20, Kolb received a telegram from Paramount News: "Have you any movies airplane search, Colorado River. Advise Collect." A week later, the Associated Press wired Kolb, saying the news organization "Will be glad to pay you liberally for any pictures from Hyde films found in scow. Appreciate having some negatives rushed here if good. Advise us collect."[13] Though this was not the means by which they meant to achieve it, Glen and Bessie were indeed becoming famous.

On the second day of their search above Diamond Creek, Francy and Harbin found what they believed to be the Hydes' last camp near Mile 210. They found women's footprints leading away from the campfire and the dim imprint of men's sneaker footprints on the beach. Lima beans were scattered on the ground near the remains of a campfire. Hyde recognized the label on the opened can of beans as the same brand his son had purchased for the trip.

While Francy and Harbin continued to search for the couple between Bright Angel Creek and Diamond Creek, the Kolb brothers, Mr. Hyde, and Park Ranger Jim Brooks repaired an old, flat-bottomed mining boat they'd found at the drilling camp. The finished boat would hold only three men, so the two Kolb brothers and Brooks headed downstream on Christmas Day, hoping to spot the couple marooned along the way. It had been close to a month since they were last seen by Adolph Sutro.

At Mile 232 the current crashed against a low cliff as high waves swirled over submerged rocks. The men decided the rapid was too dangerous to run and began lining their boat along the shore opposite the cliff. While lining, it occurred to Emery that the couple might have met their fate at this same rapid. Anyone looking upon this rapid could imagine what might have happened to the Hydes: A weary couple halts their scow to survey the next of what have become countless rapids on their journey. Bessie is exhausted from the trip but she takes her husband's orders to "hold the line" while he walks downstream to study the swirling water for the best route. A fierce wind blows through the Canyon, spitting freezing rain into their faces, whipping the sweeps, and jerking the boat to and fro. Scarcely five feet tall and weighing only ninety pounds, it is all Bessie can do to keep the boat from breaking loose in the raging current. Her eyes watering, her face stinging in the biting wind, she wraps the rope around her waist. The rope rocks and tugs at her and she digs her heels deeper into the soft bank. Her arms are weak, she can no longer feel her fingers. Tug, jerk. Bessie's knees wobble and her thighs burn as she fights to steady the boat that holds her life. Glen surveys the water, his hand to his chin, looking this way and that. He seems suddenly very far away and Bessie tightens her grip on the rope. Without warning, the angry breath of winter issues a ferocious gust. It catches the scow and jerks it into the open jaws of the current.

Glen turns to the direction of his wife's scream in time to see her disappear in the muddy Colorado, tethered to the scow that has freed itself. Glen dives toward the scream, the blast of cold water heightening his panic, and searches across rocks and current for his tiny wife. "Bessie!" he screams. He sees the boat has jerked its way farther downstream, such a distance, too far to swim. The water is so cold as he is pulled back into dark swirling silence and feels his body slam against the rocks. Then his world turns black. . . .

No matter what their imaginations might have conjured, the only hard evidence the searchers had was the scow, which they found floating peacefully at Mile 237. There was some water in it, but the mattress, stove, camping gear, and the pair's personal possessions were not disturbed. The boat had not capsized. The searchers retrieved Bessie's diary, box camera, heavy clothing, camping gear, and boots. Regretfully, Bessie's diary revealed little. Apart from a series of circles and dashes—circles for easy rapids, and upright slashes for difficult ones—the diary contained few remarks. On November 20, sickness had kept her in camp all day. On November 22 the boat got caught in an eddy, and Glen stayed up all night holding the boat in case the eddy broke. The next day they laid over at Bedrock Rapids while Glen repaired a broken plank in the scow. In the only sign of humor in the diary, Bessie noted that on November 24 they launched "Rain in the Face," her name for the boat. On November 27 she did laundry in a hot spring, probably near Lava Falls. The next day was windy. On Thanksgiving Day they saw a deer. The brevity of the entries was puzzling. It contained no comments on her reaction to the Canyon; no record of events, no reflections on the experience she was having with her husband; no hint about whether she was enjoying the adventure, no illustrations. In short, the diary contained nothing that would help her write a book.[14] The searchers surmised from the diary and from the forty-two notches Glen had etched on the gunwale that the couple had disappeared on December 1.

Glen's father found a glimmer of hope in the diary. The last entry, dated November 30, noted bad rapids but did not mention their location. Convinced that Glen and Bessie could not have taken their clumsy scow on low water against headwinds the 46 miles from Lava Falls to Diamond Creek during that short interval, Hyde decided the accident must have occurred above Diamond Creek and not at Mile 232 as the Kolbs and Brooks believed. This meant that Bessie and Glen might still be alive and waiting for help. Perhaps they had even hiked out of the Canyon. Growing more desperate, he hired Hualapai Indian trackers to cover the reservation south of the stretch of canyon between Lava Falls and Diamond Creek for any signs of the couple, and cowboys to search the desolate north side of the canyon. Both searches were fruitless. Hyde himself back-packed into the gorge below Lava Falls but found nothing.

R. C. Hyde could not give up the search for his only son. In a letter to Emery Kolb dated January 1, 1929, he wrote, "I have come here to St. George and am organizing a pack team to search this country between here and this river. I realize that this is likely of no avail but I wish to have nothing undone that can be done."[15] February 28 of the same year, he wrote, "I am planning to return to the river, sometime, to search and see if I cannot find the bodies. I do not know when would be the best time. What do you advise?"[16]

Hyde at least had the advantage of doing something. Bessie's family, however, were left to wring their hands with concern, the distance making the loss of their Bessie that much more mysterious, that much more unbelievable. Glen's sister, Jeanne, corresponded often with Bessie's mother and made efforts to comfort them. On January 8, 1929, she wrote, "We may have them back yet, Mrs. Haley, and if we don't, at least they have dared life and death, taken the sporting chance, and gotten as much out of life as any two people could."[17] Later that year, responding to a letter from Mrs. Haley concerning the possibility of the pair being held hostage by hostile Indians, Jeanne explained that now all the Indians lived on reservations and were peaceful, adding, "I cannot see any slight hope of their being alive."[18] A full year and a half later, Bessie's father joined R. C. Hyde in a seventeen-day search of the Canyon in a final unsuccessful attempt to find an answer.

April 1931 brought the only subsequent clue to what might have happened to the couple. Glen and Bessie's names were found written on a board inside the blacksmith shop at the old drilling camp at Diamond Creek. They had reached Diamond Creek after all, making it almost certain that the accident had occurred at Mile 232.[19] Although both families finally accepted the couple's death, questions about how they died and where they died would haunt them the rest of their lives.

Over the years, the legend of Glen and Bessie Hyde grew as river running became a popular commercial enterprise and river guides recounted the story of the couple's disappearance around campfires. On one such occasion in October 1971, a passenger on a Grand Canyon Expedition twenty-day oar trip—Elizabeth "Liz" Cutler, a sixty-one-year-old retired schoolteacher from Pomeroy, Ohio—claimed that she was really Bessie Hyde. She told how she and Glen argued and that to protect herself, she stabbed him and hiked out of the Canyon.

This account remained the province of river guides for fourteen years, gaining momentum and credibility when writer Scott Thybony suggested in an October 1985 *Outside Magazine* article that Bessie was indeed alive and well. This generated the interest of NBC's *Unsolved Mysteries*. A segment on the November 29, 1987, program called "Honeymoon Bones" shows Bessie reaching for a 5-inch hunter's dagger and left the impression that Bessie was living in Ohio.

The story remained "true" until Martin J. Anderson, a river historian, undertook to answer the question, Was Liz Cutler really Bessie Hyde? The answer: no. Liz was born Mary Elizabeth Arnold on December 2, 1909, in Pomeroy, Ohio. Bessie was born Bessie Haley on December 29, 1905, in Washington, D.C. Liz grew up and lived in Pomeroy most of her life. The local paper has her attending several Arnold family reunions in the late 1920s, at the same time Bessie would have been attending art school in California.[20]

Still, if Bessie isn't Liz, she could be someone else. Usually, the Colorado River gives up its victims eventually, but neither body ever surfaced. Did Bessie Haley Hyde's "bright future" end in the cold waters of the Colorado River? Or, did she in fact hike out to safety, to live out her life in obscurity?

A Ranger in Riding Habit

POLLY MEAD PATRAW

(1904–)

POLLY MEAD IN HER IMPROVISED RANGER UNIFORM, 1928. (Photo courtesy of Polly Mead Patraw.)

*P*OLLY MEAD FIRST laid eyes on the Grand Canyon in 1927, when she was twenty-three years old. Raised among columbines and daisies on a Colorado ranch, Polly was studying botany at the University of Chicago when she had the opportunity to see the Canyon and several other national parks during a summerlong field trip in the West. The trip was organized and directed by one of her professors, Dr. Henry Chandler Cowles.

"We went to Logan, Utah," Polly explained, "and then to several national parks—Yellowstone, Zion, Bryce, and the North Rim of the Grand Canyon. First we went to Zion, and I was so thrilled about Zion. I had never seen country like that. I thought, 'Wouldn't it be wonderful to live in a place like that?' never knowing that one day I would. At Bryce, Dr. Cowles had us hold hands and close our eyes as he led us to the lookout. What a thrill when we opened our eyes!"[1]

With visions of Yellowstone, Zion, and Bryce fresh in their minds, the group of young botanists arrived at the Grand Canyon, a fitting place to end a brilliant summer. They had seen the vastness of landscape and a range of ecosystems so delicately balanced it made the students marvel anew at all they had learned in the confines of a classroom. For Polly Mead, the trip was life-defining.

"Why can't you see the Grand Canyon?" Polly Mead inquired as they set up camp along the Canyon's rim. "Something as big as that, you should be able to see it."[2]

"Take a walk down that little path," Dr. Cowles said to his dubious student. After meeting the graces of Zion and Bryce, little amazement was left for her mind to imagine. Could any sight compare with the awe and wonder of those two places? Polly walked the few hundred yards to the overlook. "I walked down the path and discovered the Grand Canyon. A most emotional experience," Polly said. "It was so wonderful."

The moment she broached the Canyon's edge, Polly was overcome by the power of nature. She looked upon a canyon spread as wide as the horizon, burnt as red as an earthen clay pot, carved as deep as the sky is high. Pine trees competed with patches of aspen for space along the rim, and as the Canyon fell away, scrub oak, mountain mahogany, and New Mexican locust trees clung to the steep sides. In the slight breeze that wafted from inside the Canyon she detected the essense of the West. The Canyon has been here forever, and yet it was still created over time, by time. Whether one is conscious of it or not, the Canyon reminds each visitor that "I am evidence and proof of history, of yesterday, of change. I am here before you; I will be here long after you are gone."

Later, as the group drove along the Kaibab Plateau leaving the North Rim, Professor Cowles asked his students if they had noticed how the trees came right to the edge of the meadow and just stopped. "That would make an interesting study, to see why the tree line just stops suddenly at the meadow," Polly thought. Suddenly she had an idea. "That's the subject for my master's thesis."

With this first visit to the Canyon, Polly, a petite young woman with a broad smile and an enthusiastic nature, had found a place she would return to again and again. "When I graduated, my aunt and benefactor said, 'I'd like to give you a gift of a trip to Europe or a trip to the Grand Canyon to do your research.' I'd never been to Europe, but I knew what I wanted to do."

A young woman of Polly's upbringing would be expected to choose the European tour, but a determined Polly Mead pursued her interests and spent the summers of 1928 and 1929 doing research for her master's thesis near the North Rim of the Grand Canyon. Polly expanded her thesis topic from the narrow approach of determining the cause for the sharp division between the meadows and the forest to encompass a complete study of plant life on the Kaibab Plateau. Hers would be the first such study and would provide the basis for all further studies on the North Rim.

Polly lived at the V. T. Lodge, about 20 miles north of the North Rim, while doing her research. The 350-square-mile Kaibab Plateau boasts virgin stands of yellow pine, Engelmann spruce, Douglas and white fir, and wide mountain meadows where elk and deer graze. Summer daytime temperatures average 70 degrees Fahrenheit. By late October heavy snow blankets the plateau, making travel virtually impossible.

For her research, Polly used C. Hart Merriam's theory of life zones[3] to draw a map of the Kaibab Plateau defining each zone: the Upper Sonoran Zone ranged from 5,000 to 7,000 feet elevation; the Transition Zone, from 7,000 to 8,200 feet; and the Canadian Zone, from 8,200 to 9,200 feet. The meadows, which intrigued Polly, were in the lower depressions of the Canadian Zone. She carefully identified and catalogued the plant life in each zone.

"I had a plant press on my back, and I'd go out and collect specimens. Sometimes I'd stay overnight. All I'd need would be a canteen and a bedroll," Polly explained. She also took a little pistol with her on these overnight trips, thinking that as a woman out alone, "I might need it if a drunken man or wild animal approached me. One time I was in my bedroll asleep and I was awakened by footsteps going around me. I put my hand on the pistol, but nothing happened. The next morning I saw deer prints all around my bedroll."

Polly used a vasculum, a can with moist paper in it, to store the plants she gathered for identification. "You have to have fresh plants to work on, so I would keep the fresh plant for a day or two and then find another one just like it to be put in the plant press." She sent her pressed specimens back to the National Museum in Washington to confirm their identification.

To study climatic conditions in each zone, Polly rode on horseback to set up weather stations. First she placed a maximum-minimum thermometer inside a wooden box with an opening on one side; she would then position the box with the open side shaded from the direct rays of the sun and mount it on a post 36 inches above the ground. She'd place Livingston atmometer cups for measuring evaporation and rainfall near the thermometer and surround both instruments with a wire fence for protection from animals. She also would don climbing spikes and climb the tall pines to install and check on instruments, and she took soil samples to determine the percentage of water content present along the plateau. These she sent to the Desert Botanical Laboratory in Tucson, Arizona, for determination.

Because Polly's major advisor was a geologist as well as a botantist, he insisted that all papers contain information about the study area's geology. She decided to consult with Edwin (Eddie) McKee, Grand Canyon National Park naturalist stationed on the South Rim, whose speciality was geology. She had met him on the field trip the previous summer and knew he worked on the South Rim. "I decided to walk across the Canyon and meet with him."

At the time, Polly did not realize a "walk" across the Canyon was in reality a grueling 27-mile hike. In addition to the nearly 5,000-foot elevation loss and gain, Polly also contended with temperatures hovering near 100 degrees, wading Bright Angel Creek several times, and boots that didn't fit.

"Nobody knows how big the Grand Canyon is unless they have walked it every step of the way," Polly said. She spent the night at Phantom Ranch and then continued her climb up to the South Rim. "I crossed the bridge across the Colorado River with stiff boots and blistered feet. I went up the Bright Angel Trail. Some kind person poured a pail of water over me, and I made it. I was so tired I couldn't sleep," she recalled.

Polly spent several days meeting with McKee before hiking back to the North Rim. "I made a deal with him. I would work on a plant list of the Grand Canyon, and he would give me geologic material for my thesis."

One late afternoon, Polly returned to V. T. Lodge from a day in the field to find the owners quite excited. Stephen Mather, head of the National Park Service, had been looking for Polly. He left a note inviting her to be his guest at the dedication of the North Rim Lodge. As life's fortune would have it, Mr. Mather was the father of Polly's old school chum Becky Mather. He had learned from his daughter that Polly was living at the North Rim.

"I went down to the bottom of my trunk and pulled out a dress and got a ride down to the North Rim Lodge. I was the only woman present at the dedication." Seated with Polly and Mr. Mather were Carl Gray, president of the Union Pacific Railroad, and Heber J. Grant, president of the Mormon Church. Making their acquaintance would later prove beneficial to Polly.

Polly finished her research on schedule, at the end of her second summer on the North Rim. Her resulting thesis provided a complete study of the Kaibab Plateau. She concluded that a difference in the lime content of the meadows accounted for the sharp demarcation of the tree line. Trees do not flourish in soils with a high lime content.

Following graduation, Polly decided she wanted to remain

POLLY MEAD WAS THE ONLY WOMAN PRESENT AT THE DEDICATION OF THE NORTH RIM LODGE, 1928. FROM THE BOTTOM RIGHT OF THE PHOTO, SHE IS ABOUT FOUR ROWS UP AND THREE IN FROM THE RIGHT. (Photo courtesy of Grand Canyon National Park Museum Collection.)

at the Canyon. She applied to the Forest Service to work as a ranger-naturalist but was told that they did not hire women. She then applied for the position of ranger-naturalist with the National Park Service on the South Rim. "On my application someone had written a note: 'It will be remembered that Miss Mead was Stephen Mather's guest at the dedication of the North Rim Lodge.'" Although this no doubt helped her application receive some special attention, Polly believed she got the job because of her knowledge of the Canyon and because she wanted it so badly. She was sworn into office on August 1, 1930, by the park's Assistant Superintendent Preston Patraw and became the first woman ranger-naturalist at the Grand Canyon—and the second in the entire National Park Service.

Because an official female Park Service uniform did not then exist, Superintendent M. R. Tillotson decided that Polly should wear a riding habit. "I had rather light britches and hip boots. He wanted me to wear a hat like the courier girls for the Fred Harvey tours wore. He just liked that hat."

"I loved that job!" Polly enthused. "I worked at Yavapai and gave campfire lectures in the evening." Polly also did the auto caravan tours, talking about plants and geology, and she occasionally led nature hikes.

Her favorite assignment was to stand at the edge of the Canyon and give talks. "I loved to talk when I was standing on the edge of the Grand Canyon because I could talk about the Canyon and not be self-conscious at all." Who, after all, could be self-conscious with such a backdrop? "One time I had a large bus tour listening to my lecture. I wanted to get them interested in the Canyon, so I talked about the age of the rocks—two hundred billion years—and how it took a hundred million years for the Canyon to be carved." She had the group's undivided attention. When she finished they seemed eager for more information, so Polly asked, "Are there any questions?" Polly was shocked when a man asked, "'And how old are you?'" I told him, 'Twenty-five!'"[4] The group was apparently as intrigued with their ranger as they were with the Grand Canyon.

Polly prepared her own talks. "I found that if you're interested, people will be interested. If you enjoy it yourself, the first thing you know, people will be interested." Polly particularly enjoyed talking about the yucca plant, which shares a unique, symbiotic relationship with the penumbra moth. The two rely on each other for survival: If one were to perish, so would the other. "The relationship between the two is fascinating," Polly exclaimed. "The penumbra moth fertilizes the flower and starts the seeds, so there's an interdependency between the moth and the yucca. I would tell about the Indians using the yucca fiber for material and soap from the root to wash their hair. It made an especially nice soap for the hair."

Her love of flowers led her to attempt planting wildflower gardens at the Canyon. In preparation for this, she began an elaborate experiment to determine which wildflowers would grow from gathered seed. "Wildflowers are very difficult to transplant," she explained. Polly searched for wildflower seeds in the fall of 1930, and she wrote about her project in the December 1930 *Nature Notes*,[5] a mimeographed booklet published monthly by the Naturalist Department of the Grand Canyon National Park. She had gathered nineteen varieties of wildflowers, including cliff rose, Apache plume, globe mallow, and pink penstemon. Polly planted one hundred seeds of each variety in a hothouse under various soil and moisture conditions. In her meticulous manner, she carefully noted the percentage of seeds that germinated. She was most successful with the bluebonnet (lupine), with a 75 percent germination rate, and least successful with the Indian paintbrush and cranesbill, with no germination at all.

Polly continued her wildflower project throughout the winter. In the January 1931 *Nature Notes*, she excitedly reported that the Indian paintbrush had germinated after all: on January 18 she discovered eighteen seedlings. Her goal, as stated in the article, was to "shed light on the behavior of wildflower seeds" and to "assist in the eventual replacement of exotic plants by native wild plants in landscaping within the National Parks."

Despite her many projects, Polly found time for fun. She lived in the midst of one of the most beautiful places on earth, with brilliant moons, the milky flowering of the yucca, and the smell of hard-baked rock. The magic of the Grand Canyon is irresistible. As for the yucca and the penumbra moth, certain things attract there: water to dry earth, animals to plants, even man to woman. For Polly, that man was Preston Patraw, the park's assistant superintendent, who had sworn her in to the National Park Service a year earlier. Patraw was intrigued with the petite ranger in the jaunty hat and invited her to hike with him up Red Butte.

Before long, they were dating often, usually enjoying the attractions of the Canyon after work hours. Preston, a tall, handsome man with a reticent manner, asked Polly to marry him in March 1931 during a drive around the Canyon's rim. Few things are more magical than a sunset drive along the rim of the Grand Canyon: The shadows deepen, and the orange-red colors of the setting sun light up the sky. Preston stopped the car just west of El Tovar and walked with Polly to Hopi Point. She agreed to be his wife. "He wanted to get me a Navajo rug for an engagement present, but he wanted me to pick it out, so we stopped at Hopi House on the way back," Polly recalled. The rug is still on the back of Polly's sofa, sixty-four years later.

They were married May 1 of that year in the home of Polly's aunt in Phoenix, Arizona. Polly thought she would continue with her job, which she loved, but Preston did not want her to work. "I just said, 'Yes, dear,' as we did in those days!" Polly laughed. Her life shifted from botanist to wife overnight.

"As a bride at the Canyon I got up and built a wood fire to make breakfast," she said. "We had an icebox and running water." But the Canyon offered few other amenities in 1931. Because of Preston's rank as assistant superintendent, he and Polly were fortunate to live in a house in Grand Canyon village. Many lower-level employees lived in tent houses.

Although Polly no longer was employed with the Park Service, she continued to study botany and write articles in *Nature Notes*, now with the byline Pauline Mead Patraw. In the May 1931 issue, she excitedly reported on finding a broomrape, a small parasitic flower rarely found outside of Utah and Nevada. Upon finding the flower, Polly had at first misidentified it. "At first sight I thought recklessly, 'a member of the Indian pipe family,'" she explained. After further digging, literally and figuratively, she determined that it was *orobanche multiflora* (broomrape). "This is the first record of broomrape at the Grand Canyon and the only member of this family found here thus far," she wrote. Polly sketched the plant and explained in detail that it was a parasite, living on the roots of other plants without damaging the host plant.

Polly's knowledge of plants at the Canyon introduced her to architect Mary Elizabeth Jane Colter, a woman she came to admire. "She was a fascinating person. I helped her with plants at the

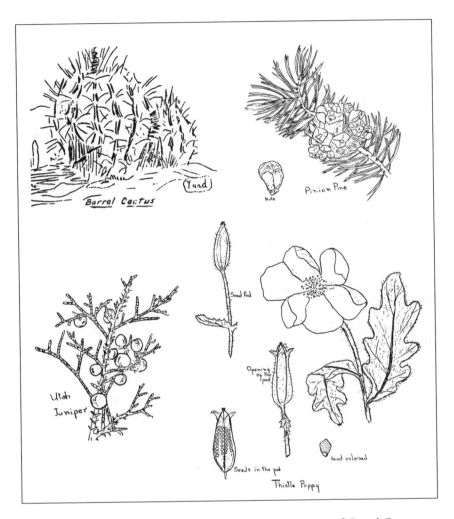

Labels in sketch: Barrel Cactus, (Yucca), Piñion Pine, Nuts, Seed Pod, Opening of the pad, Utah Juniper, Seeds in the pod, Seed enlarged, Thistle Poppy

SKETCHES FROM PATRAW'S *NATURE NOTES*. (Sketch courtesy of Grand Canyon National Park Museum Collection.)

Watchtower. She wanted some Apache bloom plants," Polly said, adding that it is sometimes hard to tell the difference between a cliff rose and an Apache bloom since they are both in the same family. "Cliff rose has a pungent odor, and the flowers are very different. Apache bloom is more delicate. The cliff rose flowers grow close together, and the Apache bloom is more spread out."

Polly and Preston started a family, and soon after their second child was born, Preston was made superintendent at Zion National Park in southwestern Utah. The Patraws left the Canyon in 1932. Polly made the transition easily, for Zion, at least, was in her beloved West. The rich red tones of Zion's earth resembled that at the Canyon and kept her from missing it too badly. Polly made sure that she and her family fit into the landscape. "The houses at Zion were built of red sandstone. You know how we like to have everything fit in with the scenery? I was a good Park Service wife: Both of our children, George and Betsy, had red hair and fit in with the scenery," Polly laughed.

Preston went on to be superintendent at nearby Bryce Canyon National Park, followed soon after by Cedar Breaks National Monument and Capitol Reef National Park in Utah and, Polly's least favorite, a short stint in Hot Springs, Arkansas. "I preferred being in the West, climbing mountains," she explained. Polly got her wish in 1947 when Preston was named associate director of the Park Service's southwest regional office in Santa Fe, New Mexico.

After having moved to Santa Fe, Polly worked on a book titled *Flowers of the Southwest Mesas*,[6] one of a series of flower books about the Southwest. Polly took nearly four years to accumulate material for the book. Five thousand copies were printed when it was first published in 1952 by the Southwestern Monuments Association. In all, there were six printings and close to sixty-five thousand copies sold.

Polly's life came full circle in 1951 when Preston became superintendent of the Grand Canyon National Park. Returning to the Canyon, she noticed a significant change. "There were a lot more people," Polly recalled. "I remember one day my husband came home from the office and said, 'We had a thousand visitors this month.'" The increase in numbers of tourists led the Park Service to discussions about providing entertainment for the visitors—which baffled Polly. "Isn't it enough enjoyment just to look at it? Why do you provide for anything except comfort? You don't need entertainment or anything of that kind when you've got the Grand Canyon to look at. I was talking to a woman from Phoenix who complained about taking visitors to see the Grand Canyon because there wasn't anything to do there. I don't feel that way at all."[7]

Polly enjoyed her role as wife of the superintendent of Grand Canyon National Park, entertaining dignitaries and making new employees feel welcome. When Preston retired in 1955, the couple moved back to their Santa Fe home, where Polly still lives today.

Polly's legacy as ranger-naturalist continues at the Canyon. In numbers that long ago put an end to any curiousity about them, women rangers give talks, lead nature hikes, assist visitors, and conduct scientific studies much in the same way Polly Mead Patraw did so many years ago.

Race to Shiva Temple

RUTH STEPHENS BAKER

EDITH KOLB LEHNERT, GORDON BERGER, RUTH STEPHENS, AND RALPH WHITE "LAY CLAIM" TO SHIVA TEMPLE. (Photo courtesy of the Emery Kolb Collection, Cline Library, Northern Arizona University, no. NAU.PH.568-512.)

HAVING A CANYON, a train, hotels, tourists, cowboys, and mules near her home seemed perfectly normal to Ruth Stephens Baker. She grew up at the Grand Canyon, and it was as familiar to her as her own backyard. Yet, for all its familiarity, the Canyon held mysterious worlds she yearned to explore. Worlds that towered above the Canyon floor with intriguing names like Isis, Wotan's Throne, Zoroaster, and Shiva Temple.

Ruth was only two when her parents left San Diego, California, in the summer of 1920 for the Grand Canyon, where her father, an accountant, had accepted a three-month job with the Fred Harvey Company to balance the books. He stayed forty years. "Mom had acrophobia, so it was amazing for her to live at the Canyon," Ruth said. "She couldn't look over the rim!"[1]

When they arrived at the Canyon, the Stephens family was shown to their new home . . . a tent house. Ruth remembered the house well. "Our tent house had three rooms with a board floor, board siding, and board struts. Everything else was canvas, the sides and everything. There was a wood fence around it, and just outside the fence, out back, was the outhouse. Exterior plumbing!" she quipped.

"Mom made the tent house a real home," Ruth recalled. "We had a proper dining room with an oak table. The kitchen had a coal range and a table, chairs, and sink. Out back was a big old tub where mother did all the washing. We brought it inside and took our baths in it too." Ruth slept in a single bed, and her parents had a Murphy bed. "My mother was a perfectionist and a proper main-line Philadelphian. It was a chore for her to live in a tent. Cleaning house was a fulltime job. The roads weren't paved, and there was lots of dust!"[2]

A childhood at the Grand Canyon was like no other. "A big 'do' for us kids was watching the Santa Fe train leave at night," Ruth says. "Also, I learned my alphabet by Pullman cars and my arithmetic by the freight cars." Thanks to the train and her father, Ruth was reading before she entered first grade in the two-room log school at the Canyon. "Dad used to read me the comics, but he would not read me *The Katzenjammer Kids* because they used the word 'ain't,' which was not supposed to be in my vocabulary. I learned to read so I could read *The Katzenjammer Kids!*" Ruth laughed.

"We played house in the caves under the rim," she remembered. "We used embossed wallpaper to make elaborate dresses for paper dolls and then wrote great stories about them. We put on plays for our parents. We wrote the plays and made our own costumes. Then we sold them hot dogs and drinks our parents had made and charged them ten cents to get in!"

There was no charge to watch the sunsets! "If Dad saw that the sunset was going to be good, he'd tell my mother, 'OK, Lil, forget about dinner and let's go.' And we'd forget about dinner and go to Hopi Point and watch the sunset. Dad and I had fun looking at clouds and seeing animals and objects in the clouds. We'd start talking about the cloud shapes, and pretty soon we'd have the dudes [tourists] doing it."

Ruth watched not only clouds but squirrels and chipmunks playing along the rim. She wanted a pet, but domestic pets were not allowed at the Canyon. She was about ten years old when, in an effort to relieve the over-population of deer on the North Rim, hundreds of deer were brought across the Canyon to the South Rim, near the village. "Everyone had a pet deer," Ruth recalled, "and I named mine Minnie. One named Smokey occasionally chased us home from school. One day Smokey went through a yard and got tangled up in laundry hanging on the line, and he chased us with laundry hanging on his antlers." Having a deer as a pet was fun at first, but later the deer became pests because people started feeding them cigarettes. "They became addicted to nicotine and were very demanding," Ruth explained.

After eight years of living in the tent house, the family moved into one of the new houses built on Avenue A (now Apache Street) in town. "We moved out of the tent house in 1928. I remember it because the next year my sister was born. Mother had toxemia, and the doctor sent her on a train to Los Angeles because there was no hospital at the Grand Canyon. If we'd been one hour later, both Mother and my sister Barbara would have died. The baby stayed in the hospital for two months. We had a new house *and* a new baby."

Just two years after moving into the new house, Ruth graduated from the eighth grade. There was no high school at the Grand Canyon, so Ruth spent her high school and college years in

California living in a home her father's family rented. She looked forward to the end of each term so that she could return to the Canyon and home. Home for a summer filled with fun and work.

"Summers at the Canyon were wonderful," Ruth said. "I fell in love every day. Every night during the summer we had a dance at Bright Angel Lodge. This was essentially for the tourists, but we joined in and danced with the dudes and each other. It was one big party. There was a program before the dance, about an hour's entertainment, cowboy songs and jokes."

At the end of the summer Ruth enjoyed a few days at Phantom Ranch at the bottom of the Canyon. "I rode a mule down," she said. "We luxuriated in the swimming pool, cold as it was. Later, the cowboys would take the girls down to see the river by moonlight. We said that it was called 'Phantom Ranch' because you had to watch out for the ghosts!"

Aside from fun, there was plenty of work to be done; for Ruth that meant the Kolb Studio. Emery Kolb had come to the Grand Canyon in 1902, and by the time the Stephens family arrived, he was well established as a photographer and considered an expert on the Grand Canyon. In his studio, built at the head of the Bright Angel Trail, Emery sold photos and gift items and gave daily lectures. Ruth knew Emery well. At age ten she baby-sat his grandson, Emery "Sonny" Lehnert, and at sixteen she began working in Kolb's darkroom. Emery took pictures of all the people who went down Bright Angel Trail on mule trips and had them developed and ready for sale when the riders returned. Ruth washed the prints and put them on pans to dry. "I had to keep an eye on them if the wind came up to make sure they didn't blow away," she said. "I had to wash off the pans to make sure they were absolutely clean so that the pictures would lift off nicely." She also hand-tinted Emery's black-and-white Canyon pictures, adding touches of color according to his instructions.

Emery promoted Ruth upstairs to the studio, where for twenty-five cents an hour she did whatever needed doing—waiting on customers, washing windows, dusting, cleaning drapes, setting up chairs for the lectures, and recruiting people to attend Emery's lectures, where he showed films and slides of his river trips and his hikes in the Canyon. "I became a regular barker," Ruth admitted. "I'd show them the telescope and get them to buy a book and come to the lecture. I had the spiel down pat. I was very shy, but I became a hard-sell barker."

As she gained experience, she took on more responsibility and learned to operate the equipment during the lectures. The film projector was a 35 millimeter Bell and Howell Peerless carbon arc projector. "Now that was some kind of monstrosity!" Ruth laughed. "I had to open the side up and line up the carbons just so, make sure I had the right height, and thread the whole thing."

Just getting the film projector going wasn't enough. "The lecture was set up so that part of it was slide and part was film. I had to know when to turn off the film and start the slide projector. Mr. Kolb stood downstairs, and he had his little buzzer and light so that I'd know when to change the slide. If I didn't get it quickly enough, buzz, buzz, buzz. I can still hear the buzz, buzz, buzz, and see the light flash! Sometimes the film would break, and I would have to throw on a slide, hurry up and patch the film, unreel it, and start over again. He was not too understanding when this happened in the middle of a lecture."

Ruth's favorite time in the studio was during the four o'clock to nine o'clock shift. "Nobody would be in there around six in the evening, and that was the most beautiful time and I had the whole Canyon to myself," she explained. It was a peaceful interlude—except when a late afternoon storm swept across the Canyon, lightning streaking across the sky, its tenacles reaching down to strike a pillar of rock or an isolated tree. "I was scared to death of lightning," Ruth said. "One time the lightning came right through the studio. It traveled right across the room. I happened to have the window open in the studio and on the porch where they had the telescope, so it was natural for the lightning to come through. I never made that mistake again."

After a storm, the Canyon would look spectacular as the

sunlight broke through the clouds. "It was like a stage, and sometimes there would be spotlights when the sun would highlight Isis, Wotan's Throne, Zoroaster, and Shiva Temple. That's when I began to dream of climbing the mysterious worlds of the Canyon, never knowing that I would get that chance."[3]

Her chance came in the summer of 1937. Dr. Harold E. Anthony of the American Museum of Natural History in New York City planned to scale Shiva Temple that September and set foot where he believed no man had ever been before. Shiva Temple rises 7,570 feet above the Canyon floor and is connected to the North Rim by a narrow land bridge. The press loved the story, and articles appeared in the *New York Times* calling Shiva Temple a "lost world" and speculating that dinosaurs might still roam in the isolated forest.[4] Emery Kolb, whose reputation as an explorer of the Canyon was well known, offered to guide the expedition but was rejected by Dr. Anthony and the Park Service.

Kolb was furious. When the Park Service refused even to let him come along on the museum's expedition, he decided to beat them to Shiva Temple. He made a preliminary climb in midsummer to find a route, and then he began to assemble his crew. Because much talk was being made of a woman going on the museum's expedition, Kolb invited his daughter, Edith, and Ruth to accompany him. Ruth's dream of climbing a part of the mysterious world of the Grand Canyon came true at age nineteen.

It was essential that Kolb's trip be kept a secret. His relationship with the Park Service was contentious at best, and he feared he might be banned from the Canyon at any time.[5] "We were all sworn to secrecy," Ruth admitted. Besides her and Edith, Kolb invited two friends, Gordon Berger and Ralph White. "My mother would never let me go down the [Colorado] River, but she let me climb Shiva Temple. Surely she didn't know what it was going to be like," Ruth said.[6]

The approach to Shiva Temple is from the North Rim, a 200-mile drive from the South Rim. To save time, Emery arranged for the group to be flown across the Canyon. Plans were made in the utmost secrecy. Kolb's wife, Blanche, made small parachutes out of gunny sacks to be filled with cans of tomatoes, crackers, and a few snacks; the pilot would drop these to the climbers after they reached the top of Shiva Temple. "When Mrs. Kolb was making our burlap parachutes she wouldn't let anyone in the sewing room. It was very hush, hush. It was all elaborately planned. Talk about scaling Mount Everest! This was the same type of thing to us."[7]

"We flew over to the North Rim one evening and spent the night on Point Sublime," Ruth explained. "We got our gear together and started our descent about 6 A.M., just about daybreak." The climb of Shiva Temple actually begins as a steep descent to a saddle. "We got down easily; it was not bad climbing at all, except in one little part where I twisted my knee, but I didn't pay any attention to it. When we got down to the saddle, there were pools of water. It had rained the night before. We got down there about 10 A.M., and here were all these great puddles of water, so we designated one puddle for drinking water, one for washing faces, one for washing feet, and one for washing socks. We left clean socks and some crackers there."[8]

Kolb worried that someone looking through the telescope on his studio porch might see them, so, although the chances that they would be seen were remote, he decided to climb up on the north side of Shiva Temple. "The climb was a bit more difficult an ascent than we had anticipated. We did use ropes once. We topped out just before noon, and they let me be the first person to be on top of Shiva Temple," Ruth said, her eyes sparkling at the memory. "I remember that the noon whistle was blowing on the South Rim. I was wearing this bright red shirt. We had decided that somebody should wear something bright when the plane flew over so we could be spotted." The pilot flew over around noon, and on spotting the climbers, tossed the parachutes out the window. "They landed in a tree, and Mr. Kolb had to climb up and get them. We had tomatoes and water and crackers for lunch."[9]

Although Kolb did not want the Park Service to know he had climbed Shiva Temple, he did want Dr. Anthony and his museum

EMERY KOLB AND RUTH STEPHENS EN ROUTE TO SHIVA TEMPLE, 1937. (Photo courtesy of the Emery Kolb Collection, Cline Library, Northern Arizona University, no. NAU.PH.568-508.)

expedition to know that someone had been on Shiva Temple. "We went over to a point we knew we could see from the studio, and we found an agave stalk and put a burlap bag on the stalk that would blend in nicely, but if we wanted to look at it, we could see through the telescope. That was our flag." But a burlap flag was not enough. "Just because we were feeling a little rambunctious and did want people to know that other people had been there and it wasn't such a great thing after all, we left a few boxes of Kodak film, obviously made since 2,000 years ago. Also, I had heard there was going to be a female on the expedition, so I had some lipstick and some tissues, and I put lipstick all over the tissues and left it on a few bushes so it couldn't be missed," she remembered. "We found that the deer had made a trail [to the top of the landform]. And we found horns, antlers locked. We found some interesting fossils, and we took a couple things back as specimens. We took pictures."[10]

By now it was late afternoon, and the group hurried to make their way down to the saddle by nightfall. "We spent the night in a kind of overhanging cave so that we could build a fire and nobody could see it. We could hear noises from the North Rim and could see the lights of the South Rim. It was the most fabulous feeling to think there was all that civilization over there, and here we were where nobody had even been before. It was the most fantastic experience." The group arrived back at the North Rim about 10 A.M. the next morning and flew back to the South Rim. "I was sworn to secrecy. Absolute secrecy. Nobody could say anything about it because of the fact that we had done it surreptitiously, and Mr. Kolb was not to be gotten into trouble. I didn't see the pictures for twenty years. It was the thrill of a lifetime. No one told for years, but the word eventually leaked out it was Emery [Kolb who had scaled Shiva first]."[11]

The following month, the museum expedition arrived at the North Rim. With great fanfare and movie cameras rolling, the group—Dr. Anthony; noted mountain climbers Mr. and Mrs. Walter E. Wood Jr.; Wood's assistant, Elliott H. Humphrey; naturalist and photographer James B. Shackelton; and George B. Andrews of the museum staff—started up Shiva Temple guided by Edwin McKee, chief naturalist of the Grand Canyon National Park, and M. R. Tillotson, park superintendent. They were supported by two private aircraft and six strong young men to carry their gear.

The September 17 *New York Times* reported that a party of scientists "tied together like beads on a string" disappeared over the rim of the Grand Canyon headed for Shiva Temple.[12] Later articles told of finding perfect arrowheads indicating that man had indeed once been on the plateau. Dr. Anthony remained on the plateau for ten days, collecting small animals and plant life.

The October 4, 1937, issue of *Time* magazine called the expedition to "treasureless island" a "scientific joke."[13] In a long account of the expedition in the October 16, 1937, *Science News Letter,* Dr. Anthony attempted to justify the expedition, although his findings must have been a disappointment to him. He noted little of scientific value, indicating only that small mammals such as chipmunks were paler than normal on Shiva Temple and that the mosquitos were "out of the practice in biting humans."[14]

Dr. Anthony alluded to finding "convincing evidence . . . that someone else had tried to jump the gun and beat us to the summit of Shiva." He referred to finding a coil of rope, a small camera, and a hooked climbing staff at the base of a steep slope on the approach to the top of Shiva Temple, and called it "mute evidence that at this point the adventurer had lost his nerve." No mention of Kodak film canisters, lipstick smudged tissues, or a burlap flag on an agave stalk. The Kolb expedition got a real chuckle out of this account.

Ruth's time at the Canyon ended soon after her climb to the top of Shiva Temple. In the summer of 1938, Ruth met her husband to be, Albert Baker Jr. "He was what we called a 'ninety-day wonder,' a three-month temporary ranger who came out for the summer." Four years after they had met, she was teaching in a three-room schoolhouse in Warner Springs, California, when she received a telegram from him. Albert was in the Air Corps and was being sent to Riverside, California, only 60 miles from her teaching assignment. They married on February 7, 1942, and subsequently lived all over the United States. Their three children were born in the East, but all have since moved West.

"To me the Grand Canyon is still home," Ruth said. "I never think of any other place but this as home. It was a closeness. I don't think we ever thought of it as anything really special. It was just a part of where we grew up."[15]

Today, Ruth returns to the Canyon occasionally to visit her mother's grave in the Grand Canyon Pioneers Cemetery. Much has changed. In 1994 at the seventy-fifth anniversary of the creation of

Grand Canyon National Park, Ruth gathered some roses from her yard in Tucson to put on her mother's grave. "There was no place to park except one spot that was marked "No Parking." I figured I would just be a minute, so I parked there and ran into the cemetery. As I was coming back I saw this Park Service car stopped at my car. "I was just here putting something on my mother's grave," I explained, and he replied, "But don't you know you're supposed to follow the rules too?"[16]

That's true, but it's the press of people that concerns Ruth. "I was walking along the rim, and this young lad said to his mother, 'Mom, I don't like this place. There are too many people'. There *are* too many people. I think people feel suffocated rather than awed. I always felt the Canyon was expansive, but now it's being pressed in, and that's too bad. I know you can't limit it, but nobody now has a chance to sit, think, expand, and enjoy. It's noise, it's people, and it's a shame. We lived here in the best of all times. We had the perfect time."[17]

7
Two Women, Three Boats, and a Plant Press

ELZADA CLOVER *(1897–1980)*
AND LOIS JOTTER *(1914–)*

ELZADA CLOVER AND LOIS JOTTER LOOKING NO WORSE FOR THE
WEAR AT THE END OF THE RIVER TRIP. (Photo courtesy of the
Belknap Collection, Cline Library, Northern Arizona University, no. NAU.PH.96.4.114.3.)

*L*ATE IN THE summer of 1937, Elzada Clover relaxed over
dinner in the Mexican Hat Lodge in southern Utah. After having
spent a hot day in the surrounding desert collecting cacti, she was
discussing a possible trip into the Grand Canyon with Norm Nevills,
thirty-two-year-old son of the lodge's owners. It was a discussion

they had had several times. Elzada, botany instructor and assistant curator of the botanical gardens at the University of Michigan, had spent most of that summer collecting specimens for the university's collection. Elzada believed the Canyon would hold a host of different or related species that would round out the collection, and she considered it a shame to miss the opportunity to explore it. She planned to go into the Grand Canyon by pack mule. Norm thought a boat trip would be better.

Norm eventually won out. A frequent "runner" on the nearby San Juan and Green Rivers, Norm now wanted to try his hand at the Colorado. He proposed a boat trip the following summer from Green River, Utah, to Lake Mead, on the Arizona-Nevada border—a distance of 660 miles. The cost of the boats—which Norm would build—equipment, and food would be shared equally by all members of the expedition. If the trip were successful, Norm planned to launch a commercial river running venture. Elzada hoped the expedition would advance her academic career. She would be the first botanist to catalog plants along the Colorado River through the Grand Canyon.

Elzada left Mexican Hat in time for the fall semester and began making arrangements for the Grand Canyon trip, securing university approval and financial support for the venture and selecting her companions. She invited twenty-four-year-old Lois Jotter, a graduate student in botany, and Eugene (Gene) Atkinson, a zoology major then working as a graduate assistant in the botany department. Both were serious students and enjoyed the outdoors. Lois, a tall, athletic woman, loved hiking and camping. Gene was an avid canoeist.

As word of the upcoming trip spread, the botanists became local celebrities. The campus newspaper, the *Michigan Daily*, headlined on Sunday, June 5, 1938, "Faculty Women to Face Danger on Stormy Colorado for Science." The women, according to the article, would traverse "650 turbulent rapids-filled miles of Colorado River—a feat never before accomplished by a member of their sex." At the botany department's spring picnic, the threesome endured unmerciful kidding about being, as the newspaper account said, "intrepid explorers."[1]

On the afternoon of June 7, Elzada, Lois, and Gene left Michigan for the long drive to Mexican Hat, Utah. Departure on the Green River was planned for June 20. They arrived in Mexican Hat on June 14. Mexican Hat was then little more than a crossroads. Named for a huge hat-shaped rock formation, the dusty "town" consisted of the Nevills's H-shaped lodge built of native red sandstone and a few other buildings.

Norm took them immediately to see the boats. Extremely well built, the boats were constructed using a new marine plywood, called Super Harbord, with oak framework. Each boat was 16 feet long, 4 feet across the stern, 5 feet amidship, and tapered to a pointed bow. Two thousand brass screws held them together.

Painted in large green letters against the gleaming white exterior was NEVILLS EXPEDITION. Individually, the boats were named the *Wen*, Norm's father's initials; the *Botany*, in honor of the purpose of the expedition; and the *Mexican Hat*, after the rock formation near the Nevills's lodge.

During the few days before departure, the Michiganites met the other adventurers who would accompany them. Bill Gibson, a soft-spoken commercial artist and industrial designer from the San Francisco Bay area, joined the trip primarily to further his photography career. He hoped to capture the adventure with his new movie camera. Norm's right-hand man, Don Harris, was a resident engineer for the United States Geological Survey (USGS). He rented a bunkhouse from the Nevills and often rafted on the San Juan with Norm. Don had helped to build the boats in his spare time, and in return Norm offered to give him one of the boats following the expedition.

By 1938, several men already had ridden the Colorado River through the Grand Canyon, but the only woman to attempt the trip until that time had been Bessie Hyde, who disappeared, presumably drowned (see the profile on her in this book). An Associated Press reporter from Salt Lake City asked Elzada and Lois what they thought of river veteran Buzz Holstrom's statement that the river was no place for a woman. Lois replied, "Just because the only other woman who ever attempted this trip was drowned is no reason women have any more to fear than men."[2] Overall, the news accounts recording the group's departure emphasized the "flora-minded women" and the "treacherous rapids" the party would surely encounter.

At 9:00 A.M. on June 20, the party started down the Green River, which had been flooded by an unexpectedly late snow melt. Family members and a small crowd of onlookers gathered to see them leave. Elzada later wrote in her diary, "The natives of Green River and Moab looked at us as if they would ne'er see us [any]more."[3] Norm and Elzada went first in the *Wen,* Lois and Don followed in the *Mexican Hat,* and Bill and Gene came last in the *Botany.* They planned to arrive on Lake Mead by the end of July.

Despite a strong upstream wind that made rowing difficult, the first day was uneventful. They camped the first evening on a sandbar near Labyrinth Canyon at Mile 84. As it was inconceivable in 1938 that a man would cook if a woman were available, Elzada and Lois became the expedition cooks. For the first evening's meal, they grilled fresh steaks.

Their few days on the Green River were peaceful. Except for contending with mosquitos and sunburn, the members voiced little complaint. Elzada and Lois took turns collecting plants, usually in the morning and evening. In the evenings around the campfire Elzada and Don played their harmonicas while the others sang.

The evening before they would meet the Colorado River, Norm grew serious. He gave the group a lecture on running rapids, beginning with a description of "holes." Water pours over an obstruction in a rapid and comes down with such force that it makes a hole in the river. The hydraulic forces in such a hole are unpredictable and exceedingly dangerous. To a group of novices, the description of this phenomenon was frightening. Norm cautioned them to avoid holes if possible, but if they couldn't be avoided, to hit them stern first. If you are thrown into the water, Norm continued, hang onto the rope on the side of the boat.

LOIS JOTTER GETTING GEAR FROM THE MEXICAN HAT. (Photo courtesy of the Grand Canyon National Park Museum Collection.)

During breakfast the next morning Norm reiterated his instructions. Nervous tension mounted among the group during the day, and remarks such as "What kind of flowers would you like?" and "It's been nice knowing you!" flew between the boats.[4] That afternoon, at 2:30 P.M., Norm stood on the forward deck of the *Wen* as they approached the Colorado and shouted, "There she is! She's a big 'un and she's a bad 'un!"[5] The Green meets the Colorado near Mile 216, three miles upstream from Cataract Canyon, so named because of its twenty-seven rapids in 13 miles.

The confluence of these two rivers is impressive. Suddenly, the calm of the Green is overcome by the frenzied rush of the Colorado's muddy waters. Lois wrote, "The character of the river changed, and slowly we realized the power of the Colorado."[6]

Norm signaled the boats to pull in at a sandbar. While Elzada and Lois took pictures, the men walked down to survey the first rapid. It appeared to be about 15 feet high, followed immediately by a second rapid with a large mushroom-shaped wave. As the men were inspecting the rapids, Bill happened to look back upriver. "My God!" he yelled. "There's the *Mexican Hat!*"[7] Lois and Don's boat had broken loose and was riding the crest of the first wave, stern first.

Norm shouted to Don to run upstream and get the *Wen*. Don ran, motioning to Lois to follow. They threw on their life preservers and shoved off in the *Wen*. Meanwhile, Norm, Gene, and Bill scrambled over the rocks to the end of the rapid just in time to see the empty *Mexican Hat* disappear in the next rapid. Norm sent Bill and Gene back to get the *Botany* and bring it down to the head of the second rapid, adding that the women should walk along the shore and catch up to them.

Bill and Gene had just set off when the *Wen*, with Don at the oars and Lois waving, passed. Aghast, Norm ran down to meet the boat as it swept into the second rapid.

"With a sinking feeling, I ran on as fast as I could. Not far to the reportedly bad [rapid] number 4 and worse than a greenhorn at the oars! Words can't tell the all-gone feeling I experienced," Norm later wrote in his journal.[8] Norm ran along the shore, trying to catch up with Don and Lois. He watched the *Wen* careen down the river, rocking like a carnival ride gone bad.

Don and Lois had a wild ride through seven rapids, finally stopping in a back eddy. Elated to be stopped and safe, they tied the *Wen* securely and walked along the shore. Lois thought she saw oars sticking up ahead. They ran, and there, floating peacefully in an eddy, was the *Mexican Hat*. Leaving Lois in sight of the two boats, Don walked upstream to let the others know they were safe.

Believing that Don and Lois were sure to capsize and drown and that the *Mexican Hat* and the *Wen* were lost, Norm had turned back at Rapid Four. Above Rapid Two he joined Elzada, Bill, and Gene, sitting dejectedly with the *Botany* tied nearby, eating dinner from cans without utensils, which were on the other boats.

As Norm sat down to eat, Don yelled from the opposite bank. Relieved that at least Don was safe, the four piled into the *Botany* and crossed the river in the strong current. "I never saw a better fight in my life than to see Norm crossing almost straight in that rough water," Elzada said.[9] Norm estimated the current at 20 miles per hour.

Now five members of the expedition were together, and they learned that Lois was safe, though alone. Don and Gene set out to rejoin Lois, but approaching darkness and the treacherous terrain prevented them from reaching her. They spent a miserable night on a large rock. Elzada, Norm, and Bill endured a cold, uncomfortable night without dry clothing or bedding. "All in all, it was a most unusual horrid night," Elzada later remarked in her journal.[10]

Though alone, Lois fared better than her companions. She had the bedding and plenty of food. She built a large fire, ate some toast and jam, and slept near the fire. Rising water forced her to move and build a new fire during the night, but as she later wrote to her mother, "Aside from a few ants, the rustling of packrats in the bushes, and the lapping and sucking of the waves, I had a lovely time."[11]

At first light, Don and Gene worked their way downstream to Lois's camp, finding her safe and comfortable. Norm brought the *Wen* through the rapids with Elzada and Gene aboard. The group, intact and safe, celebrated with a breakfast of venison steaks. They had survived their first test, but much awaited them. "This river's really showing its teeth," Elzada wrote in her journal that night.[12]

On their seventh day out, still in Cataract Canyon, they camped above a series of four rapids. Norm, Don, and Bill looked the rapids over and decided they could run the first two but would have to portage—physically carry the boats—around the latter two. The group, already fatigued, ran the first rapid and managed to get the *Wen* and the *Botany* through the second rapid, but the *Mexican Hat* had to be lined (guided with ropes) through the second rapid. They lined the *Botany* around the third rapid before, weary and exhausted, they stopped on a steep slope for the night.

Norm had trouble sleeping, worrying about the next day's efforts. He confided in his diary that the women were doing too much work whereas Gene didn't know how to work. Portgaging required tremendous effort. Tomorrow, all three boats would have to be completely unloaded and carried around the rapid. Then they would return for the supplies. It was tortuous work in difficult terrain under a hot June sun.

By this time, as will happen with small groups in trying situations, tensions were developing. Don and Gene thought Norm too cautious, that he was insisting they line rapids they could easily run. In her journal, Elzada noted that "Gene is inclined to be a little cynical of Norm's handling of lining, etc."[13]

In the morning the tired crew began unloading the boats and dragging them to the top of the slope above the rapid. This was by far the hardest day yet. Lois noted in her journal, "Painful as heck and hot. All of us pretty low, and Don feeling sick."[14] In fact, everyone but Norm and Elzada had been sick, probably from drinking river water without letting it settle, thereby irritating their digestive tracts. That evening before dinner Norm gave everyone a half-jigger of whiskey.

After a fitful night's sleep, they finished the portaging and by late afternoon were back on the river again. Spirits rose. They camped on a sandy beach, built a big campfire, and cooked a hearty meal. A light rain began to fall, and the men made a makeshift shelter. The group talked and laughed, listening to Norm's stories of his river-running escapades. When the rain turned into a downpour, they crawled into their bedrolls—but inside their flimsy shelter, they all got good and soaked.

They spent most of the next morning drying their clothes and gear. The river looked smooth as Norm headed for Gypsum Canyon, and he decided to forgo his customary scouting. He and Elzada led the way, running several rapids easily. At the mouth of Gypsum Canyon, a steep drop appeared out of nowhere. It was too late to pull for shore. Norm and Elzada hung on and miraculously stayed upright, but, as they looked back, the *Botany* flipped, tossing

Gene and Bill into the river. Gene hung onto the *Botany*, but Bill was nowhere in sight. Don and Lois made it through the drop, spotted Bill trying to swim to shore, and pulled him into the *Mexican Hat*. Norm managed to row to the capsized *Botany*. Elzada caught the bow line and pulled Gene into the *Wen*. Norm grabbed the stern rope, jumped out of the boat, and swam to shore, intending to tie the *Botany* and *Wen* together. "Got to shore as rope began to pull through my fingers. Couldn't hold it," Norm wrote.[15] The *Wen* swept out into the swift current. Gene negotiated eight rapids in the *Wen* while Elzada hung onto the bow rope of the *Botany*. Finally, 5 miles from where the *Botany* first flipped, Gene and Elzada pulled into an eddy, exhausted, but with both boats safe.

Norm ran, but unable to catch the boats, he signaled Bill, Don, and Lois to pick him up below the next rapid. The four—Norm, Bill, Don, and Lois—crowded into the *Mexican Hat*. "The worry," he wrote later, "just about shot my nerves. One boat and four passengers!" Norm feared that Elzada and Gene had drowned and lost both boats. How would he get the four of them out of the canyon? He said aloud, "This is the end of my career as a riverman."

Norm insisted on lining a small rapid in Clearwater Canyon even though Don argued that it was unnecessary. It took thirty minutes to line the rapid. A half mile downstream, they rounded the bend to the welcome sight of Elzada, Gene, and the boats, all safe. "The relief," Norm wrote later, "was more than words can describe."[16]

They made camp, Lois cooked supper, and they played a game of Hearts around the campfire before collapsing to their private thoughts. The series of mishaps had put the trip behind schedule. Norm now believed that their arrival at Boulder Dam (now Hoover Dam) would be between August 10 and 20, not the end of July as originally planned. Still, Norm refused to rush the trip and eliminate planned side trips.

On July 3, they pulled into the right bank above Trachyte Creek and walked to the Chaffin ranch, owned by a Mormon couple who had lived in the canyon for several years. The Chaffins served the river runners a feast: homemade bread and cheese, home-canned beef, fresh vegetables, and lots of coffee. Elzada recalled, "We all ate until we were nearly helpless." Lois said, "We fell to like harvest hands and had a wonderful time."[17]

They left in the late afternoon and drifted into Glen Canyon. This beautiful respite between Cataract Canyon and the Grand Canyon enchanted all who entered with its exquisite narrow side canyons, grottoes of hanging ferns, and tiny waterfalls. Today, Glen Canyon lies buried in the waters of Lake Powell, but then, for weary travelers, it meant smooth, comfortable river running. There were no major rapids for the next 149 miles, until Lees Ferry. The canyon itself was peaceful, but discontent stirred among the group. The younger members, Lois, Gene, Bill, and Don, began to float behind Norm and Elzada, comparing grievances, particularly about Norm, whom they found too high-handed and authoritarian.

Their estimated date of arrival at Lees Ferry had been July 4. The July 5 *Los Angeles Evening Herald and Express* headlined "Planes Seek Six Explorers" and announced that four daily Trans World Airline (TWA) flights would deviate from their routes while pilots looked for the missing Nevills party.[18]

Unaware that they were "missing," the group took time on July 6 to hike to Rainbow Bridge, the world's largest stone arch, standing 290 feet high and spanning 275 feet. Elzada commented in her journal that the bridge was "a breathtaking thing."[19] They all signed the visitor book kept in a galvanized box and then walked to Rainbow Camp, where people who came to see the bridge by the land route often stayed. The director of the camp had previously told Norm to use the food cache. Elzada made fifty biscuits in a dutch oven and opened several cans of food to make a delicious stew for lunch. They spent the afternoon climbing on the bridge and taking photos, and unable to resist, returned to the food cache and made more biscuits for dinner. It was dark before they made their way back to their own camp.

The next evening, July 7, as Lois cooked dinner, a small plane flew over them, circled once, and began dropping notes. One fell directly in camp. It read, "We are the U.S. Coast Guard plane searching for a party of six U. of Michigan geologists reportedly late at Lee's Ferry. If you are they, lie down all in a row, and then stand up. If in need of food, sit up. If members of party are all OK, extend arms horizontally. It is imperative that we know who you are, so identify yourself by first signal first."[20] Lois and Gene, the only ones in camp, had fun answering the instructions and waved as the pilot dipped his wings in acknowledgment.

After supper, now anxious to reach Lees Ferry, they floated on in the moonlight a few miles before setting up camp. Elzada and Don played their harmonicas as the others sang, "When It's Moonlight on the Colorado."

In the morning Don built a roaring campfire, and when everyone was up, announced that he would leave the trip at Lees Ferry. He worried that if he stayed with the trip he would not make his new job assignment in Salt Lake City on time. The group changed into clean clothes for their arrival at Lees Ferry and broke camp. Just before 10:00 A.M., they floated single file to the landing.

Reporters were sleeping and lying about in the sun. Norm shouted, "Church is out, we're here,"[21] and they scrambled awake, persuading Norm to restage their entry, which they did. The reporters then served the crew watermelon, which they ate sitting on a log, responding to questions between bites.

A flurry of activity took place during the brief layover, and the weary crew relished the chance to be landlubbers for the first time in three weeks. Bill, Gene, and Lois stayed at the Marble Canyon Lodge near Lees Ferry, and Norm and Elzada drove to Mexican Hat. Norm was anxious to see his wife, Doris, and young daughter. Enroute, they stopped at the Tuba City Trading Post to order more supplies. Upon learning that the trader's twenty-four-year-old cousin, Lorin Bell, had recently returned from a trip to the South Seas, Norm convinced him to join the expedition in Don's place. At Mexican Hat, Norm also convinced Del Reid, an acquaintance of the Nevills family then prospecting in the vicinity, to join the crew.

Back at Marble Canyon Lodge, Bill, Gene, and Lois were

HALDENE "BUZZ" HOLMSTROM GIVES A SOUVENIR TO LOIS JOTTER ON NAVAJO BRIDGE—HIS WATERPROOF MATCHCASE WITH A COMPASS. (Photo courtesy of the Lois Jotter Cutter Collection, Cline Library, Northern Arizona University, no. NAU.PH.95.3.27.)

surprised when Buzz Holmstrom, whose comment about women on the river had been widely reported, came to meet the expedition members. The three expeditioners shared their complaints about the trip with Buzz over dinner. Before leaving, as they walked out on Navajo Bridge, Buzz gave Lois a present, the waterproof matchcase with a compass that he had carried on his solo trip through the Canyon the previous year.

When he returned to Lees Ferry on July 13, Norm decided to meet the tensions head on. Believing that Gene was the major cause of the discontent, he told Gene that he had to leave the group.

A heated discussion followed, and finally Elzada convinced Gene that it was in his best interests to return to Michigan. That matter settled and new supplies loaded, the reorganized party left shortly after noon to begin the second leg of their trip. As they passed under Navajo Bridge, 467 feet above, a large crowd gathered to watch the now-famous group of river runners depart.

With Gene gone, tensions dissipated. Norm wrote in his journal that evening, "This is a swell gang and we're going to town."[22] Elzada commented, "The morale of the crowd is good,"[23] and later, "I'm glad Gene is gone. We have a fine bunch now."[24]

On July 16 they pulled into Vasey's Paradise near lunchtime. This garden paradise could well have served as a set for the movie *Jurassic Park*. Water jets out of the canyon wall 125 feet above the river, providing life for an abundance of plants. Elzada and Lois rushed to collect the red monkey flowers, paintbrush, and even the most abundant plant, poison ivy.

While they worked, the men grew impatient and hungry. Elzada remarked in her journal that the boys "wanted lunch, although it was not twelve o'clock. Finally, I suggested that they get out the lunch things. The four of them managed to round up bag number 2, but they were sitting bug-eyed and expectant under a rock when we came to them. They had not mixed the malt or anything. We have spoiled them completely."[25]

The next day they would arrive at Bright Angel Creek, but several major rapids lie in their way: Seventy-five Mile Rapid (called Nevills Rapid since 1966), Hance, Sockdolager, and Grapevine Rapids. This was the first real test with the new crew, but despite Norm's anxieties, all went well. At about 5 o'clock on July 19 the three boats rounded a curve to the left and saw the river gauging station and, 60 feet above the river, the Kaibab Suspension Bridge. Three newsmen on the bridge yelled, "Wave at us, look as if you were glad you're landing!"[26]

They camped that night on the beach near Bright Angel Creek. The next morning, everyone but Del hiked up the Bright Angel Trail. They started the 11-mile, 5,000-foot climb at dawn in an

THE "CREW" POSES AGAINST A MAGNIFICENT BACKDROP. L TO R, BILL GIBSON, LOIS JOTTER, LORIN BELL, ELZADA CLOVER, EMERY KOLB, AND NORM NEVILLS. (Photo courtesy of the Emery Kolb Collection, Cline Library, Northern Arizona University, no. NAU.PH.568-1137.)

attempt to get near the top before the intense summer sun hit the Canyon. The trail tops out at Emery Kolb's home and studio. Blanche Kolb met them with pitchers of iced tea and invited them to lunch. She offered the women hot baths, and Emery directed the men to the showers. Norm invited Emery to join them for the rest of the trip, and he accepted. Emery, already a well-known photographer and Canyon legend, had run the Colorado in 1910–1911 with his brother Ellsworth. His experience would be invaluable to the expedition.

Although it was a treat to sleep in a real bed, Lois and Elzada soon tired of all the attention. Wherever they went in Grand Canyon Village, they were besieged by autograph hunters. At 5:15 P.M. on

GRAND CANYON NATIONAL PARK SUPERINTENDENT M. R. TILLOT-
SON, ELZADA CLOVER, AND NORM NEVILLS. (Photo courtesy of the
Grand Canyon National Park Museum Collection.)

July 21, after dinner and singing around the Kolbs' piano, the group
started back down the Bright Angel Trail and into the Canyon.

The next morning, boats were loaded and a false start
staged so Emery could take movies. They had 247 miles to go before pulling into Lake Mead, the end of their journey. Norm estimated that it would take two more weeks, allowing time for plant
gathering. They ran or lined several major rapids—Horn Creek,
Granite Falls Rapid, Hermit Rapid, Serpentine Rapid. Lois and
Elzada found an abundance of cacti in this section of the river, including many large barrel cacti. Elzada noted in her journal, "Must
go now and collect plants. You've no idea how difficult it is to keep
the mind on mere plants when the river is roaring and the boats are
struggling to get through."[27]

Emery Kolb was a great addition to the trip. In addition to
being a skilled river runner, he played the harmonica and told

ELZADA CLOVER STUDIES A SUCCULENT AT THE GRAND CANYON.
(Photo courtesy of the Grand Canyon National Park Museum
Collection.)

stories. Elzada wrote in her journal, "You should see Mr. Kolb
standing up on the stern holding to ropes, riding the waves in his
BVD's, shirtail out, life preserver on, and a red hankie of mine fixed
into a knotted affair on his head. He just loves this life."[28]

Their final challenge would be the 37-foot drop at Lava
Falls. The group pulled in for lunch just ahead of the rapid, and the
more Norm studied it, the more he thought he could do it; but he
believed the chances of capsizing were great and so decided to line it.
After an extremely difficult day, all three boats were lined through
Lava Falls. That night, everyone was tired, but the worst was over.
Norm predicted they would arrive at Lake Mead in three days.

The last days were anticlimatic. On July 29 after breakfast,

Emery officiated over the River Rat Initiation Ceremony, initiating Norm, who then initiated the others. Each novice, on hands and knees, heads deeply bowed, repeated after Norm, as he had done after Emery, "I know I'm weak, I know I'm blind, I swear that I extend behind."[29] As the word "behind" was uttered, Norm gave them each a resounding swat with a life preserver.

The next day, July 30, at 5:11 P.M., Norm wrote, "We're on the LAKE."[30] They were 80 miles from the dock at Boulder Dam. With no current, unless someone came to tow them in, it would be a long, hot row. The "intrepid explorers" rose at 4:00 A.M. on August 1 and rowed four hours before pulling into a side canyon for lunch and a nap. While eating, they thought they heard a motor, and everyone ran out to the point to yell and wave. The boat turned and roared into the side canyon. It was Buzz Holmstrom at the wheel of the *Navaho,* a 20-foot powerboat. Their rowing hours ended as the three boats were tied to the powerboat. What a relief! Civilization was never a more welcome sight. Buzz wrote on Lois's helmet, "To the girl who proved me badly mistaken."[31] Women, he'd decided, did belong on the river after all!

The trip took forty-three days. Elzada and Lois claimed the distinction of being the first women to raft the Colorado River successfully through the Grand Canyon. Trip over, the group went to Boulder Dam Hotel to enjoy the comforts of a hot shower and soft bed. The next day, their history making adventure over, the group split up, returning to their normal pursuits.

This would be Elzada Clover's only trip through the Grand Canyon. She often gave talks about her adventure and always informed her botany classes that she was the first woman to run the Grand Canyon. A complete report of her and Lois's botanical findings appeared in the November 1944 *American Midland Naturalist* under the title "Floristic Studies in the Canyon of the Colorado River and Tributaries." Following her retirement in 1967, Elzada, by then a full professor, moved to the Rio Grande Valley in Texas to be near one of her sisters. She led an active life until her death in 1980 at the age of eighty-three.

Lois returned to Michigan to complete work for her Ph.D. She married Victor Cutter Jr. in 1942 and finished her doctoral thesis while her husband was teaching at Cornell University. In 1947 they moved to Connecticut, where he taught at Yale for five years; they next moved to Greensboro, North Carolina, where he became chairman of the Department of Biology at the University of North Carolina. Lois devoted her time to raising their two children, Ann and Victor III. In 1963, following her husband's death, Lois joined the faculty at the University of North Carolina as assistant professor of botany. She retired in 1984.

Lois returned to the Colorado River in September 1994 to join the Legends Trip, a group of "old-timers" whose purpose was to compare river conditions before and after the construction of Glen Canyon Dam. At the Grand Canyon River Guides Seminar in late March 1995, Lois, a tall, distinguished woman with a friendly smile, braved a harsh spring storm to tell stories and share experiences with fellow river rats. She still has the waterproof matchcase and compass given to her by Buzz Holmstrom on Navajo Bridge.

8
In Powell's Wake
DORIS NEVILLS
(1914–1949)

DORIS AND NORM NEVILLS, WITH THEIR DAUGHTERS SANDRA
JANE (LEFT) AND JOAN ELIZABETH. (Photo courtesy of the
Manuscripts Division, J. Willard Marriott Library, University
of Utah, ca. 1946.)

"I *CERTAINLY HOPE THESE* boats will do better in the water
than they have on the truck," Doris Nevills thought as she sat
hunched beside her husband, Norm, in the middle boat of a three-
boat rack in the back of Ray Lyman's pickup truck, headed for the
adventure of her life.[1] Just two years after Norm Nevills had managed the University of Michigan botany expedition team through

the Grand Canyon, he had put together a second Grand Canyon trip, this one to follow the route of John Wesley Powell's historic 1869 voyage through the Grand Canyon from Green River, Wyoming, to Lake Mead on the Arizona-Nevada border, a river journey of 1,100 miles. Doris would be joining Norm for a trip through scenery too beautiful for words—and getting soaked going through rapids, eating food mixed with sand, and coping with mosquitos, intense heat, and driving rain. But on this hot June morning in 1940, all of that lie ahead, and Doris believed that the ride in the back of the truck surely must be the hardest part of the trip.

Nineteen-year-old Doris had met Norm at a dance in Monticello, Utah, in July 1933, and she soon realized that Norm did not hesitate to pursue his dreams, which included a life with her. Early on the morning of October 19, 1933, after only three dates, they went to the General Store in Bluff, Utah, to get a marriage license and were married that afternoon.

They spent their first winter together planning, secretly, a honeymoon voyage down the San Juan River. They told no one, according to Norm, because people would think they were crazy. They planned to travel 67 river miles from Mexican Hat to Copper Canyon, without maps. They wanted the excitement of not knowing what was around the next bend.

An old horse trough and privy provided the lumber for the boat. Norm patched knot holes with tin and stuffed old undershirts into the cracks. His mother's curtain rods served as oar shafts, and "borrowed" Utah State Highway signs made useable oar blades. When a test run in February resulted in a tear in the bottom of the boat, Norm cut sheet tin into 3-inch strips and used them to cover the bottom and sides of the boat. He painted the makeshift boat white, and in March 1934, Norm and Doris set out in "Old Whitey."

Norm described their "honeymoon voyage" in a brief autobiography written in 1939.

We are but a few hours out when the little rapids and riffles arise to bar our progress. In the fast current we sweep into

DORIS AND NORM NEVILLS ON TOP OF MEXICAN HAT, UTAH, 1934. (Photo courtesy of Manuscripts Division, J. Willard Marriott Library, University of Utah.)

the rapids and more by good luck than good management we get thru them. . . . Doris and I have much fun in trying to tell [apart] a wave caused by sand and those caused by rocks. Doris is generally right. Drifting along we both suddenly sit up straighter and peer down the river. WAVES! "It's a rock," says Doris. "No, a wave," I reply. "No, no, it's a rock!" "A wave!" . . . BANG! It *was* a rock![2]

The couple survived the various rocks and waves of the San Juan and returned a week later to a quiet life in Mexican Hat, Utah. Norm loved being on the river, and he continued to experiment with boat designs over the years. Encouraged by the success of his first trip through the Grand Canyon, Norm spent the following year taking passengers on the San Juan River from Mexican Hat to Lees Ferry. He built two new boats and a three-boat rack and, two years after his first Grand Canyon trip, organized the trip that found him and Doris hunched among the *Wen*, the *Joan*, and the *Mexican Hat II*.

Norm was to pilot the *Wen*; Del Reid, veteran of the 1938 run, would man the *Joan*; and Hugh Cutler, from the Missouri Botanical Gardens, would steer the *Mexican Hat II*. Doris planned all the meals and would do most of the cooking. Paying passengers included John Southworth, a mining engineer; Charles Larabee, the trip photographer; B. W. Deason, an assayer; and Mildred Baker, a middle-aged schoolteacher whom Norm first met at Rainbow Bridge during the 1938 trip. Anne Rosner, a schoolteacher, and Barry Goldwater, a merchant from Phoenix, Arizona, would join the group at Green River, Utah. The expedition would also include some rather unusual passengers: Carrier pigeons provided by the *Salt Lake Tribune*. Doris planned to attach messages to the legs of the pigeons and send them off to carry updates of the trip to the paper's news staff.

Doris, now twenty-six years old, had worked hard getting ready for the trip. "I have worked with the food so much the last two months that I have even dreamed about it," she wrote in her journal. She was relieved to get out of the truck as they pulled into Green River, Wyoming. It was 6:00 A.M. on June 19, the day before they were to leave. She caught a short nap and a last visit to a beauty shop to get ready for the banquet given by the Green River National Community Club. They had a great time, and on behalf of the governor of Utah, the club presented Norm with three license plates for the boats. Although Doris knew she would miss their three-year-old daughter, Joan, who was staying with Norm's mother, she looked forward to the trip.

The next morning was a bustle of activity. Doris picked up the pigeons. "I immediately fell in love with them," she said. "They made such soft noises and sounded as if they are telling each other what they think about it all." The group spent the early hours loading the boats. They left Green River, Wyoming, at 10:00 A.M.

Seventy-one years earlier, John Wesley Powell had left this same point. On May 24, 1869, he wrote in his log, "The good people of Green River City turn out to see us start."[3] Doris also noted that quite a crowd came to watch them. "Everyone waves and shouts, 'Good Luck,'" Doris wrote, adding, "I imagine we will need luck at different times." The trip began peacefully—getting acquainted with one another, joking when Norm ran onto a sandbar, and swimming off the boats in calm water. In camp that evening, Mildred helped Doris with dinner. Afterwards, tired and happy to be underway, the group slept the first of many nights under the stars.

The next morning Doris dispatched the first carrier pigeons. She strapped messages to the legs of birds 714, 720, and 719 and gave them a swoop into the air. "They looked so beautiful as they circled and left for Salt Lake," she commented in her journal.

As the group entered Flaming Gorge Canyon, now submerged in the waters of Flaming Gorge Dam, they encountered the first hardships of the trip. A strong headwind blew sheets of water at them and made rowing extremely difficult. That evening, mosquitos plagued the group despite the several smudge pots they kept burning. "I have never seen so many [mosquitos]," Doris noted. "They came in clouds." After a dinner of potatoes, roast beef, peas, soup, fruit cocktail, tea, and coffee, Doris stole into bed early, hoping to escape the mosquitos. The bad introduction to Flaming Gorge notwithstanding, Doris exclaimed in her journal: "This is certainly beautiful country. I am amazed that more people don't see it. I'd love to camp and hike all over here."

The next morning, the group passed through Ashley Falls—the first really technical water they met on the trip—without incident. As they prepared to run the falls, and all the while they were running it, Doris kept thinking about Powell's experience. "I wonder what Major Powell thought as he drifted down the river and then suddenly heard a roar like a freight train entering a depot. What courage that man had and how indomitable in his purpose he was." To celebrate their smooth running of the rapid, Norm, Charlie, and Hugh carved Nevills Expedition 1940 with the group's names underneath on a wall opposite the falls.

As they emerged from Flaming Gorge Canyon, the river again calmed. To break the boredom and to get fresh supplies, they occasionally stopped at ranches along the Green River. At the Jessie Taylor ranch the group learned about the progress of the war in Europe. "We seem very far away from the turmoil of war," Doris wrote. "Somehow Hitler fails to stir us up." A few miles downstream at the Charlie Taylor ranch, Doris purchased eggs, milk, and coffee. She had figured on one pound of coffee for every two days, but Del and Charlie drank so much that she realized they would run out soon.

At Disaster Falls—so named by Powell because his boat, the *No Name*, broke in two there—the Nevills also courted disaster. Norm studied the falls and decided that by going quickly to the right of the rock in the middle of the narrow channel, they could make it easily. The *Wen* and the *Mexican Hat II* went through beautifully, but Del in the *Joan* went down the left side and got caught up high and dry on the rock with Mildred and Charlie on board. When rocking the boat didn't loosen it, Hugh and Norm crossed the river in the *Wen* and pulled on the boat's line as its passengers rocked until the *Joan* slid off the rock with a grating sound. "It made me feel awful to see a boat take such punishment," Doris wrote later. Norm feared the boat would need time-consuming repairs, but an examination revealed no significant damage.

The next day, as they approached Hell's Half Mile, they heard a deep rumbling roar. "Major Powell named this rapid most fittingly, as the river here plunges madly at first, one rock and then another," Doris wrote. Powell noted, "The river tumbles for half a mile with a descent of a hundred feet, in a channel beset with great numbers of huge boulders."[4] Norm signaled the boats to shore so he could study the rapid. He told Hugh and Del the course he planned to take, then directed the passengers to make their way around the rapid on foot. Doris felt sick with fear as she watched Norm lead the way through the water, and as she and the others slipped on rocks and fought their way through the underbrush, she worried that he and the other pilots would not make it safely. An hour and a half later, all the boats were through without mishap, and none of the walkers had more than a few scratches.

The next morning, Doris decided to send off one of her two remaining pigeons. She wrote a message, put it in the bird's leg capsule, and released the pigeon; but instead of flying toward Salt Lake City, as all of the others had done, it flew directly across the river and sat on a rock. "The remaining pigeon paced frantically back and forth in the cage. We concluded they must be mates, and since we don't care to witness such distress I hurriedly wrote another note and strapped it on the other pigeon. The pigeon that had been left couldn't possibly have seen where the other one went, yet he flew unerringly until he was within a few feet of her, and she joined him, then they flew swiftly towards Salt Lake. This was one of the most thrilling sights I've ever witnessed," she wrote.

After eighteen days on the river, the group arrived at Green River, Utah. Don Harris volunteered to watch the boats while the group spent an evening enjoying the comforts of a restaurant and real beds. "I was shocked when I saw myself in a mirror," Doris said, remembering her suntanned and wind-chapped skin. Norm's mother drove up from Mexican Hat so that little Joan could see her parents. Joan's first comments were, "Mommie, your nose is sunburned. Where are your pigeons?"

The two new members, Anne Rosner and Barry Goldwater, joined the group, and B. W. Deason left for Salt Lake City. He would rejoin the expedition at Bright Angel Creek, and Anne would leave the party there. Barry planned to stay with the group to the end of the trip. Norm purchased three outboard motors in Green River and attached them to the boats with the hope of making better time on the long, smooth stretches. They left Green River that afternoon.

Doris could barely contain her excitement when, on July 14, the expedition neared the confluence of the Green and Colorado Rivers. "I feel impatient to be off and finally in the rapids. I have heard so much of Cataract Canyon that I can hardly wait to see it." They came to the junction of the Green and Colorado Rivers about midmorning. "One can immediately feel the difference in these two rivers," Doris wrote. "The Colorado feels so strong and mighty." Powell had written at this point, "The River is rough and bad rapids in close succession are found."[5]

After the first rapid, Norm looked back at Doris and said, "Well, how do you like Cataract?" "Swell," she replied. Later she wrote in her journal, "I am so glad to be here. Cataract is a forbidding canyon with its high sheer walls, and I feel as if the canyon is embodied with a personality. It seems to offer us a challenge and dare us to conquer and yet to be too proud to stoop to notice us invading its sanctuary. I love Cataract, with its rough, wild ruggedness. To me it is the most beautiful stretch on the whole river."

Cataract showed its power at Rapid 24. "This rapid is the most terrifying thing I've seen yet," Doris wrote. "It has the most terrific roar imaginable. You can't hear a person shouting at the top of his voice even though he is only twenty feet away. The water dashes over these huge rock with an inhuman violence." Norm studied the rapid and decided that he, Del, and Hugh should take the boats through without passengers.

As Doris watched from the shore, Norm went first in the

Wen and then guided Hugh safely through in the *Mexican Hat*, but Del, in the *Joan*, missed the starting position by two or three feet. "It was immediately apparent to all of us watching he'd be wrecked," Doris wrote in her journal. Del swung to the right, nearly capsized, and then crashed between two rocks. Norm, Barry, and John jumped in the *Wen* and rowed toward Del and the boat. As they worked the *Joan* loose, it took off and turned over, exposing a 6-inch hole in the prow deck. Although everything was soaked and the boat was damaged, Del pulled through okay.

They spent most of the next day drying things out and working on the wrecked boat. "I feel almost physical pain when anything happens to our boats," Doris wrote in her journal. "They are such gallant and courageous crafts. It's all right to tell oneself they are mere wood, but when they turn in such magnificent performance time and time again, one soon regards them with affectionate concern."

Despite the upset, Doris had mixed emotions when they left Cataract Canyon on July 20. "This canyon is so beautiful," she wrote. "Its depth in places is almost unbelievable, and at every turn of the river something new in coloring and weird formations is presented." Still, she was anxious to continue downstream to see Glen Canyon, where a calm Colorado would wend its way through a labyrinth of exquisite canyons (now buried under the waters of Lake Powell). One of them was Hidden Passage Canyon, 800 feet deep and only 35 feet wide, of which Doris wrote, "A more beautiful spot would be hard to find. There is running water and deep narrow pools, regular bath tub pools."

A few miles downriver, they reached an alcove, named Music Temple by Powell. Doris commented, "Upon entering this alcove we find a small grove of box elder and cottonwood trees; and turning to the right, we find ourselves in a large room, carved out of rock. At the upper end there is a clear deep pool of water. This room is more than two hundred feet high, five hundred feet long, and two hundred feet wide." Major Powell camped at this spot, and to quote from Powell, "when 'old Shady' sings us a song at night, we are pleased to find that this hollow in the rock is filled with sweet sounds. It was doubtless made for an academy of music by its storm-born architect, so we named it Music Temple."[6] Shady, Powell's brother's nickname, entertained the group with songs nearly every evening. Carved into the wall of Music Temple, Doris and her mates found the names of all the members of the Powell expedition: P. M. Bishop '71; F. S. Dellenbough '71; J. K. Hillers '70–'71; W. D. Johnson '72; J. F. Steward '71; W. C. Powell '71; and J. W. Powell '70–'71. That evening Norm pitched camp in Forbidding Canyon, the gateway to Bridge Canyon and Rainbow Bridge. Doris wrote, "I am so thrilled that tomorrow I shall see Rainbow Bridge."

The next morning the group headed up Bridge Canyon bound for the bridge, a 290-foot-tall natural stone arch. "I shall not describe the bridge because words can't do it justice," she wrote. "Just to look at such a beautiful thing makes me feel rested and somehow at peace with everything. One forgets the pettiness of life and its worries. Out here things are so big and great [that] one feels quite unimportant in the plan of life."

A sudden rainstorm hit while they fixed lunch near Wiley's Camp at the base of Rainbow Bridge. After the rain passed, Doris, Norm, and John started out to look at Bridge Creek, curious to see if it had any water in it, when they heard a roar. "Norm and John were ahead of me and kept urging me to hurry, but I was running at top speed, and over the rocky ground it wasn't easy," she wrote. "However, we all got to the edge of the canyon just in time to see Bridge Creek come down in flood. I have never seen a more thrilling sight. There was this dry wash and the next minute a wall of water 12 feet high swept down, carrying huge timbers that would hit the walls at different bends in the wash." The expedition had planned to spend the night at Wiley's Camp, but Norm decided they should return to the river and see if the boats had been damaged by the flash flood.

After waiting several hours for the creek to go down, they started back. "The wash was terribly deep in spots where the pools were," Doris wrote, "so Norm would go ahead with a stick, feeling his way, and then he'd toss the rope to Del if the water was too swift, and Del would secure the rope, and then I'd go across holding the rope." They hurried, trying to beat the impending darkness. "We crossed and recrossed the canyon and the stream. Got in at 7:30 P.M. Six miles in two hours and 35 minutes!" she wrote. Fortunately the boats were not damaged, and so the group decided to relax another day.

Doris and Norm spent most of the next day alone, exploring a canyon Norm had heard about. They expected to find pools of water, but as they continued to hike up the narrow canyon, all they found was dried curls of mud. Norm kept saying, "Just around one more bend, honey." Finally Doris rebelled. "No, not one more bend. I'm going to lie right down here in the middle of this wash, and you go on for another five minutes. Then if you find it, yell and I'll come." As Norm walked on, Doris felt very much alone in the dark, narrow canyon. "I kept thinking what would happen if a flood came down it. There was absolutely no place to climb out," she said later.

Back on the river, they left beautiful Glen Canyon and floated the short distance to Lees Ferry. There Norm borrowed a truck and drove to Marble Canyon Lodge, where Doris and Norm learned that Doris's mother had a broken ankle. They rushed to Mexican Hat and found that things were running smoothly. After a brief reunion with little Joan, Doris and Norm drove back to Marble Canyon. Doris wrote, "I have never seen a more magic night. As we rode along we could see the lights from the Navaho fires dotting the desert. Norm and I sang all the songs we could remember."

They were back on the river again by August 4, heading into the Grand Canyon. "It's simply perfect to be back in fast water and have the feeling of exhilaration and accomplishment and then at the end of the day to have the companionship of one's brother 'River Rats,'" she wrote.

Norm's experience was evident now as he guided the boats through Unkar Creek, Hance, Sockdolager, Grapevine, and 83 Miles rapids in a push to get to Phantom Ranch. They pulled in at Bright Angel Creek at 5:30 P.M. on August 9 and hiked the mile up to Phantom Ranch. There they rested for two days. "Showers, iced tea, a swim in the swimming pool, a bed. In short, heaven!" Doris commented in her journal.

As Anne Rosner hiked out on Bright Angel Trail, B. W. Deason rode down on a mule, ready to rejoin the group. "I can't help but compare our party as it is now and as we were when we started out," Doris wrote that evening. "Our gaiety and light-heartedness is gone. We have a job to do now—get thru this canyon. We wouldn't have it otherwise—none of us would abandon this trip. The thrill of seeing new country as we go on, and the sense of real accomplishment, is something we would not trade for all of the ease and comforts of civilization—however, we are tired." It had been twenty days since she had left Wyoming.

The party left the comforts of Phantom Ranch on August 12 and three days later came to a small rapid that was not even on their map. Norm asked John how it looked; he stood up on the stern deck to be able to see better, and replied, "Doesn't look like anything—may be a hole there." Doris lay on her stomach to hold on better and took a good grip of the ropes. "I was watching Norm's face when all of a sudden a wall of water came over my head, making it impossible for me to see him. The next second I felt my body floating. I still had hold of the rope but I was in the river. My first and only thought was 'what a funny time to be without life preservers.' Because no bad water was indicated on the map, we didn't have them on. Then I felt a real tug and the boys pulled me in the cockpit of the boat and dropped me like a sack of meal," she wrote. Doris Rapid, as it has since been known, is now noted on most maps of the river.

In the days following the excitement of Doris Rapid, the expedition coped with more tricky rapids, bailed out boats, marveled at the scenery, and on August 23, sixty-three days after they put in at Green River, Wyoming, arrived at Lake Mead. In her final comments written during the trip, Doris noted, "We have come 1,100 miles—hard, yet beautiful miles. . . . One learns more of the true value of things. In the canyon only the essentials count. . . . Some day I'll go again."

Reflecting on the trip, she expressed admiration for Norm's skills. "Our intentions were to follow the path of Major Powell, and we have accomplished that. To me it is a very remarkable and praiseworthy deed to have gotten nine people down this river without a mishap. Nine people, and each one having his own ideas as to how an expedition should be run. Heaven deliver me from ever being an expedition leader! I know I will often have a feeling of nostalgia for this canyon and the river."

As the trip came to an end, the group signed each other's hats. Barry lost his and asked everyone to sign his air mattress. He later gave talks about his trip, and in part because of his reception, he decided to run for political office. It was the beginning of a long and successful career in the United States Senate.

This was Doris's only complete trip of the Colorado River through the Grand Canyon. She and Mildred Baker earned the distinction of being the first women to retrace Powell's expedition from Green River, Wyoming, to Lake Mead.

After World War II ended, the Nevills established a full-fledged commercial river running business, heralding the beginning of river running as we know it today. Doris was responsible for meals: she reprovisioned trips at Hite, Utah; Lees Ferry; and Phantom Ranch and cached food at several places for the San Juan River trips. She and Norm added a fourth boat to their fleet, the *Sandra*, named for their youngest daughter, Sandra Jane.[7]

Because roads were often impassable in the remote desert country, Norm in 1946 bought a Piper Cub airplane. He named it *Cherry*, his affectionate name for Doris. By 1949, with a new airplane—the *Cherry II*—and a fleet of sturdy boats, the Nevills had a successful river running operation. In September of that year Norm closed a deal with the Sierra Club to escort seventy-five people through Glen Canyon, and he finalized plans for a movie-making run for Walt Disney Studios. Supplies were ordered to build new boats for the Disney trip. Norm and Doris's future was as bright as a Canyon dawn.

Then late one September afternoon, Doris received a telegram with news of the unexpected death in California of her favorite uncle. She was deeply saddened by the news and wanted to be with her aunt as soon as possible. Norm offered to fly her to Grand Junction, Colorado, that night to catch a commercial flight to California, but Doris said she could wait until the next morning.

As dawn spread across the desert in its rich red hues, Doris and Norm made their way to the *Cherry II*. Sandra waited expectantly in the front doorway as she watched the plane take off and grow smaller in the brightening sky. As always, the plane turned and made its way back, high in the air, toward the house. Little Sandra waved at her parents, but when her father dipped one of the plane's wings to wave back as he always did, the motor coughed and fell silent. It glided over the house, sputtering and flailing in the air like a broken bird as Norm tried desperately, without success, to restart the motor. The plane crashed into the side of a draw behind the house and burst into flames.

Three years later, on July 11, 1952, a group of Doris and Norm's friends gathered for the dedication of a memorial plaque to be placed on the rim of Marble Canyon below the western end of Navajo Bridge, overlooking the Colorado River. Joan and Sandra Nevills unveiled the plaque, which reads:

They run the rivers of eternity
In memory of
NORMAN D. NEVILLS
April 9, 1908–September 19, 1949
and—DORIS—his wife
March 11, 1914–September 19, 1949
Who sought & ran & mastered
The wild and secret waters
San Juan River—Green River
Colorado River—Grand Canyon
Salmon River—Snake River

By the river they loved so well
In the desert that was their
Home, this record is placed by
The Canyoneers.

Today, on any summer day, visit Lees Ferry, Arizona, the put-in point for boat trips through the Grand Canyon, and you will see the legacy of Norm and Doris Nevills: People getting onto boats, heading down the Canyon to meet the adventure of their lives.

9
A Canyon Trailblazer

GALE BURAK

(1918–)

GALE BURAK AND HER GRAND CANYON. (Photo courtesy of Gale Burak.)

G*ALE GARDNER BURAK* was twenty-four when she first saw the Grand Canyon in May 1942. Like the blink of an eye where strangers fall instantly in love, she knew with her first breath of Canyon air that it had become part of her and she had become part of it. Through the dissolution of one marriage and the embrace of the next, across the births of three children, moves from place to place, and managing a business, Gale would return again and again to the Canyon like a homing pigeon. She would live, hike, visit, and work there in the course of her life; its expanse gave her the three greatest gifts her independent nature craved: solitude and freedom in a setting of stupendous beauty.

"Everyone thought I was crazy," Gale said of her earliest days in the Canyon. "After all, I was one of the few nuts, male or female, who hiked in the '40s. Everyone rode a mule in those days. Hiking! Imagine!"[1] And hike she did, usually alone, across more trails and to more remote places in the Canyon than any other woman. The Grand Canyon became, as her daughter Pam would say years later, "mom's backyard."

Gale was born, she said, "with wanderlust in my blood." She learned about seeing new places early in life as her father, who worked for a large chemical company headquartered in Boston, helped start up new plants. "Each time he was sent to a new city, we went too. I'd moved ten times by age twelve," Gale explained, "but mostly I grew up in the suburbs of Boston." She loved the outdoors and as a teenager joined the Appalachian Mountain Club, where she was introduced to hiking, white water canoeing, skiing, and rock climbing in the White Mountains north of Boston.

"By the time I graduated from high school, I really had itchy feet and was ready to move," Gale said. But she married Reuel "Mac" McLaughlin instead, a man much older than herself. "I shouldn't have. It wasn't a very happy marriage. Mac contracted tuberculosis and had to be in a sanitarium for a year and then needed another year of convalescence. The doctor advised us to go out West."

Gale contacted a married school friend who lived on a ranch east of Springerville, Arizona, and made arrangements for them to live there for a few months, helping with the chores, while they decided where to settle. "It was wonderful," Gale said. "I hiked from one end of the Penasco Valley to the other. . . . [There was] such beauty to this barren country that it just was immediately home. When we left the ranch we decided to take a look at the

BURAK, SPORTING HER SIGNATURE PIGTAILS, STANDS BEFORE A MAGNIFICENT BACKDROP. (Photo courtesy of Gale Burak.)

Grand Canyon before settling down. I was overwhelmed. I tele-phoned my mother and said, 'Send me my clothes and my bicycle, I've found Utopia.'" Gale wanted the bicycle for exploring around the South Rim of the Canyon.

Gale and Mac, by now well again, both enjoyed the Canyon and wanted more time to explore. They found jobs at the Fred Har-vey Motor Lodge—Gale as a waitress, and Mac as a maintenance man. The nation was in the midst of World War II, and most busi-ness at the Canyon involved soldiers on "R and R"—rest and relax-ation. "The army had a big mechanized unit outside of Kingman, Arizona, and the men were brought up to the Canyon for R and R," Gale explained. "The Motor Lodge was one of the places they came because they didn't have much money. I got a lot of proposals of one kind and another," she laughed.

The Air Force came to the Canyon, too. "In the morning we would hear a rumble to the south, and it would be pursuit planes from the Phoenix bases," Gale recalled. "They would come in for-mation, a few at a time. They would aim for the flagpole by the El Tovar Hotel and dive-bomb down just above it, then just keep going on down into the Canyon, zooming out north, east, or west, once they got down. A normal sound in the Canyon is amplified, whether it's a voice, a bird, or the roar of a river. When you add mechanical noise, it is certainly not conducive to serenity in the Canyon!"

The serenity of the Canyon did not help Gale's relationship with Mac, and a few months after getting jobs at the Canyon, they agreed to divorce. "He took the car, and I kept my bicycle and the Canyon. I got the better deal for sure," Gale said.

After Mac left, Gale usually ate dinner with the Fred Harvey wranglers who took "dudes"—Eastern tourists—into the Canyon. The wranglers gave her the nickname "Pigtails" in reference to her preferred hairstyle. "It was fun to have dinner at the transportation dining room in the back of El Tovar," Gale said. "I used to listen to them try to outdo each other with 'trail tales.' I enjoyed these stories, and the men were good to me. I never really minded when they called me 'that doggone crazy Pigtails.'"

GOOD FRIENDS EMERY KOLB AND GALE BURAK. (Photo courtesy of Gale Burak.)

During this time Gale became friends with Emery Kolb, the famous photographer and Canyon explorer who had been living at the Canyon since 1902, and his family. In his younger days, Emery had hiked all over the Canyon, so he was a wellspring of information about areas Gale could explore. In return, she would visit Emery after her trips and share stories about what she did and what she saw. Unable to explore the Canyon as deeply and fully as he once could, Emery relished the opportunity to compare notes with this intrepid, pigtailed explorer. "He hiked vicariously through me," Gale explained.

She arranged her work schedule so she'd have a few days off in a row. "Sometimes I'd pop down to Phantom Ranch after work for an exploring trip up Phantom Creek, up to Utah Flats, over to Clear Creek, or to the North Rim for a few days," she said. Gale especially enjoyed moonlight hikes where she felt herself float down the thin, white thread of trail into a breathless shimmering void. "I can still feel the thrill of those night hikes. Cliff walls dipped away in successive waves of looming then lessening glow and shadow, indistinctly softening into nothingness away from me."

Midnight might find her taking a quick swim in the Phantom Ranch swimming pool before going to bed in the little stone cabin that her friends Phil and Em Poquette, ranch managers, kept open for her. "It was bliss just to stretch out and breathe in the Canyon night as sleep gradually stole over me. There'll never be better nights than those; never be times of feeling so sublimely alone yet so completely part of that wonderful world."

Come daylight, Gale would head out with some leftover hotcakes, a chunk of cheese, and an apple or two given to her by Em or Phil. When she got out of sight of Phantom Ranch, off came most of her clothes. "I am, I must admit, by nature a nudist, and even though the theory is to be sure to cover and conserve the moisture of your body, I am much happier when I'm freer," Gale said.

Gale would pull off her hiking boots along Bright Angel Creek, for in the 1940s there were no bridges in Box Canyon, and she had to wade. "Eventually my feet got so tough that I'd go barefoot between crossings. I had the Canyon to myself. It was bliss."

Gale often hiked from the South Rim to the North Rim and back, seeing no one save an occasional fisherman in Bright Angel Creek and the staff at Phantom Ranch. "I'm so sorry that people can't experience that today," she said. With over five million visitors each year, of which perhaps a quarter are either day or backpacking hikers, it is quite impossible and not even permissible for one to find such solitude there now.

When time permitted, Gale headed out for several days of more distant backpacking. "At first, I had a heavy wooden pack that I'd made myself. Then I started using a blanket roll. I put my food, spare socks, a long-sleeved shirt, and a canteen in the center of the blanket. I'd tie it on [to myself] different ways, either over one shoulder like the doughboys used to do in World War I or else I had it around my shoulders and dangling in front of me, and then I tied it to my waist. I would just decide which direction I was going in and I would tell either a friend or a ranger on the rim or Phil and Em where I was headed. I would establish a base camp and hike out from the camp." These were days and nights of pure solitude. Time was limitless, and Gale would spend hours exploring side canyons for hidden waterfalls or Indian ruins. At night she'd watch millions of stars ignite the sky as she fell asleep atop her bedroll.

Gale's initial time at the Canyon was too short. She was transferred to Fred Harvey's Escalante Hotel 30 miles south of the Canyon in Ash Fork, Arizona, at the end of the summer tourist season. She worked there until the following spring, when she quit to hike down Havasu Canyon to Supai, a village in the western end of the Grand Canyon that was home to three hundred Havasupai Indians. Havasu Canyon is an oasis in the desert—striking blue-green foaming waterfalls tumble through red sandstone cliffs to form deep blue bathtublike pools. Over a mile below the village, Havasu Falls cascades about 90 feet, and a mile farther down the Canyon, spectacular Mooney Falls drops nearly 200 feet, forming a large pool at its base.

Unlike today, when helicopters fly daily into the Canyon and electricity and satellite dishes connect the Havasupai with the outside world, in 1943 they lived an isolated life deep in the Canyon. Although some of the tribe worked at the South Rim of the Canyon, most remained on the reservation, growing their own food and eeking out a meager existence, either by farming or working for the small lead and zinc mine halfway between Havasu and Mooney Falls. They were well known for their peach orchards and each fall celebrated the harvest with a rodeo and Peach Festival. Although many visitors came each year for the festival, few tourists came at other times during the year.

BURAK AT HAVASU FALLS. (Photo courtesy of Gale Burak.)

Anyone going down to Supai then caught a ride with Foster Marshall from the South Rim post office out to Tocopoba Hilltop. Marshall hauled the mail and other supplies to the hilltop every two weeks, meeting a Havasupai packer, Lorenzo Sinyella, and his strings of horses there. As Gale climbed in the back of Marshall's pickup and found a seat on a mail sack, she met two women who were also traveling into Havasu Canyon. Gladys Broderson and Sonia Buchholz had already explored Supai on horseback on several previous trips. The three women got acquainted during the bouncy 35-mile ride to Tocopoba, at which place the two women mounted horses for the trip, and Gale set off gaily down on foot to the village. They spent the late afternoons that week together comparing their separate adventures, Gale on foot and Gladys and Sonia on horseback, as they swam and relaxed in the pools below Havasu Falls.

Later in the week, the mine owner, Mr. Sanderson, came up to the village frantically looking for a new cook. His cook was seriously ill and leaving for medical care. Never shy in the face of opportunity, Gale agreed to take the job for one week. "I had never done any cooking for other than my immediate family in my lifetime. But I figured, 'Well, he'll have pans and he'll have food and if they don't like it, I am just as happy not to be doing it anyway.'" The week lasted three months.

Gale's new living quarters lacked any amenities. At first she slept in the cook shack beside the table; that ended when mice started falling out between the overlapping corrugated roofing and landing with a thump beside her. "I had visions of them falling in my open mouth," she laughed. "One night I caught a little spotted skunk in one of my mouse traps . . . and that settled it. I slept out under the cottonwoods from then on."

The cooking conditions would have challenged even the most experienced cook. Only someone like Gale—flexible and resourceful—could have managed so well. The tiny shack had a kitchen area on the left with a counter and some cupboards. At the end was a small woodstove vented through the roof. The stove had no oven, so Gale was unable to make bread. "I made spider bread," she explained. "That is, corn bread made in a 'spider': an old-fashioned heavy skillet." The heat in Supai in the summer is intense, and Gale had no refrigerator, but she did have a pair of old-fashioned double soapstone tubs. "I put water in the tubs and kept vegetables in there. In the spring I had a little frame box with netting—a refrigerator-type frame box on legs. It had netting on all four sides and hemp sacks hanging down all around, letting water from a pan on top drip down with the wind blowing through to keep food fairly cool. There was an old prospector's dugout I used for a cold cellar. A big bullsnake lived in there and kept the mice down."

The men she cooked for worked hard and ate heartily. They wanted three square meals a day and always insisted on onions. "Onions three times a day proved a little difficult until I realized that I could pickle them and keep them on the table," she said. "The noon meal would usually be a beef stew or sow belly and beans and was the main meal of the day."

Havasupai packers carried out the lead ore five days a week to Hualapai Hilltop. They also hauled down mine supplies and food for the camp. Gale made a list once a week and sent it to be filled at the grocery in Seligman and packed for horse-transport. Gale ordered enough meat for fifteen men, a case of eggs, several heads of cabbage, bunches of carrots, many pounds of potatoes and onions, apples and oranges, rice, and oatmeal. "I'd always get candy for the village children, and ribbons, rickrack, sugar, and other notions for the mamas, not to mention the latest newspapers for the miners. It took quite a few horses to lug it all down each week!" Gale said.

All was not work. With a day off each week she found much exploratory fun up side canyons or on the redwall rim about the creek. On workdays, Gale took time in the afternoons, usually from two to four, to go down to the creek to enjoy the combination of the sun, heat, and cool water in the pool below Havasu Falls. She became friends with several of the Havasupai women, most of whom spoke English. "I couldn't figure out why the children were such good swimmers and their mothers would never get in the water," Gale said. "I would lie in the creek nearly every afternoon and read and write letters, and Effie Hanna, who became a good friend, would come down to the bank to talk and giggle, but she wouldn't take off her Mother Hubbard dress and enjoy the sun as I was doing. She wouldn't even go in the water."

In the evenings everyone in camp sat under the cottonwood trees. "I enjoyed listening to the stories of these fellows and the jokes, which would be a bit off-color sometimes but never really raunchy. The stories usually involved either narrow escapes in the mine, some drinking escapade, or some other tales that made good listening. But you knew there was a borderline of truth and fancy in the stories." Being the only woman did not present a problem because, as Gale said, "I wasn't the sweet, helpless little doll-baby that perhaps they might have had different ideas about."

After she'd been cook three months, Gale and Sanderson had a disagreement. She agreed to stay one more week, until he got a new cook. When word of her impending departure spread, many of the Supai, especially the women and children, expressed their sorrow that she was leaving. They had grown to love this unusual young woman who clearly enjoyed being with them and their canyon. Effie invited her to take a sweat bath with the women before she left. This was an unusual honor and one that Gale could not refuse.

A Havasupai sweat lodge is a small igloo-shaped hut formed with bent willow branches and covered with green hides, built beside a creek to allow for quick cooling-off afterwards. Rocks are placed on hot coals in a pit in the center. Water poured over the rocks creates intense steam. "There were four of us using this particular lodge, and I was nearest the door. You had to crouch in the fetal position around the edge of it with your head well down because it was so low and rounded that there was no chance to sit straight up," Gale explained. "When you figure the condition of the old hides as affected by the heat, plus the accumulation of both smoke and strong perspiration odor, the effect of it all was pretty strong."

"In about fifteen minutes I was praying silently but very fervently, 'Please Lord, don't let me faint because I'll fall flat on my face on these hot rocks and scar myself for life.' Between the heat, the humidity, and the 'fragrance,' it was just more than I could stand for a longer period than that. And so I just got out and jumped in the creek, which is cold and deep. The shock is tremendous, and you do feel like a million after that, but once was enough."

On the day Gale left, Jim Crook, the Supai village minister, sent his favorite horse down to the mining camp for her to ride out to the hilltop. "As I went up past the village, past the homes and fields and gardens, past the [Indian Affairs] Agency and rodeo grounds, everyone, even the kids, was out. They all said, 'Good-bye, good-bye,' and it was really very traumatic for me. I felt happy that they felt that way."

Though her time there was short, Gale's experience at Supai and the mining camp was meaningful. The openness of the Havasupai people and their acceptance of her despite their differences lent a human edge to the Canyon walls and water she loved so well. She had become a richer person for having been there.

Gale was again struck by the familiar pangs of wanderlust, and she set out to explore more of the West. Living the carefree life of a vagabond, Gale spent the next couple years of her life hitchhiking to Los Angeles, Reno, and Yosemite, visiting old friends and making new ones, exploring the countryside and mountains. She worked odd jobs as she needed to get from one place to the next, often hitchhiking along lonely stretches. "I looked like a fellow," Gale laughed. "I had a slim body. I had Levis on, I had a big pack and a cowboy hat on. My braids were tucked up under the hat, and invariably when someone stopped, they said, 'My God, it's a woman!'"

During the summers of 1944 and 1945 Gale worked in Yosemite National Park for the Yosemite Park and Curry Company, the park concessionaire; and as she had done at the Canyon, she spent her days off hiking in the high country. When the summer season of 1945 came to a close, Gale decided to take one last backpacking trip. "I headed up out of Yosemite Valley to Merced Lake, where the cook was closing up camp for the season. He gave me a big piece of hot apple pie, and I went on up the trail with it in my hand covered with a napkin."

Just before the junction with the Half Dome turn-off, she came across a fellow bent over, drinking from a brook. "He looked up and grinned, and, oh, what a grin!" The grin was on the face of Ted Burak, a Rhode Island man who'd gone west in an old jalopy in the late 1930s. He'd worked in Yosemite Valley until he was drafted into the army and sent to Alaska, where he worked on the construction of the Alaska Highway. When his term with the army was over, he returned to Yosemite to visit friends. "We climbed up the trail to Vogelsang Camp, where he polished off most of the food I'd planned to use for several days." This meant that they both had to return the next day to the valley; Ted treated Gale to a sumptuous home-cooked dinner in his small, rented cabin. That's when they really got acquainted.

With a mutual love of mountains and hiking as a start, the two soon married and settled in Sonora, California, where Ted opened a service station. Their three children, Lance, Susan, and Pam, were born there.

In 1955, when Gale developed an acute allergy to poison oak and Ted's service station fell victim to an interstate, the couple decided to move to New England to be nearer both families. They settled in Lincoln, New Hampshire, in the White Mountains, where Ted ran a service station and Gale managed a grocery and gift shop, cabin rentals, and campground. Over the next eighteen years they carried their beloved West deep in their hearts as they led a very busy life, working seven days a week during the tourist season, which began with fishing in April and didn't end until after the fall foliage faded in early October. It was not until 1973, when the children were grown and on their own, that Ted and Gale consolidated their holdings and sold all but their home and garage. Although Ted still had to tend the garage, Gale was now free to return to the West to work.

While on a hiking trip in Utah's Capital Reef National Park, Gale, then fifty-five, met an older woman behind the visitors center's information desk and learned that she was a Volunteer in the

Park (VIP). She thought, "If she could do it, I jolly well could too!" She contacted the personnel director at the Grand Canyon about the program and, as fate would have it, was hired for the following season as a VIP in the Backcountry Information Office.

Gale and other qualified volunteers received a small stipend for expenses and an RV campsite with hookups to live in during the summer tourist season. That fall, with Gale's service at the Canyon complete until the next spring, Ted turned the supervision of his garage over to his manager and headed west for a "honeymoon" winter with Gale, roaming the deserts of Mexico and the Southwest. For the next several years, Gale spent long summers at the Grand Canyon as ranger in charge of Inner Canyon campgrounds, and she and Ted were reunited each winter for their travels about the West.

These later years at the Canyon had brought Gale full circle. Some thirty years after she'd first laid eyes on it, she was back again, working as she had before—but this time for the National Park Service. She worked three seasons as a VIP and then spent most of the next eight years employed as an Inner Canyon Seasonal Ranger, working six to seven months of the year. Still slim, fit, and eager to explore, Gale spent her off-duty time hiking in the Canyon.

Once, on a return hike from the Inner Gorge near the lone pine overlooking Horn Rapids, Gale noticed an elaborate spider web and pulled aside a small bush to get a better look at the web. There, behind the bush, lay the corrugated, coiled base of an earthenware jug. "What a thrill!" she said. "Normally, something like this should not be touched, but right along the bench below the cliff, I had seen the recent tracks of man-sized boots, traipsing along. They served to remind me that others go far off the beaten trails now too. I didn't dare leave this bit of history." Gale carefully drew the pot out and examined the treasure. It was whole and in perfect condition except for a small hole on its down side with a ring of caliche stain around it. The jug was empty with no evidence of a lid, pollen, grain, or charcoal, and no black widow spider either!

Finding the heavy pot was one thing, but getting it safely up to Indian Garden was another matter. "I had a long-sleeved cotton shirt in my daypack," the ever resourceful Gale recalled, "and by tying opposite tails and sleeves together I made a fine sling to carry it. It was tricky, swinging it carefully from arm to arm as I scrambled hand and foot up the slickrock gully to the plateau, but at that point I'd rather have broken an arm than that pot." Luckily, she met Ranger Wayne Paya, who carried the pot on horseback to Indian Garden. From there it was helicoptered to the South Rim.

Robert Euler, then Park Service archaeologist, told Gale that her find was a utility jug, probably a thousand years old, and had most likely been used as a water storage pot for hunters who had hidden among the boulders waiting for bighorn sheep to come down for water in a *tinaja* (small rock pool). Today the pot is in the research collection at the Grand Canyon Visitor Center.

Gale found the pot while on a hike that her longtime friend Emery Kolb had suggested. Emery, an ailing ninety-five years old, had lost his wife, Blanche, several years earlier and was alone in his studio and home on the edge of the Grand Canyon. Gale stayed with Emery that summer of 1976, sleeping in the same bed that Theodore Roosevelt once used. "Emery needed somebody that could supplement his lack of sight, lack of hearing, and a pair of hands as well," she explained.

Leaving the Park Service temporarily, Gale worked for Emery for five months, May through September, helping him sort through his memorabilia and photographic collections. "He was such a packrat!" Gale said. She would describe an item, and he would say, "Yes, that's something I want to save," or "This is something that is nobody's business. I want you to destroy it." Gale sorted papers according to subject material and date and put them in boxes. She found piles of photos garnered from every shelf, closet, and drawer. "There were hundreds of duplicates," Gale exclaimed. "I saved the best for Emery's files and then sent the rest up to the studio to be sold at many times their original price. This pleased Emery to no end!" She felt her work was a labor of love. "It was of great importance for Emery as well as to me, and one of the most exciting times of my life," Gale said.

GALE BURAK

Kolb died that December, only two months after Gale had left for her winter trip with Ted. They were in Tucson for Christmas with friends when Gale received the phone call about Emery's death. Because she had so recently acted as his secretary, housekeeper, chauffeur, and companion and knew not only about his affairs but of his wishes concerning certain matters, she was asked to return to the Canyon for a few days to help sort out his estate. "It proved to be a fitting farewell to Emery, in a way, as there were many things he and I had discussed which put a bearing on decisions. I was glad to do it," she said.

Gale helped pave the way for women rangers to work in the Inner Canyon posts—stations that were traditionally given to men—when in the spring of 1978, she became the second woman ever stationed in the Canyon, replacing the supervisor at Phantom Ranch. The following summer she was stationed at Hermit Camp, a popular wilderness camping area at the foot of the Hermit Trail, but it was Cottonwood Campground that Gale came to call home.

She spent four seasons (1980 to 1983) in the tiny residence in the shade of the tall cottonwoods as the ranger in residence. She was responsible for all maintenance, law enforcement, and minor medical work, as well as assisting hikers and campers, checking permits, patroling the North Kaibab Trail, and answering questions. She especially enjoyed giving interpretive talks in the early evening. She liked to let hikers headed for the North Rim know what to expect. "Near the end of the talk, I emphasized to everybody that if they were going to the North Rim they'd best get started by 4:00 or 5:00 A.M. I would stand right beside a big rock in the group campsite where I could look up Transcept Canyon and see the Grand Canyon Lodge while lecturing. I would keep my eye on it, and as soon as the light came on up in the lobby, I'd say, 'I see that the eye of the North Rim is on us, so it's time to get to bed.' They'd look up too, and the light looked almost straight overhead. Shocked, they would say, 'My God, you mean we have to go up *there?*'" The North Rim was a 6.7-mile hike away—and nearly a 5,000-foot climb!

THE INTREPID RANGER AT COTTONWOOD CAMPGROUND.
(Photo courtesy of Gale Burak.)

Gale often stopped hikers she thought were headed to the North Rim too late in the day. Late one afternoon, she stopped two men to warn them they didn't have enough daylight left to reach the top. As it turned out, they were only going another 3 miles, to Roaring Springs, where they planned to turn around and go back to Bright Angel Campground. One of the men, Abdoul Balsharoff, told her he had decided he would like to spend more time in the Canyon, and Gale arranged by radio for him to spend two nights at Indian Garden on his way out to the South Rim. While they were talking, Gale commented that they had on identical hiking shoes: men's size 8 Nikes of the same color. Even the Canyon has room for small co-incidences. The three finished their conversation, and Abdoul, his friend, and Gale went their separate ways.

Glad to have met and helped the young men, Gale's attention turned to her upcoming hike to Phantom Ranch, where she would meet Ted after their long summer apart. They would hike the Canyon together for a week before closing Cottonwood Campground for the season. When she arrived at Phantom Ranch, she found a scene of unusual excitement. Before even saying hello, Dave Bucchello, head ranger for Bright Angel and the Colorado River, asked Gale if she planned to stay at Phantom.

"Yes, tonight and tomorrow night," Gale replied. "Why?"

"We're getting ready for a manhunt. It's a kid that was supposed to get up to Indian Garden last night and didn't get there," Dave explained.

"Anybody I should know?" Gale queried.

"He went up the Canyon a couple of days ago, Abdoul Balsharoff," Dave said.

"Oh my Lord!" Gale exclaimed. "I'm the one that gave him his permit to go to the Gardens." Gale described Balsharoff, including what he was wearing, and the size and style of his shoes. Gale maintained the base at Phantom Ranch during the search, handling the helicopter traffic, answering the radio, and providing any information she could, such as the various trails she had recommended to him.

Two days after he disappeared, searchers found a footprint from a size 8, Nike-type sole near the mouth of Clear Creek, headed downstream. This led the rangers to speculate that Balsharoff had gotten disoriented and tried to follow the river back to Phantom Ranch. A Huey helicopter with sophisticated infrared equipment came in from an airbase in California and searched the river and side canyons for two days but found no sign of him. The search was called off, and he was never found. Gale could not help but wonder what had happened to Balsharoff. She knew full well the dangers that await even experienced hikers like herself.

In 1983 Gale left her work in the Canyon to spend more time with Ted. He sold the business in New Hampshire, and he and Gale bought a house in Moab, Utah, to be close to the canyon country they both loved. Gale worked as a VIP interpretive guide at Arches National Park while Ted golfed. A year after making Moab their home, Ted was diagnosed with cancer. They returned to the East so that he could spend his remaining time near their family. He died in 1987. Gale returned to Moab for one more year before moving again to New Hampshire.

She came back to the Grand Canyon again to work the winter of 1991–1992 as a VIP interpretive ranger at Phantom Ranch. She would hike in and work ten days on with four days off, staying at the Phantom Ranch Ranger Station along with two other employees.

"The first thing I did in the morning was to call dispatch and get the weather forecast. I had to write up copies of this for the various display cases, including two at Phantom, one down at the lower bridge over Bright Angel Creek near the river, and one in the campground. I also put up the title of that evening's talk and a notice of the 4:00 P.M. informal gathering under the cottonwoods by the dining hall, both of which I would give."

Once again Gale especially enjoyed delivering the afternoon talks. She prepared and presented a variety of programs about Canyon history, including accounts of the Civilian Conservation Corps building the River Trail during the Great Depression, early days at Phantom Ranch, or evidence of prehistoric Indians that lived in the Canyon. Each group of visitors had questions. "They'd invariably start by saying, 'Do you mind if I ask you a personal question?' and I'd know what was coming. 'How old are you? How did you get down here? Did you get flown in?' I'd say, 'I'm seventy-four, I hiked in, and I'm hiking out,' and then get on with the program."

Gale had completed her winter at Phantom Ranch in early March and had set out on her hike back up the Bright Angel Trail.

AT HOME IN THE WHITE MOUNTAINS, FALL 1995.
(Photo by Betty Leavengood.)

She was to meet her friend Myla at the top, and the two would spend a few days together on the South Rim. The weather looked forbidding that day. "I shouldn't have tried to go out," Gale later reflected, "but I thought that the next day might be worse. It was raining down at Phantom, and by the time I got to the Gardens it had turned to slush. In the redwall [section] the slush turned to ice." As any true Canyon hiker, Gale measured her progress in terms of geologic layers. The redwall, about 5 trail miles from the Colorado River, is one of the more difficult sections of the trail. It is hard enough when the trail is dry, but on rainy days—and, especially, snowy days—the trail is treacherous.

"My feet were wet, and by the time I got up to somewhere in the upper Hermit layer, it was snow. Just when I got to the tunnel in the Coconino layer I heard way up above, 'Gale! Gale!' and I didn't have enough wind to answer. By the time I got to Kolb's Corner, I could tell whose voice it was; it was my friend Myla. She was up there in the snow waiting to give me a ride home. When I hadn't shown up earlier, she had called down to the Gardens and knew that I was on the way. Here I was hiking out of the Canyon, snow swirling around me, ice and slush on the trail, with no one else around, and I wondered if I would ever be doing this again."

She never has. In fact, Gale has not hiked to the bottom of the Canyon since, though she has returned to the Canyon to visit friends and take walks part way down. She lives now in North Woodstock, New Hampshire.

In June 1996 at the Grand Canyon Pioneers annual picnic, Gale stood on the rim of the Canyon at Shoshone Point side by side with Harvey Butchart, a legendary Canyon hiker. No one yet has come close to hiking the Canyon as much as these two "pioneers." Now, one nearing eighty and the other ninety, the two talked animatedly of their experiences in the Canyon, laughing, remembering, and wishing they could do it all over again.

Woman of the River

GEORGIE WHITE CLARK

(1910–1992)

GEORGIE WHITE IN ACTION. (Photo courtesy of the Delphine Gallagher Collection, Cline Library, Northern Arizona University, no. NAU.PH.93.5.120.)

W*HEN GEORGIE WHITE CLARK* first saw the Colorado River in 1945, she said, "I'd always been restless, but when I saw the Grand,[1] I knew I was home. It had everything I wanted. It was beautiful beyond words, like nothing I'd ever dreamed of, and it was wild, and at the same time you had the parts that were peaceful."[2]

Born Bessie DeRoss in Guthrie, Oklahoma, on November

13, 1910, she quickly acquired the nickname "Georgie," probably after her father, George DeRoss, a sometime miner and general n'er do well who abandoned the family when Georgie was very young.

Georgie grew up too fast. She married Harold Clark, an all-American-looking 6-foot blonde, at sixteen and gave birth to her only child, Sommona Rose, a year later. Unprepared for the responsibilities of parenthood, Georgie and Harold left their daughter with Georgie's mother and moved to New York City. There Georgie worked as a comptometer operator (a pre-calculator device used to tally receipts and keep books), and Harold took on part-time jobs; together they did their best to make ends meet during the Depression.

Partial to open spaces, Georgie didn't like New York. She thought the city to be too expensive and far too crowded. The turning point in her life came when she met some professional bicycle racers training in Central Park. Intrigued by their unusual lifestyle, she learned to ride a bike and decided to cycle to California. In August 1936, a determined Georgie quit her job and announced to Harold that they were going to ride bicycles to the West Coast. Now twenty-six, Georgie had a fierce, independent nature. She rarely let anything or anyone stand in her way—not even her husband. When he hesitated, Georgie informed him that she would leave without him. Unwilling to let her go alone, Harold agreed, and they started across the country. They ate at farmhouses along the way and picked up odd jobs where they could. When the couple reached the West Coast they flipped their last quarter to decide whether to go to Los Angeles or San Francisco. Los Angeles won. They spent the quarter on waffles and syrup, then set off to pawn Georgie's diamond wedding ring for $75.

Georgie found a job again operating a comptometer. She convinced her mother to move from Oklahoma to Los Angeles, bringing her brother Paul, her sister Marie, and Sommona Rose along. Older, wiser, and more interested in mothering, Georgie now found time for her daughter. Sommona Rose at twelve had taffy-colored hair and blue eyes and the same fearlessness and love for adventure that drove Georgie. They were kindred spirits, "peas in a pod," as Georgie said.[3] Georgie and Sommona Rose climbed nearby mountains, skied in the winter, and rode their bikes along the coast to Santa Barbara. As Georgie and Sommona Rose grew closer, Georgie and Harold drifted apart. They were divorced "by reason of his absence" in May 1941.[4]

Georgie did not remain single long. On February 6, 1942, she married a man eleven years her senior, James Ray White, a driver of oil tankers. Friends warned her that he had a drinking problem, but Georgie insisted that the jovial "Whitey" was only a social drinker. Before their marriage, Georgie told him that she would not be a dutiful wife: If she wanted to go on skiing trips or long bike rides, she would do it. And this would prove true. In return, Whitey would disappear for lengthy periods, and increasingly Georgie seemed to prefer it that way.

Soon after she and Whitey married, Georgie learned about the Ferry Command, a group of female pilots who delivered planes to airbases around the world during World War II. With Sommona Rose in tow, she went to a training facility in Quartzite, Arizona, to learn to fly. Sommona Rose flew with Georgie on several occasions and once landed the plane while sitting on Georgie's lap. Georgie completed her training with the 318th AAF Flying Training Detachment in Sweetwater, Texas, on February 12, 1944, but the war ended before she received an assignment to deliver a plane.

Disappointed, Georgie and Sommona Rose returned to Los Angeles and Georgie began working as a real estate agent, again spending her free time with her daughter. On a June afternoon in 1944, the two were biking on Highway 101 to Santa Barbara when a drunk driver hit Sommona Rose. "She was singing a song, and it quit right there," Georgie said.[5]

Georgie remembered vividly and painfully the events of that day, the sound of screeching brakes and the dull silence of her daughter's body. She had memorized the license number of the car that hit her daughter. The driver, a U.S. Coast Guardsman stationed at Santa Barbara, was later arrested, but Georgie chose not to press charges against him, saying, "It wouldn't bring her back."[6] But

Sommona Rose's death affected Georgie profoundly. Not only had she lost her daughter—an inexpressible grief for any mother—but she had also lost her best friend. The two had become inseparable companions and, as true kindred spirits, shared a particular understanding of life and of each other. Georgie was rudderless without her daughter. Any sense of purpose or direction she may have had bled from her with Sommona Rose's passing. She had lost interest in her own existence.

Trying to both console her and reawaken some interest in her life, her friends brought Georgie to a Sierra Club meeting. There, she met Harry Aleson. It was he who would help her get back on her feet—quite literally, in fact. Aleson was scheduled to lead a Sierra Club trip to the Grand Canyon where participants would hike from the Canyon floor to the top of Mt. Dellenbaugh, a 7,072-foot peak on the Shivwits Plateau. Georgie signed on. Along with Aleson's only other recruit, Gerhard Bakker, a biology instructor from Los Angeles City College, they left Boulder City, Nevada, on August 20, 1944, and crossed Lake Mead by powerboat. They continued up the Colorado River to Quartermaster Canyon, where Aleson had a camp he called "My Home." Now on foot, they began the long, treacherous climb out of the Canyon. They went up Burnt Springs Canyon and then turned up into Twin Springs Canyon, which turned out to be a dead end. They retraced their steps back to Burnt Springs Canyon, eventually pulling out on the North Rim and heading toward the town of St. George, Utah. Their blisters festering, they decided not to take the extra day to climb Mt. Dellenbaugh.

Georgie and Aleson became close friends. They hiked together in Canyon country several more times. In her book Georgie writes that the strenuous hikes were good for her. Indeed, they provided a unique kind of therapy that was just the right ointment for her grief. "Much of the time right after my daughter's death, I hardly knew where I was or what I was doing. Thoughts of Sommona completely occupied my mind. All I knew out there on those desert trails was that I had to keep putting one foot in front of the other," Georgie explained. "Looking back now, I know that the best thing I could have done at the time was to take those long hikes with Harry. While they did not take my mind off of Sommona, they acted as therapy to cleanse and renew me."[7]

Some people criticized Georgie, a married woman, for spending so much time alone with another man. Georgie explained that there was never a romantic attachment between her and Harry. "I became determined to explore the desert and Canyon country," she said, "and Harry was the only person who would go with me." Whitey, she said, understood her need for these trips.

During her trips to Aleson's camp, Georgie enjoyed swimming in the Colorado River; in fact, she loved being in the water and became determined to raft the river. "I knew nothing about the deep Canyon country, the sheer walls, the turbulent water, or the tremendous power of the rapids," she said. She and Harry discussed all the possible problems they might meet, including what would happen if their boat capsized and fell apart. Could they swim out with their life preservers? And then there was the problem of securing a boat, which neither could afford. Finally one day Georgie said, "Harry, instead of waiting to save the money to buy a raft, why don't we swim the lower Canyon in our life preservers?"

Just a year after Sommona Rose died, in June 1945, Georgie and Harry decided to do just that. They drove to Boulder City, took a bus east to Peach Springs, Arizona, stripped down to swimsuits, tennis shoes, light jackets, and their life preservers, and hiked 20 miles to the Colorado River. Once on the river, they gasped in disbelief at the raging water swelled by an above-average spring run-off. They had originally planned to take the river by sections—swim a bit, then rest, and swim again. But looking at the river, they realized it would be impossible to stop once they got in the swift current. They stood a few minutes and stared into the rushing, roaring current. The river's voice was deafening; yet, if it was shouting "Turn back, fools," it did not shout loud enough. The two swimmers looked at each other and exchanged a sly grin.

Harry waded in first. Without a moment's pause, the current caught him from behind and pulled him out of sight. Georgie stepped in next. "The current grabbed me and swept me downstream at breakneck speed," she said. "What a helpless feeling! As I shot along I had the feeling that I had passed Harry in the current, but I wasn't positive." When the current finally swung her toward the shore, Georgie climbed out and waited. No sign of Harry. She thought he had drowned—and then she heard him shout from downriver.

They decided it would be better if they stayed together in the river, and so they spent twenty minutes devising a wrist lock. "We stepped into the river then. The current caught us and shot us downstream," Georgie said. For six hours, Georgie and Harry were carried through rapids and bounced around like two bobbing corks. "It was like riding a roller coaster made of water. But the wrist grip really worked, and we stayed together as if locked in a vice. Time after time, Harry and I tried to make the bank, but the raging water kept forcing us downstream."

At one point they were sucked into a whirlpool. "Round and round we went. All afternoon that wrist lock worked well. But now it proved to be a terrible handicap. The whirlpool plunged me under head first, dragging Harry feet first. Then it threw me out and pulled Harry under head first." Georgie thought she would die. "The whirlpool caught both of us and threw us violently against a rock wall. I grabbed the rock desperately and held on." She and Harry eventually pulled themselves up on the rock and on to a narrow ledge. "It was turning dark fast. I knew we couldn't get back in the river again because we had no way to know when we could crawl back out again. Besides that, I didn't even know that we could swim through the whirlpool." Wet, hungry, and alone in the Canyon, the two spent a cold night on the ledge, unable to build a fire, unable to sleep, and unable to keep from worrying about the whirlpool that awaited them at daybreak.

At dawn, they locked wrists and prepared to go into the whirlpool. It was gone. The whirlpool had vanished in the night. "Later I learned that this happens frequently on the river," Georgie said. "A whirlpool will form right under you, then travel to high water or disappear completely." The rest of the trip seemed un-eventful after that, even though the water remained as fast and furi-ously unpredictable.

Arriving at Pierce's Ferry on Lake Mead, they found them-selves completely alone, 70 miles down a rough dirt road from the main highway. They came upon a recluse living in a shack nearby, but he had no transportation. As the likelihood of anyone coming in the next few days was remote, they resigned to walk to the highway. With some food given to them by the recluse, they hiked for three days across the desert to the highway, where they flagged a bus for Boulder City.

Back in Los Angeles, Georgie and Harry assured each other that they would never swim the Colorado again. But as time went on, the bad parts faded into memory's black hole, especially for Georgie. She began to wonder what it would be like to cover twice the distance. "Finally, I made up my mind that I wanted to try swimming again," Georgie said. Harry at first refused, but Georgie kept mentioning it on their hikes in and around the Grand Canyon. Finally Georgie told Harry, "Okay, I'll go by myself. I can find my way down to the river." Harry responded, "Okay, Georgie, you win. We'll try the river again."

This time they planned what they called a "raft-drift." They would build a raft of driftwood and, if that didn't work, use the one-man collapsible rubber air float designed for rescue at sea, which they purchased at an army-navy surplus shop. The shop also provided United States Navy kapok vests, Army Air Corps Mae West life preservers, and backpacks to carry equipment and food.

Two summers after Sommona Rose died and one summer after their first "expedition," the two met in St. George, Utah, in mid-June. The next day a friend drove them the 100 miles from St. George to the 6,000-foot Shivwits Plateau, where they strapped on their supplies and set out through a vast, roadless, unmapped land to where the Parashont Wash empties into the Colorado River. Four days into the trek, their canteens were empty. Georgie remembered that the barrel cactus contains water. "I cut one open and started to chew," she said. "I made a big mistake. It tasted like a mouthful of hemp, and I spit it out immediately." Finally, Harry spotted a few yellow jackets buzzing around a pothole in the limestone. An hour's digging produced a little muddy water, enough to get them down Parashont Wash to the Colorado.

Once there, Georgie and Harry built a makeshift raft using driftwood and old timbers, only to have it capsize after four hours. They inflated the air float, which barely held both of them. It capsized in an hour, tossing them into the river. And so they struggled for 76 miles, one person using the float, and the other swimming. Often, they thought the river would win. Swirling rapids sucked them under, tossed them out, then pulled them under again. After six days on the river they arrived on Lake Mead. Harry wrote in his report in the Sierra Club newsletter, "Under no condition must others plan a similar raft drift, unless it be to save your, or other's, life."

"Harry told me if I wanted to go again I had to go alone," Georgia said. "People often ask me how I could have done something so foolish. Actually, those two swims proved invaluable. I learned more about water and the Colorado River on those two trips than I could probably have learned in ten years any other way. I came to understand how the currents acted both on and below the surface. I saw firsthand how rocks affect the water, and I learned some important lessons about controlling myself in high water."

The hours and days Georgie spent swirling about the waters of the Colorado did more than teach her about its rocks and currents. The river got under her skin and into her veins, coursing through her body like her own blood. It became part of her. Whether she knew it or not, the river had become inextricably linked to her life. Her longing to be near it, on it, in it, meant the difference between simply existing or utterly living life. She would return to it again and again, until she found a way to make it her life.

At this point, however, she needed only to find a way to convince Harry to return with her; whenever she would mention the Colorado River to him, he would say, "Don't you ever say 'swim' to me again, because I'm not going! I'm going to shoot you if you mention it!"[8] Georgie then suggested they get a larger raft, one large enough to carry both of them and their supplies. Army surplus stores in Los Angeles carried all sizes of rafts, so Georgie purchased a ten-man raft, and Harry bought a seven-man raft.

In early November 1946, when Georgie's real estate business was at a seasonal low, the adventurers headed again for the Colorado River. Georgie took a bus from Los Angeles and met Harry in Richfield, Utah, where together they caught another bus to Green River, Utah. "I can still see the look on that driver's face when he saw Harry's seven-man, 250-pound raft sitting there on the sidewalk," Georgie said. They convinced the driver to put the raft in the baggage compartment and hurriedly boarded before he had a chance to change his mind. This time they planned to launch on the Green River, join the Colorado, run Cataract Canyon, and take out at Hite, Utah, a distance of 150 river miles.

Neither had been to the high desert in November, and they were sorely unprepared for the cold. Harry wanted to turn back, but Georgie said, "No way, I've come this far. I'm going the rest of the way." Reluctant to leave her alone, Harry went against his instincts, and the two pushed the raft into the Green River. For three days they drifted in the swift water, suffering from the cold, with snow and wind swirling about their heads. When they joined the Colorado, the nature of the trip changed.

The steep, narrow walls of Cataract Canyon channeled the Colorado through narrow chutes and over huge boulders. "We shot suddenly through one of these chutes, banging against the rocks as water pounded us from all sides. We were now literally bouncing from rock to rock. The raft suddenly flipped upside-down and—with Harry and me hanging on—banged through the rest of the rapid," Georgie recalled. They managed to work their way to shore, climb out, and build a small fire to ward off the miserable cold. For two more days they ran the rapids of Cataract Canyon—Satan's Gut, Dirty Devil, Dark Canyon—before reaching the tiny town of Hite.

There they caught a ride to the highway from an older couple who'd walked down to the river to watch them land. Nineteen miles north of Hite, the car stalled; the battery was dead. Although they were tempted to leave the couple and walk on to the highway, Georgie and Harry headed back to Hite, retrieved a new battery from the couple's shed, and walked back to the car. With the car working again, they reached the highway and caught a bus home.

The cold temperatures, freezing water, treacherous rapids, and nearly 40-mile hike of this trip was enough for Harry. Although he and Georgie remained friends and he described her as "a most courageous person, a woman without fear,"[9] Harry refused to run the Colorado with Georgie again. Perhaps he secretly feared they might not survive another trip. Georgie had no such fears. "If you believe in yourself and you know what you can do and can't . . . I wasn't foolhardy. I figured I could hike out of the Canyon because I had really good legs. And I felt positive about my swimming."[10]

Georgie returned to the Colorado alone for the next three summers, experimenting with her own ten-man raft. In 1950 she worked for a Mexican Hat river running expedition as chaperone for five young starlets being featured in a Capitol Enterprises feature film, *Six Girls Against the Colorado*. Georgie had to keep running the same "riffle" below Lees Ferry. They would ride down the rapid and then helicopter the girls back to the beginning.

Following the filming, Georgie decided that if she could take care of those "dingalings" (her word for the young ladies in her charge), she could lead anyone through the Canyon. In 1952, she took her first passenger, Elgin Pierce, on a raft trip. They put in at Lees Ferry in midsummer with Georgie's trusted ten-man army-navy surplus raft. She managed to get through Badger Creek and Houserock and other rapids with little trouble, but on her third day out, she hit Hance. "The water, frothing and white, rolled in full boil, with huge waves crashing sideways into the big rocks. The holes that day were the wickedest I think I've ever seen," she recalled. "Suddenly a huge hole loomed directly in front of us. I couldn't possibly avoid it . . . woosh . . . the front end of the raft dipped, a giant wave loomed above us, and all at once the raft tilted sickeningly and hung there suspended!" Elgin panicked and jumped from the boat. Georgie saw him out of the corner of her eye, climbing onto the shore. "A swift back current caught the raft, taking me forcefully toward a rock wall," she said. The raft flipped upside down, but Georgie managed to hang onto the rope running around the raft and get a grip on a rock. Elgin rushed to help her, and together they tied the boat to the rock. This was the first of several upsets, but they made it successfully to Lake Mead. The trip gave Georgie the confidence she needed to run river trips.

Georgie's long-gone husband, Whitey, reentered her life about this time. Possibly deciding that if he were ever to see Georgie again he would have to join her on the river, he agreed to drive a truck loaded with rafts to Lees Ferry, where she and a group of customers set out; he then met them at the end of the trip. He learned to handle a raft and occasionally joined Georgie on the river. The rest of Georgie's family also got involved in the business. Her brother, Paul, became an expert boatman, and sister Marie did the bookkeeping, logistics, food purchases, and even the laundry after trips.

In 1953 Georgie led her first "Share the Expense" trip on the Colorado. At a time when other outfitters were charging from $850 to $1,000 a trip, Georgie charged $300. Many men, including her longtime friend Harry Aleson, were outraged at a woman guiding trips on the Colorado. Georgie was far more interested in refining her skills than responding to such unfounded criticism. And she had plenty of customers, to boot—both women and men. The trip was exciting except for the required portaging at major rapids, done to ensure the safety of novice river runners. Hating the tiring process of carrying boats and supplies around the rapids, Georgie began thinking of ways to make portgaging unnecessary.

Halfway through a trip in 1954 she got the idea to lash three ten-man rafts together, side by side. A ten-man navy life raft is 17 feet long, 8 feet wide, black in color, and shaped like a paper clip. If one section got into trouble, she reasoned, the other two would pull it along. It worked. After Georgie lashed the boats together, she ran every rapid but the dreaded Lava Falls, a 37-foot drop that roared like a freight train as the rafts approached.

THE CELEBRATED "G-RIG." (Photo courtesy of the Grand Canyon National Park Museum Collection, Grand Canyon, Arizona.)

Georgie had stumbled onto something workable, but she wanted to run all the rapids this new way, even the notorious Lava Falls. Plus, she wanted a craft safe enough to carry small children and elderly people. She reasoned that if the 17-foot rafts would work, larger ones would do even better. Georgie purchased three 27-foot bridge pontoons and lashed them side by side. Each pontoon had a Johnson outboard motor, but she used only the middle motor, saving the others for emergencies and spare parts. After further experimentation, she placed inflated rubber tubing in the oval center of each pontoon, giving the passengers a convenient back rest and eliminating much of the bailing because there wasn't room for as much water to stand. The contraption became known as the G-Rig—or Georgie Rig—by other boatmen.

It had only one limitation. It was so large that occasionally the leading raft folded and flipped over onto the rest of the rafts, making what came to be called a Georgie Sandwich. Georgie explained that people just think it is a sandwich, but it really isn't. "When you go up on a wave, because they're so high they're looking down on the other people who are down in this trough . . . so they *think* it's coming on them; it isn't."[11] There were many who disagreed with Georgie's analysis.

Her 1955 trip carried the largest group of people ever down the Colorado: twenty-eight. The entourage included Whitey and her brother Paul. Also on the trip was Park Ranger Dan Davis, the first river ranger in the Grand Canyon, whom Georgie had invited. "I almost quit the Park Service and began working as a boatman," Davis said. "It was the greatest trip. Georgie was the toughest woman I have ever seen. She could pick up two Johnson outboard motors as if they were nothing." Georgie enthralled Davis with stories about swimming the Colorado, climbing sheer canyon walls, and cycling across the country. "She kept us spellbound," he said, "but I sometimes questioned the details."[12]

The big boat exceeded Georgie's expectations; she had found her mode of operation. For nearly forty years Georgie's big boat was on the river. For fifteen of those years Whitey helped sporadically as a driver and guide, but his drinking worsened over the years. By 1971, Georgie could no longer tolerate his excesses, and they divorced.

Georgie's true love was the river, and she conveyed that love to the people who accompanied her on her river trips. A "Georgie trip" started with a list of instructions mailed well in advance of the event. Bring an air mattress with three compartments, a rainsuit, colorful clothes for pictures, bathing suits, a plastic bowl, a plastic cup, two stainless steel spoons, and two can openers.

Canned food was a vital part of Georgie's food supply. "Every night we had a slightly different version of 'Georgie Stew,'" explained Delphine Gallagher, a Georgie regular. "All kinds of canned vegetables were dumped in a big kettle and heated. Then we each received a small can of some kind of meat, which we mixed into our bowl of stew. So our dinner would be Georgie stew with meatballs, or Georgie stew with chicken, or Georgie stew with ham."[13]

Georgie's river runners also knew to expect boiled eggs every morning. Delphine recalled Georgie putting thirty eggs in a large kettle to boil for breakfast. "Shortly she would yell, 'Anyone who wants soft-boiled eggs, come and get 'em.' A little later, 'Anyone who wants medium eggs, come and get 'em.' Still later, 'Anyone who wants hard boiled eggs, come and get 'em.'"[14]

Her trips put in at Lees Ferry. Loading seemed chaotic but was actually highly organized. Two Los Angeles firemen once joined her on a trip, and Georgie told them how her boatmen often argued with each other. The firemen suggested she should use firemen because they worked together as a team. Word spread among Los Angeles firemen that Georgie needed boatmen, and for years many firemen spent part of their summer vacations on the river with Georgie.

Loading complete, Georgie would launch the boats, dressed in a leopard-skin bathing suit and flying a leopard skin flag from the big boat. A mile or so below Lees Ferry, when the raft would bounce over a ripple and invariably a newcomer would say, "Is this a rapid?" Georgie would laugh and say, "That? That's a miscellaneous!"[15] In Georgie talk, this could be interpreted as "You ain't seen nothin' yet!"

First-timers soon learned that whatever they were in life—doctor, company president, lawyer, bus driver—on the river they were all equal. Georgie had no use for pretentious people. The only people that weren't allowed along were sourpusses. "One sourpuss can ruin an entire trip," she said. Nor could she tolerate whiners. When she asked a passenger how things were going, she expected them to answer, "Everything is just the way we like it!"[16]

That response was critical in the initiation that took place near the end of each run. Georgie decided that if you made it through the Grand Canyon, you should be dubbed not simply a River Rat but a Royal River Rat. The initiation ceremony was held after dinner, as the sun left the Canyon. The new "rats" were blindfolded, led to a

ORVILLE MILLER AND GEORGIE WHITE INDUCT DELPHINE MOHRLINE GALLAGHER (CENTER) TO THE ROYAL RIVER RATS WITH THE TRADITIONAL SHOT OF BLACK-BERRY BRANDY. (Photo courtesy of the Delphine Gallagher Collection, Cline Library, Northern Arizona University, no. NAU.PH.93.5.173.)

beach, and seated in a circle. "Then we'd throw some cold water on them and tell them that's just to clear their memory," Georgie laughed. "Then we would say that this was an educational experience and that if they got the correct answer, they didn't get a bucket of water thrown on them; but if they were wrong or answered out of turn, they would get a bucket. We'd ask all sorts of questions about the geology and where we camped. Then we'd crack an egg over the person's head, give them a crown, and tell them they were going to take an oath."

Those who passed the test (everyone passed) were brought over to Georgie, where they kneeled down, still blindfolded, to listen to Georgie's speech. "On the river, you know, by this time, that no matter what happens to you, the main thing that you must learn is a slogan that everything is just the way you like it." She then asked, "How is the trip?" to which a chorus of would be Royal River Rats replied, "Everything is just the way we like it!" They would get a whack with a paddle, then they would stand up, their blindfold removed, and they would receive the congratulations of all. They had become Royal River Rats.[17] Doctors, lawyers, and professional men and women throughout America proudly displayed their Royal River Rat Certificate on their walls next to their degrees.

The morning after the initiation, headed downriver, the River Rats sang, "I'm a river rat, you're a river rat, we're all a river rat, and when we get together we like to sing our song." Then everyone would go "Yak, Yak, Yak" and clap their hands three times, and then repeat the verse as long as they wanted to and, when the song was finally over, give a loud yell, "Yah."[18]

Georgie became as famous as John Wesley Powell, in part because she engineered that fame. She put modern-day public relations firms to shame. The well-known photographer Josef Muench went on fifteen trips with Georgie; his photos appeared in publications around the country, particularly *Arizona Highways*. And then there was *Call of the Canyon*, a ninety-minute documentary filmed by Roger Bowling and narrated by Georgie, billed as "a dramatic, educational chronology of a twenty-one day expedition in rubber life rafts through 330 miles of the Eighth Wonder of the World." Thousands of viewers saw Georgie in action.

Georgie appeared on some of the most popular television shows of her time. When Art Linkletter of *House Party* asked her, "Aren't you afraid of anything?" she replied, "Oh you bet! I'm afraid of anybody driving me on the freeway!" To Groucho Marx, who said, "You know, Georgie, with all those horrible things that happen on the river, what you really need on trips is an undertaker," she quipped, "Oh no, you just take a shovel along and bury the bodies right there on the spot." This comment, a reference to the time Georgie found and buried a body along the river, left the audience in stitches.

On *To Tell the Truth,* where a panel of four celebrities had to guess who the real "Georgie" was, she fooled all but Bill Cullen, who pointed to her and said, "She has to be the real Georgie; she is the only one that came down the steps without looking or holding the handrail. I'm sure that's the kind of confidence it takes to run a raft through the rapids."

Georgie had her critics. Her boats were too big, she took too many people at once, she grabbed the best campsites and then left them littered with opened cans, there was too much horseplay, too much Coors, not enough attention to safety. In her long career, three people drowned on her trips. When Georgie didn't cry, people accused her of being heartless.

Still, Georgie made rafting the Colorado River affordable and safe for the ordinary passenger. The rafts she pioneered, at first ridiculed by boatmen, became the accepted mode of river travel. Although she hired only men for her crew, she led the way for women to work on the river. Her spirit was indomitable, and her love for the Colorado River of the Grand Canyon was fierce. People would ask her, "When are you going to retire?" and she would reply, "I'm retired to the river."[19]

In November 1990 over two hundred people gathered at the Hatch Warehouse in Marble Canyon to celebrate Georgie's eightieth birthday. Georgie danced like a teenager that day, and it seemed like she could live forever, running the river, but a little over a year after the party, she was diagnosed with stomach cancer and became so weak she could barely walk. She longed to go back to the river. "How I wish I was running that river," she wrote to friends in April 1992. "I could be dressing to go put on coffee water for early coffee hounds before dawn. I used to love that early hour."[20] Georgie died a few weeks after she wrote the letter, on May 12, 1992. One imagines that Georgie didn't mind dying so much. If she couldn't live on the river, she wouldn't want to live.

Cataloging a Canyon

LOUISE HINCHLIFFE

(1922–)

LOUISE HINCHLIFFE AND THE LIBRARY AT GRAND CANYON NATIONAL PARK. (Photo courtesy of the Grand Canyon National Park Museum Collection, Grand Canyon, Arizona.)

*A*s a child growing up in Massachusetts, Louise Hinchliffe would stare longingly at the painting of the Grand Canyon hanging in her parents' living room. The painting depicted a landscape that was utterly unfamiliar to Louise. Layers of rocks plunged to hidden depths, a mystery, and she could only imagine what beauty lay beyond the painting's frame. She dreamed of one day stepping into that scene. The artist was her uncle, Hans Kleiber, a forest ranger in Wyoming.

"I'd look at that painting and think about going out West," Louise recalled, "but during the Depression, money was scarce, and I went to work right out of high school."[1] Although she'd learned typing and shorthand, she found her first full-time employment with the American Optical Company, assembling eyeglass and goggle frames. She advanced steadily through the company—and through World War II—over the next eight years. It was then that her mother suggested she take a vacation trip out West.

"In 1947 I went on a tour of several national parks, including Union Pacific's 'Utah Parks' tour, which branched out beyond Utah and gave me my first look at Grand Canyon from the North Rim," Louise remembered.[2] The painting in her childhood home had not prepared her for the Canyon's vast reality. Its beauty was immense, inarticulate; and its grandeur touched and quieted her soul. She knew she would return to this place some day.

Two years after her visit to the North Rim, Louise took a "packaged tour" of Yellowstone National Park and went, by bus and train, to spend ten days with her Uncle Hans and the aunt she had never met. "They took me on a lot of 'local' trips, places like Sheridan and Custer battlefields, dude ranches, and up into the Bighorn Mountains," Louise recalled.

Fascinated with the West, especially the Grand Canyon, Louise came back again and again. "I made another trip in 1949 through Zion and Bryce and to the North Rim again. Then, even though I couldn't afford it, I came back again in 1951." Louise began corresponding with people in the parks about finding a job. "I learned that there were openings for women in the National Park Service," she said, "and that was rather a revelation, because you didn't see very many women in those days employed at the national parks. You knew there were families living with the rangers, but you didn't find very many women actually working for the Park Service."[3]

Louise passed the Civil Service examination and began receiving offers from various places, but none at the Grand Canyon. "Finally I wrote to Grand Canyon Park Superintendent Harold C.

Bryant, and I was very fortunate because my letter arrived just about the time the Naturalist Division was looking for a new secretary, so on the basis of the qualifications I described in my letter and my experience, they decided to take a chance on me."

Visiting the West was one thing, but the sudden prospect of moving there made the West seem remote and far from Massachusetts. "My mother encouraged me to take the job. I'd always lived at home," Louise said. "It was the hardest decision I made in my life." Feeling very much alone, but determined, Louise boarded a train headed west and into a new life. "I was on the train headed for the Grand Canyon on Thanksgiving Day, 1951, and it was the loneliest Thanksgiving of my life," she said. "I'd given up a pretty good job and a very good home. The only thing I regret is that my mother didn't tell me how ill she was. I never saw her again."[4]

Louise arrived at the South Rim of the Grand Canyon the weekend after Thanksgiving. Although she had been to the North Rim several times, this was her first visit to the more populated South Rim. Her living quarters proved disappointing. "They called it the 'stenographer's cabin.' It had two rooms—a living room/bedroom combination and a kitchen. There also was a 3-foot by 5-foot bathroom," she recalled.[5]

Although Louise admitted she was a bit "let down," she understood the reasons for her meager quarters. "You had to work your way up the housing chain based on your pay rate, longevity, and size of family," she explained. She mustered her resolve and worked to make her house her home. "I saw it as a chance to 'make the best of it,' so I made curtains and slipcovers for the steno's cabin."[6]

Her first year at the Canyon was rough for Louise. Alone, really for the first time in her life, she grew homesick and a bit scared. The Canyon can either amplify or mollify loneliness, depending on how one opens up to it. Louise was fortunate to take comfort in the Canyon's grandeur, which softened her loneliness, and soon grew to love being at the Canyon. "I didn't get tired of looking at the Canyon. I think some people do. There were people who worked here, who lived here, who never went out of their way to go out and look at it. . . . I can't quite understand anybody having so little interest or curiosity, and about things right on their doorstep."

Louise lived in her tiny cabin nearly four years, until after her mother's death. "My father wanted to sell the house, and I wanted to keep some of my furniture, a bedroom set and a drop-front desk, and some keepsakes of my mother's. I told the man in charge of housing assignments that I needed a bigger place to live in so I would have some place to put the furniture, and eventually I got an apartment in an old CCC barracks," Louise said. "The walls were like cardboard, but at least I could have my furniture. I stayed there for about three years, until the Park Service built some new apartments for single employees, and by then I had enough seniority that when the eight apartments became available, I had my choice."[7]

As she grew used to living at the Canyon, Louise looked increasingly forward to her time alone with the geologic wonder. "Weekends or whenever I could, I'd go out there," she recalled. "Some mornings I got up extra early and walked along the rim to come to work. . . . Simply because it was different every time. And it wasn't just the Canyon. I mean, it wasn't just that big beautiful view out there. It was the little things that I'd notice along the way. I keep discovering something I hadn't noticed before about the way the pine trees grow or some flower that I hadn't seen before, or some bird comes along that I hadn't seen for a long time and I think, 'I used to remember what your name was' . . . It just continued to be exciting to me, and I kept discovering little places that I'd never walked before."

She also made friends in the small community. "That helped through the rough parts. There was a church group, and I met the wives of the men I worked with."[8] She participated in community activities such as the Square Dance Club, picnics at Shoshone Point, softball games, movies in the community building, and a local amateur theater company. Grand Canyon Village in 1951 had only 300 people, compared to over 1,600 in 1998.

Although many women lived at the Canyon and several worked for the Fred Harvey Company, only three women worked for the National Park Service in 1951: Louise and two secretaries, one in the superintendent's office and the other in the engineer's office. "It was strictly a man's world," Louise commented.[9] Even so, Louise enjoyed her job, which turned out to be much more than the "clerk-typist" designated on her employment form. She worked for Louis Schellbach, head of the Naturalist Division.

"When you think of Schellbach, think of a turtle who carries his shell on his back," Schellbach told Louise, then he added a bit of advice. "When you think of the turtle, remember he never gets anywhere unless he sticks his neck out." Louise liked and respected "Louie," as everyone called him, and later, when she disapproved of some of the changes made at the Canyon over the years, she would remember Louie saying, "Nothing is permanent except change." Schellbach would prove to be a tremendous influence on Louise. She would work for and with him over the next seven years. It was from him that she would gain a deeper understanding of the Canyon's plants, animals, and geology.

Schellbach laid the foundation for much of the interpretive program in place at the Canyon today. He wanted visitors not just to look at the Canyon but to understand and appreciate it. Consequently, he built a large study collection and developed interpretive programs to teach people about the Grand Canyon. He believed that when people understood the Canyon they were more likely to protect it.

Louise, Schellbach, and his assistant, Ernst Christensen, plus a few seasonal employees in the summer months made up the Naturalist Division in 1951. Their office was in a three-room school building that had been earlier condemned before Schellbach convinced the Park Service to refurbish it. The study collection, an assortment of specimens from preserved animals to rocks to pressed plants, filled one room. The largest room, where Louise worked, contained a combination office, workshop, and library. "If somebody was running the power saw, you got sawdust all over your desk," Louise laughed, "but, at the same time, it was a very pleasant working arrangement in that everybody took part in everything that was happening. You felt very much a part of the team."

This little building comprised all the Canyon had in the way of a Visitor Center in the early 1950s. "We were so much off the beaten track that most visitors weren't aware we existed," Louise said. "People would come around and knock on the back door. We'd greet them enthusiastically and show them around and, if they wanted to stay in the exhibit room for a while and look around, fine. If it was somebody that was quite interested, as often they were, we'd spend some time giving them a tour of the study collection. And if they were really interested, they got the rare treat of perhaps spending an hour listening to Louie." Schellbach was a riveting speaker, and his dedication to the Canyon was clear. Louise said that listening to Schellbach's enthusiastic talks helped her get through the early parts of the job. "When I was feeling pretty homesick, the realization that there were such dedicated, interesting people in the Park Service helped my determination to stay."

As the primary contacts with the public, the naturalists gave talks on various topics, including daily geology lectures at Yavapai Museum on Yavapai Point. Louise assisted with talks whenever one of the men was ill, on vacation, or too busy to appear that day. Before Louise was hired they had sometimes asked one of the rangers to fill in, she explained, "but there was always a friendly rivalry between the two groups; the rangers were the 'cops,' and in their view the naturalists were 'butterfly chasers' or 'fern feelers.' To avoid asking favors, my boss got the idea that I should do it."[10]

Louise had been listening to the talks on her days off or by occasionally closing the office to attend. "Geology was my favorite, and often, when they did a nature walk, I would go along. My first talk was on geology, and it went pretty well. It was forty-five minutes long, and I'd prepared a few three-by-five-inch cards as reminders in case I forgot what came next. In the second talk, I unexpectedly had real stage fright for the first time, but after that I was OK. At first I didn't wear a uniform, but soon they decided that because I was before the public representing the park, I should obtain a uniform."[11]

Louise gave talks when needed for about five years. "It was a challenge because I was shy and had a limited background. Occasionally we'd get a crank in the crowd, but I got so I could deal with them. Louie taught me how to handle the people who objected to the statement that the Colorado River made the Grand Canyon. When someone said, 'God made the Grand Canyon,' Louie would pull out his pencil and draw a line in his notebook. Then he would say to the group, 'Did this pencil make this line, or did I make this line?'"[12]

Louise also helped design and build exhibits. "I learned how to mount plants and spread butterflies. I just did whatever needed doing. I even skinned birds for the study collections." Skinning birds was a complicated process that Louise learned by observing and using a handbook. "It's like taxidermy, except that you don't strive for a lifelike pose." Louise removed the perishable 'innards,' taking care not to injure the skin or feathers, then treated the cavity with preservatives to avoid insect infestations. She filled the cavity with cotton, smoothed the feathers into place, and after it had dried, placed the bird in a sealed cabinet.[13]

Louise pitched in whenever she was asked, even if it meant hiking 9 miles down the Bright Angel Trail in the heat of summer to repair damage done by vandals to the River House (a trail shelter near the Colorado River) exhibit. Louise designed the exhibit, organized the specimens and labels, and, with the help of two seasonal employees, hiked down the trail to install the exhibits. One of the panels Louise designed had a relief map of the river's course, another explained the geology of the Canyon, and the third depicted exploration of the river. Exhibits today are made by professional artists, and though topnotch, they lack the personal feel of the early homemade designs.

Often Louise drew the morning chore of driving out to Yavapai Museum (now a bookstore and information center) to "open the doors," which involved more than simply turning the key. "There wasn't any glass around the front of the building. It was an open porch out there. The binoculars had to have covers tied over them every night and taken off every morning to protect them from the weather," Louise explained. "Plus, the exhibits that explained the binoculars had tin lids over them that had to be placed each night and removed in the morning." The job proved more difficult in the wintertime. "If there had been some snow, you'd have to shovel the snow off the porch and fling it over the edge into the Canyon. The oil stove had to have oil carried to it from a tank down by the parking lot."

All the talks, exhibit preparation, and snow shoveling came second to what would eventually be Louise's primary responsibility: managing the library that supported the Naturalist Division. When she arrived at the Canyon, 2,320 entries were recorded in the library accession book. The library was in a little corner room, about 10 feet square, and on some additional shelves in the workshop. "Part of my job was cataloging anything that came in, so I learned the Dewey Decimal System," Louise said. "We were a specialized library, and the Dewey system hadn't expanded to its present levels—it tended to lump together, under one number, every book about the Grand Canyon."[14] Louise improvised a more detailed system that would let her categorize books about the Canyon into specific subjects, so that as the collection grew, library users could find what they wanted more readily. As the Natural History Association increased the library's budget, Louise bought books and subscribed to more periodicals.

In 1957 the Park Service built a new Visitor Center near the entrance to the Canyon. More emphasis was placed on visitor interpretation, and the name of the Naturalist Division was changed to Interpretive Division so as to better reflect its purpose. The "new" Interpretive Division, including the extensive study collection and the library, moved to the new center. Although Louise excelled at her job and adapted easily to her many unexpected duties, she had grown accustomed to her cozy office and the close working relationship with the small staff, and she had difficulty adjusting to the new Visitor Center. Moving the library proved especially frustrating.

"At the time that we were ready to move into the new building, the library shelves hadn't arrived yet, and all we had was a big, empty room. Fortunately it wasn't raining on moving day, since they sent an open, flat-bed truck," Louise explained.

Louise waited at the Visitor Center. It was her plan to direct placement of books on the floor by the windows so she would have an easier time shelving them in order. "When they arrived with the books, they didn't have enough manpower to carry them all in carefully. So, to cut down on the number of trips they had to make, somebody said, 'Let's pile them up in the wheelbarrow! We can carry more of them that way,'" Louise recalled. "So they came in with wheelbarrow loads, books just piled in, helter skelter. To make it worse, somebody had been mixing cement in the wheelbarrow, so it was a little bit gritty." The books were piled all over the floor in no particular order, and Louise faced the demoralizing task of having to reorganize and shelve the books when the shelves arrived, as well as clean bits of cement from many of the volumes.

Thankfully the move was easier for the study collection. "Everything had to be moved: the insect and butterfly specimens, geology samples, and archeology artifacts," Louise said. Because someone on the staff had to drive to the Yavapai Museum at least three times a day to open, give a talk, and close, Louise decided to utilize those trips to assure that the delicate butterflies and insects reached the new Visitor Center, which was midway on the route, safely. "We would put a few drawers in the car and drive very carefully. It took a lot of trips, but was worth it," she explained.

The move to the new Visitor Center brought added responsibilities to Louise's job description. The tiny department was now charged with staffing the Information Desk seven days a week, in addition to their other responsibilities. "It was a bit of a job to provide that much service with just three staff members," Louise said. "At first, there weren't too many visitors, so we kept a bell out front on the desk so that when somebody came and wanted something, they'd ring the bell and we'd go out."

The most difficult part of the move, however, was that it

brought with it the retirement of Louie Schellbach. Louise feared that some of Schellbach's beloved study collections and exhibits would be dismantled once he was gone, but that was not to be the case. The new director, Paul Schulz, did attempt to upgrade the exhibits with mechanical devices: "There was a little map showing the trails, exhibits, and museums, and there was a light on each one. Kids tried to see how many of the lights they could reach with one hand and make them all light up at the same time—and that usually short-circuited the whole thing and blew it all up," Louise recalled.

Schulz's recorded roar of the Colorado River also caused problems. "It was activated by lifting up an ordinary telephone receiver and holding it to your ear. But when people finished listening they would just drop the thing, and it would bang against the wall and break," Louise explained.

The most popular exhibit was not mechanical, but a piece of schist from the Inner Canyon with a file attached to it. Vishnu schist, at 1.7 billions years old, is the oldest rock in the Grand Canyon and virtually indestructible. "People were supposed to file the rock or at least attempt to file it, and, of course, in their frustration when they found they couldn't file it because it was just too hard and the file was wearing out, they'd start pounding with the file . . . we broke a lot of files that way."

Needless to say, the once quiet, smooth workdays of the old Naturalist Division were gone forever, giving way to the increasing pressure of the growing attendance at the Grand Canyon. By 1960, half a million visitors came to the Grand Canyon annually, most of them making the new Visitor Center their first stop.

Louise now devoted most of her time to the library and study collection. She responded to the increase in visitors by offering tours of the study collection and an open day in the library. "Most tourists were content with a chance to just enter the library, hear a little of its history and purpose, and get back to more interesting activities, but the study collection tours were rather popular," she said. "I explained the purpose of study collections, some of the history of our collection, and why it smells so awful in here—it was the preservatives; and after some cautions about not handling anything unless I passed it around, we toured the whole room, exploring cupboards and drawers from anthropology to zoology, hummingbirds to eagles, skunks to skinks."

Louise recognized that the nature of the Canyon tourists was changing. No longer were the majority English speaking. "Sometime in the early 1960s we recognized the need for a condensed version of the Yavapai guide booklet, translated into the most often requested languages. At first we mimeographed them—no photocopiers then—and did French, German, and Spanish. Japanese was a greater challenge—we had to have it printed in California." Today on the South Rim, the number of foreign visitors makes up over 50 percent of total visitorship, thanks in part to the one-day flights from Las Vegas to the Canyon that are a regular part of many foreign tour packages.

By 1975, as the staff of the Interpretive Division increased, Louise became full-time librarian. As such, she was often enlisted by writers doing research on the Canyon. "I've worked with many authors who have come here to write books about the Canyon," Louise admitted, "and while I don't mean that I've had any impact on what they've written . . . it has been an interesting opportunity to add to the accuracy of some of the books that were published by helping them with their research, by reviewing their manuscripts, and pointing out things that they really shouldn't say because they weren't accurate or they were misleading or they might cause people to get a wrong impression about what could be done here in the park." Many authors have mentioned Louise's invaluable assistance in their acknowledgments.

After nearly thirty-four years at the Grand Canyon, Louise retired in August 1985. At her retirement party that September, Superintendent Richard W. Marks renamed the park library in her honor. It is now the Louise Hinchliffe Library, a tribute to how she built the library's small collection to a comprehensive 7,000-volume collection.

A BELOVED LOUISE HINCHLIFFE (CENTER FRONT) IS HONORED BY COLLEAGUES AND FRIENDS ON HER RETIREMENT. (Photo courtesy of the Grand Canyon National Park Museum Collection, Grand Canyon, Arizona.)

Why did she stay at the Canyon so long? "People often ask me, 'Doesn't it get tiresome to see the same place and the same people and the same buildings for such a long time?' The answer to that is you don't see the same people. They are always coming and going. . . . You keep getting your batteries charged by meeting new people." Louise compared her long tenure at the Canyon with being married to the same person for a long time. "It may not be quite as exciting as a lot of turnover in jobs or partners, but that doesn't mean there isn't any chance to grow and to develop and to have new experiences. . . . There's always been a challenge."

Part of the challenge for retired Grand Canyon National Park Service employees is giving up their Canyon home. Many, as did Louise, stay nearby so as to be able to return occasionally. At her home in Sedona, Arizona, looking at a dramatic view of the red rocks through her living room window, Louise offered a bit of advice: "I think maybe what I might say I've learned is that if you have a dream, for goodness sakes, do something about it. Don't say,

LOUISE HINCHLIFFE AT HOME IN ARIZONA. (Photo by Betty Leavengood.)

'That's impossible, that's too difficult or it involves too many changes, too many chances to take.' Follow it—because you only get one chance. You only get one life, and if you don't do those things that seemed a little bit out of reach, what was the point of living?"

My Heart Knows What the River Knows

KATIE LEE

(1919–)

KATIE LEE SERENADES A MOST SPECIAL PLACE. (Photo by Frank Wright; courtesy of Katydid Books and Music.)

≈

My heart knows what the river knows
I gotta go where the river goes
Restless river, wild and free
The lonely ones are you and me[1]

IMAGINE A SUNRISE in the southwest section of the North American continent, sometime in the early twelfth century. The brilliant ball of fire rises slowly in the east, bringing the day. Its first light heightens and defines shadows. Before long, everything is bathed in a fiery red, and the baked stone of the earth begins heating. This is the light that funneled into Glen Canyon for millennia, lending depth and nuance to countless natural arches, river-carved walls, ledges and alcoves, and the yellow sand on the canyon floor. It is the light by which groups of people collected water, hunted and gathered, and carved their stories and histories into rock. The cycle of day is evident in the constancy of this place, a place so sublime that its existence is reliable, unequivocal.

Fast-forward now to the twentieth century, where the same sun rises upon a dramatically altered landscape. No natural disaster, no ice age, not even the hand of God turned this remarkable canyon into the underbelly of a deep artificial lake. This was the handiwork of the U.S. Bureau of Reclamation.

It was this, and a score of other unfathomables, that left folksinger Katie Lee aghast.

Katie Lee grew up in the desert east of Tucson, Arizona. She is an accomplished singer and songwriter, but she is more famous for her unyielding devotion to a certain river and its canyons. She turned her fame and talent to a worthy cause: saving Glen Canyon and the Colorado River.

She was introduced to the Colorado River in 1953, when she took her first trip down the Colorado through the Grand Canyon. The trip left her spellbound. "It was just the most awesome, magnificent thing," she recalled. "You could see the way the whole world's put together, by looking at how it's been cut away millennium after millennium, and then you'd feel just like what you really are—a grain of sand in all this creation."[2]

Katie returned to the Colorado River the next year, this time to Glen Canyon, 164 miles upriver from Lees Ferry. Her arrival there was preceded by many other visitors, the earliest of whom was

KATIE LEE IN GROTTO CANYON, ONE OF THE MANY SMALL CANYONS THAT
BRANCHED OFF GLEN CANYON PRIOR TO THE BUILDING OF THE DAM
(1956). (Photo by Frank Wright; courtesy of Katydid Books and Music.)

John Wesley Powell. Upon first seeing the canyon in 1869, he noted,
"We have a curious ensemble of wonderful features. . . . Carved
walls, royal arches, glens, alcove gulches, mounds, and monuments.
From which of these features shall we select a name? We decide to

call it Glen Canyon." Writing in his expedition logbook, Powell described "mounded billows of orange sandstone," "fern decked alcoves," and rocks that are "chiefly variegated shades of beautiful colors—creamy orange above, then bright vermilion, and below, purple chocolate beds, with green and yellow sands."[3] Like Powell, Katie was enchanted with Glen Canyon. "It was utterly the most beautiful place I've ever seen in my life," she said, "with its marvelous rock formations, gorgeous little canyons, and waterfalls, and every single one of them had water in them. Nooks and crannies and pools to swim in. It was inspiring, that's all." On that first trip in 1954, Katie and her fellow boaters heard about the proposed Glen Canyon Dam. "I didn't believe it. None of us did. We said, 'They'd never do that, they won't dam this.'"[4]

But Katie and her friends were wrong. By the close of 1954, the idea to build dams in the West had been around a long time. President Theodore Roosevelt advocated "reclamation of the arid lands in the West" in his State of the Union message in 1901. He said, "The western half of the United States would sustain a population greater than that of our whole country today if the water that now runs to waste were saved and used for irrigation." In other words, developing ways to collect and store the West's water was critical to the region's settlement. In June 1902 the Reclamation Act created the Bureau of Reclamation. In 1916 and again in 1922, E. C. LaRue, chief hydrologist for the United States Geological Survey, proposed dams that would flood Glen Canyon, providing water for irrigation and hydroelectric power.

Just thirty-two years later, the bureau had built over fifty dams, including the spectacular Hoover Dam (originally named Boulder Dam, completed in 1935). In the spring of 1956, President Dwight D. Eisenhower signed into law the Colorado River Storage Project act (CRSP), which authorized eleven irrigation projects, including the Glen Canyon Dam. Blasting would start in mid-October.

As the "Wreck-the-Nation" Bureau's[5] designs on Glen Canyon deepened and solidified, so did Katie Lee's devotion to the river and the canyon. She worked out a deal with Mexican Hat

Expeditions, a local river running company, to help keep her on the river. "I would take my guitar . . . I sang on the beach every night for passengers, and that way I got my passage for nothing," she said.[6] "What is greater than being on this river?" she wrote one evening, after playing her guitar and singing for the passengers. "To be able to sit and talk about things with the magic roar of the water in your ears and the smell and spell of the Canyon all around you . . . the night a blanket of stars . . . oh, river . . . you put all problems to shame!"[7]

The river became her refuge. It grounded her. "It was just necessary for me to get out with nature and be in this most beautiful place. It was just like having a soothing balm rubbed into me for two or three weeks or a month when I was there. And I would go back just completely cleansed and feel like a whole new human being." She was fortunate, for river runners who came after Katie did not and will not know the depth of soul to be found in Glen Canyon. "I know who I am now, and that river helped me find out—especially Glen Canyon helped me find out—so that there isn't any question about it."[8]

For many, especially those who called the Colorado River and its canyons "home," the damming of Glen Canyon was unthinkable. The project grew more controversial as awareness increased. "I started fighting," Katie said. "At first, I did everything wrong. I got mad and angry and everytime I opened my mouth, I insulted somebody. The only way I could get anything across was to shut my mouth and sing. People listened to music. I wrote songs, and I sang them everywhere I went, all over the country, singing in nightclubs."[9]

By 1957 she'd written five songs of protest, including "The Wreck-the-Nation Bureau":

> Three jeers for the Wreck-the-Nation Bureau!
> Free loaders with souls so pure-o
> Wiped out the good Lord's work in six short years.
> They never saw the old Glen Canyon

Just dammed it up while they were standin'
At their drawing boards with cotton in their ears!

(Chorus) Oh, they're gonna dam the Frying Pan
You're next, old Roarin' Fork.
And when they build Glen Canyon dam
The San Juan got a cork!
No river's safe until these apes
Find something else to do
So have your fun in Cataract
'Cause after that, you're through!

Three beers for the Wreck-the-Nation Bureau
For them I know there is no cure-o
All the waters of the world they would impound.
I'll tell you now of their latest whimsey;
To fill Grand Canyon to the brimsey
While Rainbow Bridge comes crashing to the ground!

(Chorus) Oh, they've gone and dammed the Frying Pan
The Muddy and the Blue
If we'd left it to Half-Aspinall,
He'd got the Crystal River too!
These little hard hats with their toys
Of dynamite and drills,
Won't rest until each mighty gorge
Is choked with cement fills.

No fears have the Wreck-the-Nation Bureau,
In their ignorance secure-o,
What's a few more billion? . . . ain't that nice?

KATIE LEE
187

'Bridge Canyon for the Havasupai'
Dams and trams and tacky-poop, I
Wonder at my river's slow demise!

(Chorus) They've gone and dammed the Frying Pan
The Yampa, Green and Bass,
In Steiger's book a ripplin' brook
Was a place to drowned your ass.
He'd rather shoot a burro
Than a rapid, anyway—
And leave a dam down in the Grand
To mark his cocky way!

No ears have the Wreck-the-Nation Bureau,
Blind as well you can be sure-o;
Domminy, old Floyd, was their head *fink*.
They'd drowned the wildlife of Alaska,
Build Rampart Dam, not even ask ya
If you want the world's most useless skating rink!

(Chorus) They've gone and dammed the Frying Pan
The Gunnison and the Snake.
For them, all rivers of the world
Have got to be a lake!
So busy with inundation
They can't unsalt the sea . . .
'Cause that would mean an end
To their Pork Barrel Revelry!

A pox on the Wreck-the-Nation Bureau
Down with the Wreck-the-Nation Bureau

Up the Wreck-the-Nation Bureau
And their little cousins,
Hard-hats by the dozens,
The stupid Army Corps of Engineers![10]
(© Katie Lee; reprinted by permission of Katydid Books & Music.)

Others joined in the fight, all believing that if people knew
what was being destroyed, surely the dam would be stopped. Ken
Sleight, a river runner, formed Friends of Glen Canyon, a loosely organized group of river runners who sought to educate the public
about the beauty and historical significance of Glen Canyon. David
Brower, executive director of a fledging conservation group called
the Sierra Club, started a campaign to save Glen Canyon. William
L. Thompson, a member of the National Parks Association, was
quoted in the October-December 1955 issue of the *National Parks
Magazine,* "There are others (canyons) that are more grand and
more violent, but none that is more beautiful."

Despite the growing protest, the public's eye was fixed fast
on the benefits of the dam. Two powerful Arizona politicians, Stewart Udall and Barry Goldwater, argued in favor of building it; cham-
bers of commerce in Utah, Arizona, and Colorado saw dollar signs.
Boaters and fishermen wanted a lake in the desert, and even conser-
vationists, who believed in maintaining a balance between reclamation and conservation, supported the project.

In October of 1956 the first blast of dynamite struck the
canyon walls.

"When I think ahead," Katie wrote in her journal, "I begin
to choke. . . . This will all be under water. Why? Why? I know why
. . . man's stupidity, his greed and thoughtlessness. . . . The canyon I
stand in now will be full of slime and stink from lack of free
drainage, and the beauty and mystery of the incredible Glen will be
gone forever."[11] It *was* unthinkable, and Katie grappled with what
she couldn't fathom.

"That mile through Labyrinth—It just isn't believable that
there could be such a place! Six hundred feet high and an average of a

foot or two wide, winding like a snake through solid rock! Oh, how I cry in anger against these imbeciles who will build a dam to cover this." Katie and some friends visited and boated down the canyon early in the construction of the dam. She noted: "At Sentinel Rock there is the horrible scar on the wall where the bloody business of beginning the dam is evident. They have white lead paintmarks all over the walls for several miles upstream and below the site itself. A big gaudy sign, which is an infringement on the constitutional rights of American citizens (since this part is a navigable river) shakes its fist:

WARNING
No travel beyond this point to Lees Ferry
Blasting on Canyon walls is dangerous to
boat travel.

Katie and her companions disregarded the sign and continued down the river. "A mile below, little men were crawling over the walls from the top in little rope chairs, all silent and busy, marking the wall for blasts. On Monday, President Eisenhower presses a button in Washington, and the first explosion begins construction officially. Back in the boat and down our river, I cannot hold back tears of anger and resentment against this wrongdoing."12

Two days after she wrote these words, on October 15, 1956, President Eisenhower pressed a ceremonial key in Washington, D.C., and a roar filled Glen Canyon, catapulting boulders into the air. As they tumbled into the river, a cloud of dust rose from the canyon. The Glen Canyon Dam project was a reality. It would be seven years before the dam was completed and the canyon flooded.

The realization that Glen Canyon would soon be gone forever led many other people to flock to the area. River companies advertised, "Last chance to see Glen Canyon," and many people came on their own to wonder why such an exquisite place was being destroyed. Two well-known photographers, Philip Hyde and Eliot Porter, spent time capturing the images of Glen Canyon. Hyde's

LEE RELAXING ON ONE OF HER MANY TRIPS DOWN RIVER. (Photo by Frank Wright; courtesy of Katydid Books and Music.)

1955 photographs became a fourteen-page photographic essay in the November 1958 Sierra Club *Newsletter*. Porter photographed Glen Canyon in 1960 and again in 1961. He brought his photographs to Sierra Club Director David Brower, and together they planned to publish a book.

Katie and her friends Frank Wright and Tad Nichols had their own private plan; they set out to explore the hidden canyons of the Glen. "We didn't set out particularly to name them, but we went down there so much that we needed to know where we were, and when we got off the river we would try and remember, 'Now was that Mile 64 or what?' That doesn't stay in your mind as long as a name, and, for our own reference, we started naming the canyons," Katie explained.[13]

Their efforts brought forth names like Cathedral Canyon, Dangling Rope, Dungeon, and Wishbone, which made a wishbone before it emptied into the river (the United States Geological Survey called it Oak). Naming these special places helped Katie and her friends imprint them permanently on their minds. "There are twenty-five names left on the canyon by us; names that we gave them from 1955 to 1960. My last run was in 1962," Katie said.[14] During the construction of the dam, diversion tunnels carried the water of the Colorado past the site, allowing Katie and her friends the chance to do their work. In January 1963, the diversion tunnels were closed, and the Colorado River began to fill Lake Powell.

The extra trips to the canyon, protests, letters, articles, and Katie's songs did little to impede the inexorable progress of the dam. A town—Page, Arizona—was developed to house the workers. Millions of tons of concrete were poured into massive footers. Nothing—not a six month strike by construction workers, weather, or changes in administrations in Washington—stopped the steady rise of the dam.

Growing increasingly defeated, opposers of the dam held out one last hope. "From the beginning we knew that Rainbow Bridge National Monument was supposed to be protected," Katie said,[15] referring to a key sentence in Section One of the Colorado River Storage Project Bill, which says, "No dam or reservoir constructed under the authorization of this Act shall be within any national park or monument." Section Three of the bill further stated that "the Secretary of the Interior shall take adequate protective measures to preclude impairment of the Rainbow Bridge National Monument." If they couldn't save Glen Canyon, perhaps they could save the monument. In legislation dating from 1910, 160 acres surrounding the stone arch were included in the designated monument area. However, if the new lake were backed up to its maximum height, an elevation of 3,711 feet above sea level, water would be 15 feet deep beneath the bridge.

Katie's suggestion was simple: make the water level lower. Other suggestions included building barrier dams around the monument to protect it. In the summer of 1960, as the campaign to save Rainbow Bridge National Monument escalated, Stewart Udall, U.S.

Representative for Arizona and member of the House Interior and Insular Affairs Committee, went to inspect the monument.

Frank Wright and Tad Nichols took Udall up Forbidding Canyon to Bridge Canyon and finally to Rainbow Bridge. He climbed on top, cooled his feet in the creek, and later met with the chief project engineer, Lem Wylie. Wylie said the monument could indeed be protected with two barrier dams, a pumping system, and at least 15 miles of new roads.

Although Udall believed that the wording in the CRSP act called for the protection of the monument, he came away convinced that the resulting construction would do more damage to the area than letting water intrude on the monument. If the barrier dams were built, Rainbow Bridge National Monument would be sitting in a box, its dramatic impact destroyed.

When in the spring of 1961 Congress again refused to allot money for the protection of Rainbow Bridge National Monument, the Sierra Club's David Brower called for construction on the Glen Canyon Dam to cease until funds were provided for its protection. His call fell on deaf ears.

Time grew short. Late in 1962 the National Parks Association filed suit in United States District Court on behalf of several conservation organizations against Udall, by then President John F. Kennedy's secretary of the interior, to prevent him from closing the diversion tunnels until Rainbow Bridge National Monument was protected. The court ruled that the National Parks Association did not have the right to sue the government.

The final blow to the monument was struck on January 18, 1963, three days before the scheduled closing of the left-bank diversion tunnel. Interior Department lawyer Frank Barry reported to Udall, "the provisions originally included in the Colorado River Storage Project Act calling for protective measures at Rainbow Bridge National Monument have been suspended by the Congress and are no longer operative."[16]

Brower flew to Washington in a last-minute effort to persuade Udall to change his mind. Udall wouldn't see him. He was holding a press conference to announce plans for two new dams—downstream from Glen Canyon. Brower left in shock. They were going to dam the Grand Canyon!

On January 21, 1963, the tunnel was closed, and the reservoir began to fill. The battle for Glen Canyon and Rainbow Bridge National Monument was lost, but Brower vowed to save the Grand Canyon.

Katie's songs became a lament. In 1964, Folkway Records released her album *The Folk Songs and Poems of the Colorado River,* some collected from years on the river, many written by her in protest of the Glen Canyon Dam. In the liner notes, she wrote, "To those of us who love the river for what it is, who have found the Glen Canyon to be one of the most beautiful, unmolested, clean, fascinating areas in the country, packed with scientific information, with ancient history and ruins, and who have experienced adventure unparalleled amid its winding side canyons, the damming of its flow seems an appalling waste of everything."[17]

Lee's liner notes warned about future dams proposed for the Grand Canyon. She asked, "Is it progress to destroy beauty, wildlife, ancient ruins, solitude? And now, though nobody will be able to tell you why, it is progress to destroy one of the wonders of the world—your Grand Canyon."

Eliot Porter's Glen Canyon pictures were collected in the book *The Place No One Knew*, edited by David Brower and published by the Sierra Club in 1963. Stewart Udall received an advance copy. Brower clearly blamed Udall for the destruction of Glen Canyon. In the introduction he wrote, "The man who theoretically had the power to save this place did not find a way to pick up the telephone and give the necessary order."

Katie believed the title of the book explained why we lost Glen Canyon. "There weren't enough of us who knew anything about it. It really was the place no one knew." But she likened solving that problem to a snake eating its tail: "The more people you get to fight for the rivers, the more people you have to take to the rivers, thereby ruining them in order to save them from destruction. You get a lot more people on the rivers than many of the rivers can take. The river's a very delicate ecosystem. Those little canyons in the Glen, if there had been more than ten footprints in there a year—some of those hanging gardens—they'd have been gone."18

The Glen Canyon Dam marked the end of an era for the Bureau of Reclamation. Now people knew that dams destroyed. The Sierra Club took out full-page ads in the *New York Times, Washington Post, San Francisco Chronicle,* and *Los Angeles Times* stating, "This time it's the Grand Canyon they want to flood. The Grand Canyon." And later, "Should we also flood the Sistine Chapel so tourists can get nearer the ceiling?" The Sierra Club published a coffee table book, *Time and the River Flowing,* about the Grand Canyon. Hundreds of thousands of letters arrived at the Bureau of Reclamation, at Congress, and at the White House. All said in effect, "Keep out of the Grand Canyon." On July 31, 1968, House and Senate conferees specifically prohibited the future construction of dams on the Colorado River between the Glen Canyon and Hoover Dams. The Grand Canyon was saved.

Although there would be no more dams built in the Grand Canyon, the Glen Canyon Dam continued to fill. Those who opposed the dam's creation stumbled on something they hadn't considered before: The river might save itself by destroying the dam. "Geologists said, 'This is not the place to build a dam. The sandstone is too porous,' but they went ahead. They work constantly on the right bank beside the dam to hold their cement plug in place, so it's going to go. It will happen," Katie believes.19

And it almost did in 1983. Heavy snowstorms in May, followed by a sudden warming, swelled the run-off to flood level. Lake Powell had not been drawn down enough to accommodate the unanticipated run-off. When operations manager Tom Gamble directed the east spillway gate to be opened, the river spewed house-size boulders. The tunnel ripped apart, and Gamble quickly ordered the spillway closed. Workers lowered into the tunnel the next morning found the concrete eaten away, and huge, gaping holes in the sandstone.

The spillways could not be used. The dam's engineers would have to wait out the run-off.

When the crest reached 3,700 feet, however, the water would automatically spill over and into the damaged tunnels. Time was critical. Gamble installed temporary plywood flashboards on top of the gates to hold back the rising water. The water level in Lake Powell reached 3,708.4 feet on July 14 and then began to recede. Amazingly, the plywood held, and the dam was saved. Both spillway tunnels were repaired using new technology that would theoretically prevent the destruction from occurring again.

The Glen Canyon Dam still stands. There are those who say we lost a beautiful canyon but gained a beautiful lake. And there are those who say we lost a beautiful canyon, period. But problems with the lake and dam continue. A November 19, 1995, headline in Tucson's *Arizona Daily Star* read, "Filth in Lakes Powell, Mead Prompts Health Concerns." The accompanying article noted that "Water quality in spots along both lakes has tested dangerously high for fecal coliform bacteria associated with human wastes." Glen Canyon National Recreation Area (GCNRA) is the National Park Service's number one destination for overnight visitors. According to Stephen Dubois, chief interpreter at GCNRA, there were 2.5 million visitors in 1997. Many laud these statistics and point to the use of Lake Powell as justification for the building of Glen Canyon Dam.

Not Katie Lee. Her home in Jerome, Arizona, is filled with artifacts and photos from her days on the river and in Glen Canyon. Her personalized automobile license says "DAM DAM." There's no question where this outspoken defender of Glen Canyon stands. Her book, *All My Rivers Are Gone* (1998), describes her experiences in Glen Canyon, her transformation into protest singer and environmentalist, and the failed movement that she helped lead against the building of the Glen Canyon Dam, an action she describes as "trying to put out a wildfire with a teacup."[20]

She took her boat, *Screwd-River,* on Lake Powell a few times. "I spent all my time crying and looking down into the water, trying to find the places that I knew were so beautiful."21 Instead, she found the lovely little side canyons that once were so enchanting to explore now choked with rotting logs, drift, orange peels, and floating beer cans and bottles.

She doesn't go back anymore. "And when I drive across the dam I put the blinders on so I can't see the reservoir. I can smell it; it doesn't smell like a river." She refers to the "poor, castrated thing down there called the Grand Canyon." She'll never see it again, either. "You couldn't pay me to go down in Grand Canyon now. . . . And I think that the blue, stinking, bloody cold, freezing ice water is an unnatural sickness, and all the long, clean beaches and bars that were down there are gone. The happiest day of my life will be when the 'Wreck the Nation' Bureau screws up one more time and the river cleans that place out again."22

It's always hard to reconcile memory with change. But at least we *have* memories, and Katie has many of the sandy beaches in Glen Canyon. She recalled, "We would build a fire at night with driftwood. Where'd this one come from? Well, this piece of wood, this came from the Colorado. No, this one came from the Green. This is the tree that grows up on the Green. No, this is . . . you know, all these pieces of wood from all over, all washed down over the years. May take a tree two, three years to go down the river. Depending on what you knew about wood, you could just about tell where it came from."23 Those days are gone, as is the driftwood. Gone too is the Driftwood Burners Society, whose claim to fame was lighting a driftwood bonfire with one match. The warm, red, silty Colorado—too thick to drink, too thin to plow—is gone, and with it, Glen Canyon.

Katie's anger remains strong, and the sentiments of her song "The River . . . to the Dam Builders" still encapsulate what many feel about the dam:

You've silenced me! You've cut my chattering string!
Are you glad that I no longer sing?
Are you proud, now in my millionth year,

Proud to see my journey's end so near?

And when you've covered o'er my secret carvings back beyond,

Will you feel might at having laid my restless waters still?

I'm sure you will!

You never knew, nor took the time to find

What strange and wondrous scenes I left behind.

Nor felt the blanket pressure of the stars

Hold you against the warmth of my sandbars.

My deep and winding crevasses you've never climbed with
   pounding heart

To turn, and, down the fluted sides in wonder let a tear fall
   through.

No! Not you!

You have no tears! You've dollar signs for eyes!

Not one of nature's wonders made you wise.

Your only thought was how to cloak the facts.

Which men can we buy? Who'll get the fat contracts?

I nearly flipped my stream that day I saw my face in *Life*

You had me growing corn on rock where even God had never
   tried!

Again, you lied!

Only a few who've stood with me alone

In the twilight bottom of a bowl of stone

Only those who've followed me in wild elation

Will feel each drowning inch with suffocation!

To them I leave a gift you dam builders will never own.

It can't be bought, or sold, nor spit upon, nor torn apart.

The music in my heart!24

(© Katie Lee; reprinted by permission of Katydid Books & Music.)

Today there is hope that Glen Canyon may be restored. In November 1996 the Sierra Club Board of Directors, at the urging of eighty-four-year-old David Brower—who has carried the destruction of Glen Canyon in his heart for forty years—voted unanimously to drain Lake Powell, to "pull the plug" and let the Colorado River run free through Glen Canyon once again. When Richard Ingebretsen, president of the Glen Canyon Institute, called Katie to discuss the proposal, Katie said, "That call was the first glimmer of light at the end of an incredibly depressing tunnel."[25]

Katie Lee is a key player and board member in the newly formed Glen Canyon Institute, a nonprofit organization that is battling to drain Lake Powell and restore the natural ecosystem and beauty of the Colorado River and its tributaries. The Glen and Katie were featured in the PBS special *Cadillac Desert,* based on Mark Reisner's best-selling book. She also was quoted in a 1997 feature story on Glen Canyon in *National Geographic* magazine. And in *All My Rivers Are Gone*, Lee tells the story of her "lost rivers," including the Colorado.

And so it has begun again—the Congressional hearings, the debates, the studies. This time the question is not, "Should a dam be built?" but, "Should a canyon be restored?" Who will win? Time will tell, but for Katie Lee, there is finally hope. There will be a new song!

Rowing a River, Rowing a Life

LOUISE TEAL

(1946–)

EXPLORING A SIDE CANYON OF THE GRAND CANYON. (Photo courtesy of John Annerino © 1998.)

W*HEN LOUISE TEAL* talks about the Grand Canyon, her eyes glisten and the shadow of thoughtfulness washes over her face. A river guide, or "boat woman," over the past twenty-five years, Louise has spent countless hours on the portion of the Colorado River that snakes its way through the Canyon. With each trip she has taken on that river, the essence of it has penetrated her soul more deeply.

When Louise was in high school in the San Francisco Bay area, her father introduced her to the Colorado River on a commercial trip through Glen Canyon. That trip affected Louise profoundly. "Being in Glen Canyon was a spiritual experience for me," she explained. "I was raised Presbyterian, but it always had seemed so limiting in that it didn't cover all the bases for me. Seeing the Canyon walls, immense, awesome, awe-inspiring, full of possibility and mystery, I lost any belief that I had been taught in church. I mean that. I distinctly remember the time and place where this happened, sitting alone, looking straight up at the walls in a narrow, now flooded side-canyon of the Glen. My dad would have died on the spot," Louise admitted, "if he'd known that the trip, which he took me on, had had that effect, but I know that today he'd be glad of where that realization eventually led me back to spiritually."[1]

It would be another seven years before Louise returned to the Colorado. "My husband, Roger, and I were living in Seattle under grey skies, when I saw a magazine article about the Grand Canyon. Some of the pictures showed boats, and I wrote to the park to see who ran river trips. I signed Roger and me up for the longest, cheapest trip," Louise recalled. "When it came time to go, Roger couldn't go, so I went alone. The Canyon was beautiful and intense, a completely fulfilling place to be. I wanted to stay. Simple," she thought. "I'll convince Roger to become a boatman."

And so she did. It helped immensely that Roger had burned out at his job as a stockbroker and was as ready to leave Seattle as Louise was eager to head to the Southwest. Louise observed that the women working on the river during the early 1970s were more or less assistants to their river running husbands or boyfriends. "I later realized that for most women, breaking up with their boatman boyfriend meant the end of going down the river."

It turned out that no one wanted to hire a former stockbroker as a river guide, so Louise and her husband enrolled in the American River Touring Association's (ARTA) first river running school. "The next year, Roger was running motor trips down the Grand Canyon, and I was working as his assistant, a soul in bliss."[2] Louise found she didn't like motors and wanted to learn to row. The following summer, she and Roger purchased a raft and helped other boatmen give free trips to kids on the Stanislaus River in California. "I learned to use oars that summer," Louise said. At the end of the summer, Roger went fishing in Alaska, and Louise managed to get on a Grand Canyon "snout" boat trip. A snout is a 22-foot, one-ton boat equipped with 13-foot oars. They are configured from a 4-foot-wide steel and wood frame set between two inflated military surplus pontoons. Learning to row a snout is hard for anyone, man or woman. "I learned to use the current as much as possible," Louise said, "looking way ahead in order to have time to make any needed maneuvers. Making tight eddies right above a rapid like the small entrance to Matkatiba Canyon was the biggest challenge."

Louise got the chance to row her own boat when Rob Elliott and his wife, Jessie Youle, bought ARTA and changed the name to Arizona Raft Adventures (AZRA). "They wanted to start women rowing. I was a likely candidate because I was already working there as an assistant and I had learned to row in California. Then, although Roger and I broke up, I continued rowing."

As with anyone who is an outsider of sorts, Louise did feel left out some of the time during her early years on the river. "After years of being a tomboy, of playing fighter pilot instead of house, it was still pretty obvious that I wasn't a guy. When I worked on crews as the only girl, it could get a little lonely. It took me a while to realize that I didn't want to be a guy anyway! Being in this great place surrounded by these vibrant men was a great deal. . . . They were superb, intelligent, and caring people, and how they made me laugh!"

Apart from a brief stint in real estate in Los Angeles in 1979—a bad career move brought on by a panic attack, where Louise convinced herself she had to work a "real" job in order to live a meaningful life—Louise was lost to the Canyon. Talking with her, it is hard to picture her in a business suit and high heels, clutching a clipboard and steering clients from one ranch-style house to another; she seems at home sitting in a boat, oars in hand, rowing river-soaked passengers between cavernous Canyon walls.

Louise enjoys the exhilaration of river running, including reading the water correctly, maneuvering into a tight eddy successfully, and surviving a dowsing at Lava Falls without flipping. But the quiet moments are equally gripping, and it is those moments she holds sacred. The beauty of the Canyon astounds Louise continually. It is what keeps her there, what she wants to share with her passengers.

"When I first started working here, I was beyond eager to learn everything about the place. I'd go to libraries and read old journals and books. I still find the science and history fascinating, but more and more, it's the feeling of the place that astounds me, the beauty. The shape and color of a rock, the flowing water, and always, the light . . . the light. The light down there is like nowhere else. The Canyon has a glow, salmon, rose, and orange."

It is important to Louise that her passengers experience this glow. "All a guide ever asks from the passengers is that they are blown away by the Canyon, that they appreciate the place. That's all. I don't care if they ever help in the kitchen, leave a great tip, or whatever. Just so they fall in love. So they realize where they are and aren't just floating through the Canyon sitting on the boat, talking about the next vacation they're going to nab." And more often than not, passengers do fall in love, they do connect on some level with the ineffable beauty of the Canyon. Much of this may well have to do with Louise's own profound connection to the river, for she is always encouraging her passengers to take notice. "I joke sometimes about telling the passengers to shut up and look at the Canyon. Like when they want to know how far, when will we get there, what mile, and so on, reasonable questions, but sometimes asked just to fill the air with distracting facts. Distracting from what they are feeling and seeing and hearing."

Yes, the Canyon has a voice, too, and Louise bids her passengers to listen for it. Its voice is the roar of the rapids, but it is also the soft bubbles that follow to tell you calm is restored, giving the listener permission to rest and think. And it is everything in between. "On my last trip with a group, we were being quiet and we heard a deer rustling in the reeds before we ever saw him. He was a big buck, and we would have missed him entirely if we'd been jabbering."

Louise Teal's devotion to the river is evident the moment she begins talking about it. She has a profound respect for its beauty and its power, both of which she has experienced firsthand. "You're not going to realize the power of the river until something goes wrong," a veteran boatman once told her, "and he was right," she said knowingly. "It is not until you're up against a rock and the river is folding your boat, or you've flipped and you are rolling around like a washing machine in the water, and the water is pounding you, and then you will realize the power of the river."

On a trip several years ago, after a particularly strenuous day of into-the-wind rowing, Louise set up a tarp because it looked like rain and collapsed, exhausted. When she awoke sometime later, she realized immediately that something was different. "I was in the middle of the river, with another boat tied to me, heading downstream toward Lava Falls. My story would have a different ending if I'd stayed sleeping until the jet engine roar of Lava Falls woke me up. As it was, I managed to pull the boats to shore well before that noisy 37-foot drop. Still, it's a story I always tell as we row down to run Lava, and I always mention that I was naked, in the thunder and lightning, except for my life jacket. On one trip, this gave a group of women riding on my boat an idea: 'Let's run Lava naked!'"[3]

Despite some initial concerns, Louise agreed to go along with her passengers. "At the scout [the place where the guide studies the rapid] above Lava, we parked a little away from the other boats so they wouldn't see us until we pulled out to run it. We put our life jackets on, and at the last minute I realized that I was going to slip all over the seat without pants on, so I put a scarf on the seat.

"We had a wild run and slammed into the top wave, slid down into the V-shaped wave and just got pummelled. Even with the scarf, I almost slid off the seat. I lifted myself back into some semblance of control over the boat, but we weren't going to be straight for the first big wave. I yelled, 'High Side.'" (High side means that everyone on the boat gets on the high side of the boat to prevent it from flipping.)

"We all leaned into the big wave and went up and over it. Then we just got absolutely hammered by the second wave behind it. It was like trying to hold on with a fire hose blasting you, and it was absolutely incredible. But, amazingly, no one fell in. The wave finally spit us out. We looked around and couldn't even see our boat. The tubes were literally under water, but they slowly wallowed up as we started bailing," Louise remembered. "One girl had blood all over her face because she'd been hit, probably by someone's elbow, but she didn't realize it. She was OK. I've decided it was a safety measure not to have clothes on, because no one was about to let go and get picked up naked. We were about as high and happy as you can get. We'd felt the full force of the river."

A river that can toss and pummel you is not a force to be reckoned with but to respect. People lose their lives when they fail to discern this one fundamental distinction. But when people meet the water's force for the first time, especially when their lives are in danger, they often perform remarkable feats. "People perform way beyond their capabilities—or what they perceive as their capabilities," Louise explained. "There was a sixty-year-old lady named Grace on a boat that flipped in Sockdolager. She got caught under the boat, but she did exactly what she was taught—looked for the light and walked her way out with her hands from under the boat. All this in the middle of a big rapid! She was so excited. Grace said she'd always wondered how she would react in an emergency, and she was really proud of herself. It was great to be part of her excitement."

In 1978, Louise and AZRA planned the first all-women's trip through the Canyon. "A passenger on one of my trips came up with this idea," Louise explained. "Pulling an all-woman crew together for the trip was tough. That's how few qualified women were Grand Canyon guides then." Louise was to lead the trip though she'd only led one other trip before. Her boss, Jessie Youle, and fellow guide Suzanne Jordan would run two other snouts, and Barbara Thomas guided the smaller paddle raft.

LOUISE TEAL MASTERFULLY NEGOTIATING CRYSTAL RAPIDS. (Photo courtesy of John Annerino © 1998.)

"We finally got it all organized and were at Lees Ferry with our snouts tied up to the shore," Louise said. "We had three snouts and one paddle raft to carry twenty-two women. I'd just finished my introductory/safety speech, and we began to untie and shove our high and dry boats into the river, when the ranger decided we needed another spare life jacket. We had to stall while our truck driver went to borrow one from a nearby river company's warehouse. I took the group back to the shade of the tamarisk trees and talked more about safety tips and taking care of the Canyon, totally forgetting that the water was due to come up thanks to the workings of the [Glen Canyon] dam.

"We hung out under the trees for a while and then started walking back to the river. Whale, a Hatch River Expeditions motor boatman who was also putting in, grinned at me and said, 'Louise, I

tied up your boats for you. They were starting to float away.' So . . .
oh, my God . . . the first Grand Canyon women's trip in history
came pretty close to—instead of being pulled off without a hitch,
which it was safety-wise—came close to becoming a great river
story in which all our boats floated downriver without us!" After
telling this story, Louise suggested that all boatwomen working
today should be glad that Whale wasn't one of those boatmen who
thought women shouldn't be guides in the Grand Canyon. He could
have had a heyday by letting their boats drift away. Instead, he had
the good grace to cut the women a break—Louise in particular. She
learned from Whale and others like him.

Louise arrived on the river at the time Americans—indeed,
people across the globe—were at a cultural crossroads. Women
were just beginning to assert themselves in the male world, and she
unwittingly championed the role of women working on the river
not as assistants but as full-fledged river runners and guides. She
recognized early on that her opportunites were possible because of
the courage of her contemporaries, both men and women.

"I wanted to honor the women I'd worked with and met on
the river," Louise said, and she did so by writing *Breaking the Current: Boatwomen of the Grand Canyon*, a compelling collection of biographies of the Grand Canyon's boatwomen. Writing the book, she
said, "was a way to show my love for the people and the place."
Though the issue of sexism was not the motivating factor to write the
book, it necessarily surfaced in her research because it was a sizable
part of the experience of those she interviewed. "The book became
not only a story of people in love with a place, which I feel it primarily is, but also of women struggling to be in a place they loved. I
wanted to honor that struggle." As Louise wrote in the preface to her
book, these first boatwomen "were only following their hearts amidst
the pressures and possibilities facing all women in our particular era."

The evolving role of women on the river has been the hallmark of the quarter century Louise has spent on the river. Boatwomen have made incredible strides, with more working as guides
today than ever before. "They're no longer oddball or working jobs

on the periphery. They're acknowledged contributors. In 1869, John Wesley Powell made his first exploration in the *Emma Dean*. Robert Brewster Stanton's survey crew rode the rapids in the *Sweet Marie* and the *Bonnie Jean*. Now we're rowing the boats!"

Louise has witnessed a lot of changes in the Canyon and among the people who visit, some not so agreeable. The days of high adventure and the thrill of the unexpected have been diluted by movies, books, and magazines. The clientele has changed as the trips become more and more expensive. The river has become increasingly crowded, more and more regulations have been established, and (thanks to the Glen Canyon Dam) beaches have disappeared and the riparian habitat considerably altered. Most disturbing to Louise, however, is the growing popularity of "interchange" trips, where visitors run only short sections of the river. "It takes folks three or four days to really be there," she explained, "and if they leave on day five or six, they miss the opportunity to immerse themselves in the experience, to become a tribe traveling through the Canyon." Without this complete immersion, visitors are missing the true magic of the place, the mysterious effect it has on body and psyche. It is a rare gift, she says, to disappear into one of the earth's deepest crevices and to escape cars and phones and televisions.

Louise laments the passing of earlier days, where adventure and discovery of the unknown were what drew people to the Canyon. She wishes she could have gone down the river before the Glen Canyon Dam controlled its flow. "Can you imagine being with Elzada Clover and Lois Jotter? Being the only trip in the Canyon? Never knowing what was around the next bend? What an adventure that would be!"[4]

Despite the less agreeable changes, Louise's connection to the Canyon and the spiritual renewal she finds and shares there remain constant. And she plans to keep on "rowing the boats." She says, "It's still absolutely the coolest thing to be down there. Even with the changes, the place is always there . . . the beauty and magnificence is solid. I can't imagine not being there. I plan to keep doing it as long as the body's willing."

Saddle Up! Lady Mule Wranglers of the Grand Canyon

MULE WRANGLING AT THE CANYON SPANS GENERATIONS FOR
SOME FAMILIES, INCLUDING EARLY SETTLERS WILLIAM AND
EDITH BASS AND PRESENT-DAY WRANGLER PATTY KNOX,
PICTURED HERE WITH HER FATHER BUD DUNAGAN.
(Photo © Sue Bennett, 1999.)

*F*OR MORE THAN a century, wranglers—folks who work
with mules and horses—have guided dudes—city folk pretending
they are cowboys—into the Grand Canyon. Mule rides are a favorite pastime for Canyon visitors, and most agree that exploring
trails while atop a mule is the most exciting way to see the Canyon.
Not only have they been brought face to face with the Canyon's exquisite beauty, the "dudes" have had a true Western experience.

Mules are crafty animals, known for being sure-footed and stubborn, yet safe. In the more than one hundred years that mule wranglers have been taking dudes into the Canyon, they've never lost a dude! That's because mules have a special set of breeding requirements. A male donkey is called a jack, and a female donkey is a jenny. In horses, the male is a stallion, and the female, a mare. Breed a jack with a mare and you have a mule. (Breed a stallion with a jenny, and you get a hinny.) The result of this breeding is an animal with the shape and surefootedness of a large donkey and the disposition of a horse, making it an ideal animal for trips along steep, narrow ledges like those found in the Canyon.[1]

Mules were the work animal of early prospectors like John Hance and William Bass (see chapter 1), who used them to haul ore from their mines in the Canyon. Both men soon learned that putting a dude on the back of a mule was more profitable than ore, and by the mid-1890s both men offered trips into the Canyon. In the early years, women rode into the Canyon wearing long skirts and proper hats, but none were counted among the ranks of the wranglers. That is until William Bass's daughter Edith came along. She rode her own mule down to Shinumo Camp at age three and a half, and by age thirteen she could wrangle a mule better than most cowboys. Edith's outgoing personality and skill with mules made her a natural with dudes, and she can rightly be called the Canyon's first woman wrangler. Edith married Bert Lauzon, a Fred Harvey guide, in 1917 and lived at the Canyon until her untimely death in 1924 after appendix surgery.

Wrangling was incredibly hard work, and it remains so even today. No modern devices substitute for the personal touch of the wranglers. Today at the Canyon, a mule wrangler's day begins much the way it always has: with a cold splash of water on the face at 4:00 A.M. and a quick, hearty breakfast. The Grand Canyon mule wrangler is in the stables before the sun crests the horizon. Stalls are swept clean, and fresh hay replaces the matted, day-old pile. The wranglers haul grain for the mules' breakfasts and then brush, comb, and check the animals head to heel for cuts, bruises, or other injuries

EDITH BASS, THE CANYON'S FIRST FEMALE WRANGLER. (Photo courtesy of the Arizona Historical Society, Tucson, Arizona, Bass Collection.)

that may not have been apparent the night before. All are then sad-dled, cinched, and led off to the corral to await the day's dudes.

Guiding dudes requires more than being a good rider. First and foremost, the wrangler is responsible for each rider's safety. In addition, the wranglers give talks about the Canyon in an entertain-ing style, put up with every personality type known to the human race, react in a split second to an emergency, and do it all with a smile. Not much has changed in the past hundred years. There is one difference: The mule wrangler of today is just as apt to be named Patty, Bernice, or Kitty as Joe, Curley, or Carl. Today nearly half of the wranglers at the Canyon are women.

Ron Clayton, livery manager for Fred Harvey and an admitted chauvinist, was at first reluctant to hire women wranglers, but he now says, "My women wranglers are great. You don't need brawn to be a wrangler—it's the knowledge of the animal and skill with people that counts! Patty is one of my best wranglers."[2]

Patty Knox was in her sixth year of wrangling dudes when I met her on the South Rim of the Canyon. "My mom always told me, 'Don't learn to cook or type,'" Patty laughed as she explained how she came to the Canyon, "but I didn't listen and worked as a legal secretary in Flagstaff for several years. Finally, when my kids were out of the house, I decided to do what I'd always wanted to do, and I came here to work. My dad worked here as a wrangler in the 1960s before becoming a deputy sheriff. I've been around horses and mules all my life."[3]

It's hard to imagine Patty, a petite blond with a long ponytail and soft voice, working as a wrangler. "I do have a problem being female sometimes," Patty explained, a bit annoyed. "Although I have the most seniority here, the male dudes will walk right by me and ask the male wranglers a question!"

Patty also has trouble convincing men that she can get them on the mule. "They'll come up to me and say, 'You can't possibly get me up there.' It's real easy. You just use your brain instead of your back. I drop the stirrup down real low so they can reach it, then I get down and lift with my shoulder at the same time they are pulling themselves up. It works perfectly," she explained.

The concern doesn't end once the dudes are saddled up. "For about the first twenty minutes of the ride they are really nervous about whether I can take care of them or not, but I have this sense of calmness when I go down the trail because I have done it for so long," Patty said. Her weekly schedule is one overnight trip to Phantom Ranch, two day rides to Plateau Point, and a day in the barn sweeping, cleaning, and loading hay into the chutes. "I love it," she said, sweeping her hand toward the Canyon and patting her mule. "I have the greatest office in the world and the best desk."

What could be better than having a movable desk that takes you where you want to go—into the Grand Canyon?

"I love the Canyon, and I love to show it off. All I ask is that people really look at the Canyon and love it too," Patty commented. "I hate when I am with people who signed up because it was the thing to do or because someone else insisted." However, people who don't want to do the ride are usually willing to follow instructions, unlike "experienced" riders. Of the latter Patty pointed out, "They may be experienced, but they are not experienced in the Grand Canyon. One morning I was tightening cinches and came to a man wearing a movie logo jacket. He told everyone that he was working on a movie and that he was famous, but I didn't recognize him. He also said he had done a lot of trail riding and told me, 'Young lady, if you need any help today, you just let me know.' I thanked him politely and cinched him up, and we took off down the trail."

The Bright Angel Trail starts off gradually but quickly becomes steep, with some abrupt turns and sheer dropoffs. "Everyone else was a little nervous and was sitting up straight and paying attention and doing what I had told them to do, but this guy was hanging back and taking pictures. He had his bridle reins over the saddle, and the mule stumbled a little, and this guy bounced off into the ditch because he wasn't holding on," Patty recalled. "We were near the top, and I could have called someone to come after him, but he insisted he could go on—but he was terrified after that, and he swore everytime the mule made a little stumble and yelled, 'Patty, he's bucking on me.' On the way back up he got off and led the mule."

When an accident like this happens, it's nearly always the dude's fault. Patty explained that the mules that carry dudes are very trustworthy. "We get new mules once a year, and the guides ride the new ones to see how they will do. They come broke to ride, but they have to get used to the Canyon and the hikers. If they scare us, we turn them over to the packers. It is a common myth that the mules pack first and then go to the dudes. This is not true. We pack them when we don't trust them. Our duders—the mules that carry guests—are solid gold. I have seen people get off, catch their foot in the stirrup, and fall, and the duder mule just stands there and looks bored."

Pack mules, said Patty, are a different story. She should know. Her husband, Ross, is head packer for the Fred Harvey Company. "Ross says leading a pack train is 'hours and hours of boredom intermingled with moments of sheer terror.'" A pack mule can suddenly turn ugly. "It is really scary when a pack mule throws a fit," Patty explained. "Pack mules are more dangerous since they are tied together, and we have lost pack mules."

Patty joked that she was introduced to Ross by a mule. "After my dad retired from the sheriff's department, he came back to the Canyon to work as a wrangler again. Ross was a wrangler then too, and Dad was showing him some pictures of his family. Ross said, 'Who's that?' pointing to me. Dad, who wasn't anxious for me to get tangled up with a mule wrangler, said, 'That's Patty. She's in Florida.' Now, I've never been in Florida!"

Patty and Ross have been married eight years. Ross is a published cowboy poet, well known in cowboy poetry circles. He and Patty always go to the annual cowboy poetry gathering in Elko, Nevada. Patty sings and has written several original songs, including "The Grand Canyon Pack Mule Waltz." They've produced one tape—Ross recites poetry, and Patty provides vocal background—and have plans for others.

Patty is considering adding cartooning to her many talents. "I run into so many ideas every day. One day a man told me that old joke, 'What do you get if you play country music backwards?' The answer is 'You get your wife back, your car back, and so on.' In my cartoon sketch, I'd have a lady wrangler say to the mule, 'Did you get that?' and the mule would look back and say, 'I'm into jazz myself.'"

Mule wranglers seem to have a special sense of humor. Like Patty, Bernice Reeves, a wrangler on the North Rim of the Canyon for 11 years often sees the humorous side of the job. I first met Bernice when I went on one of her mule rides several years ago. "Don't let your horse eat," Bernice instructed us firmly. A dude asked, "Why not?" In her most serious manner, Bernice replied, "There's a lot of buckin' weed down there." She starting laughing, and we realized that Bernice was kidding. She had me fooled. I've watched too many Western movies not to believe in "buckin' weed."

Becoming serious, Bernice explained, "The real reason we don't want them to eat is that we want them to stay bunched up because it's safer. Plus, if you let them eat, they will eat all day." Keeping the mules close together is so important that Bernice told us to give the mules a whack with our whips if they stopped. When someone asked, "Why do I have to hit the mule?" Bernice explained patiently, "This is what mules understand. It's for the mule's safety and yours."

Bernice has been giving instructions to dudes on the North Rim for sixteen seasons. "It wasn't my life's ambition to be a dude wrangler," she said, when I asked how she came to the North Rim of the Canyon. "I came out here under protest. I was in college, pre-vet [the veterinarian program], and training horses in the summer. One summer when I got out of college, the man I worked for didn't have anything for me to do. He knew the man who did the mule rides off the North Rim, so he sent me to the Canyon to work," she explained. "When I got here, I liked it. I've been here ever since. This canyon has a draw; it has some type of magical draw to it. You see the same things, but there is always something different that you haven't seen before that you notice."

For the five months the North Rim is open, Bernice rides almost daily into the Canyon. All day rides go to Roaring Springs, a 3,200-foot drop over 4 miles of steep terrain. Half-day rides end 1.8 miles into the Canyon at Supai Tunnel. "People from all walks of life and all different backgrounds come to ride. You never know what will happen," Bernice said. "We had a guy with an artificial leg just below his knee. We got him on the mule, and the wrangler walked around to adjust the stirrups—and the leg fell off. So we got him all back together and sent him out of the corral, and he got one hundred yards away and that leg fell off again! So we gave up and tied it on the mule. Everyone was laughing, including the man with the artificial leg!"

BERNICE REEVES' DAY INCLUDES GIVING TOURISTS A HEALTHY
RIBBING ALONG THE TRAIL. (Photo by Kitty Marr.)

Bernice is good at making people laugh, as I discovered as
we rested at the Supai Tunnel during our half-day ride. Someone
asked, "Where do you get the mules?" In her most serious manner,
Bernice replied, "These mules come from Tennessee, but some owners get their mules from Missouri." After a pause, she asked, "Do
you know the difference between a Tennessee and a Missouri mule?"
When no one responded, Bernice explained, "About 600 miles!"

It's not all work at the North Rim. Everyone celebrates the
Fourth of July. "At the end of the work day a parade is organized by
the Park Service in which all the North Rim employees participate,"

Bernice noted, "and the wranglers come loaded with all the water pistol firepower they can pack on their mules to ambush dudes and each other during the parade." Bernice remembers an exceptionally hot Fourth a few years ago. "We wranglers developed a mighty thirst and, with no place to tie our mules, we rode up the steps and into the saloon and ordered beers. My mule, Elvis, and I, were right in the middle of it," she laughed. Tourists watched in awe, cameras clicking, but the Park Service did not see the humor in the situation. "We pleaded for forgiveness and headed for the barn," Bernice said, "and then Judy, the head ranger, 'lightened up' and ambushed us with the fire truck. One of the other wranglers yelled, 'Bernice, rope her!' I jerked down my rope and built a loop. By this time Judy was at the other end of the fire hose, aiming at me and Elvis. Elvis pulled his ears back, and I ducked my head and let the loop sail. When I pulled my slack, all of a sudden the water stopped. I looked up to see that the rope had settled on my intended target—Judy—who was calling a truce!"

Bernice's sense of humor gets her through the season, but by mid-October, when the North Rim closes, she is ready to return to her family's ranch in Cedar City, Utah, and train horses, not people. When spring rolls around and the snow melts on the North Rim, back she goes to the Canyon, the dudes, and another summer with her friend and fellow wrangler, Kitty Marr.

Kitty is in her eleventh year at the North Rim. Like Bernice and Patty, Kitty loves the Canyon. "I think the Grand Canyon has a hold on me. I really love it here, and I enjoy working with the mules and meeting new people. It's fun taking people from all over the world [down into the Canyon], but mostly I love the Canyon itself."

I first met Kitty in 1992, when I'd arranged a backpacking trip across the Canyon from the South Rim. Our packs were to be picked up at Roaring Springs and carried to the North Rim. We were happy to drop the packs by the hitching rail after the long haul from Phantom Ranch. When I saw a woman—a short, slender woman to boot—coming into camp and leading three mules, I'll admit I was a bit worried, but without cause. Kitty made sure we

THE CANYON HAS A SPECIAL HOLD ON WRANGLER KITTY MARR.
(Photo by Bernice Reeves.)

had the packs properly packed and then lifted and arranged those
30-pound packs like they were bags of groceries. She took time to
chat with us and answered our questions about the trail ahead, and
then, with a wave and a smile, left us to climb out of the Canyon,
thankfully without the packs.

I could tell by the way Kitty handled the mules that she was
no stranger to riding. "I've been around animals since I was a kid,"

she said, "showing horses in breed shows in all classes and in 4-H. I still enjoy teaching kids how to ride." Kitty worked at a livestock auction for a few years before she started wrangling mules.

She's grown to know the individual personalities of the mules in her care. "Some are very affectionate and love to be petted. Some prefer to be left alone. Some mules like being ridden by women, others like men, and some are good for children." Some of the mules even have a sense of humor: "I've seen them go around a corner on a switchback and pause just to see if they can get a thrill out of people." And, Kitty added, they're usually successful. "I've taken hundreds of people down in the Canyon, and every trip is different. The youngest we take is eight years old. I took a woman who was eighty-three years old. Once, I had this lady who was wearing sunglasses and a baseball cap, and I wondered if she was television star Sandy Duncan. When she started to talk, I knew it was her. She was a really neat lady, and I enjoyed taking her into the Canyon."

Kitty enjoys answering questions, even the ones that are comical. "We have a half-day ride down to the Supai Tunnel. Once, I had a lady ask, 'When we get there, is there a shuttle bus that brings us back to the top?' I laughed to myself and explained to her that there are no roads into the Grand Canyon and that she would have to ride a mule both ways." When she works at the sign-up desk inside the lodge she is frequently asked, "How long does the hour ride last?"

At the end of the season, when there are no more questions to answer, Kitty, along with Bernice and the other North Rim wranglers, celebrate with—what else?—a 27-mile ride across the Canyon to meet the wranglers on the South Rim. "We have a great party!" Kitty said. The next day they ride back, close up the barn, and leave the North Rim for the winter.

Kitty usually goes home to Flagstaff, Arizona, where she works at a variety of jobs. "I like to do something totally different," she said, and has worked as a hotel registration clerk, a secretary, and a store clerk. By mid-March, she's ready for mules and dudes again, this time at Zion National Park in Utah for a couple of months while waiting for the North Rim to open in mid-May.

It's the Canyon, the people, the camaraderie of their fellow wranglers, and the mules that keep Patty, Bernice, and Kitty throwing saddles on their mules for another day with the dudes. No longer a curiosity in the Canyon, women wranglers have risen to the call of the Canyon's beautiful surroundings amidst hard work and skill.

With a Pack on Her Back

DENISE TRAVER

(1956–)

READY TO HIT TRAIL. (Photo by Mike Buchheit.)

"**Y**OU WON'T NEED this!" laughed Denise Traver as she pulled a hammer out of Jane Marshall's pack. "We'll use rocks to pound in tent stakes." Jane, New York City born and bred, was on her first backpacking trip ever, and like most people in her situation, she was seriously overloaded. "Most people come with more equipment and food than they need," Denise explained. "That's why I spend an entire day in orientation."[1]

Denise, a slender brunette with a ready smile, runs back-packing classes for women for the Grand Canyon Field Institute. The classes are her own invention and design, and she has been running them since 1992. She prides herself on introducing women to the outdoors and relishes the camaraderie that develops among the women she leads on trips.

Contrary to what one might think upon first meeting her, Denise did not grow up outdoors. "The closest I came to outdoor activities when I was young was that my grandparents had a cabin in the mountains of Washington state," Denise said. "We would visit, and I would always pretend that I was a deer running through the trees. I loved it!"[2]

Denise's parents divorced when she was only twelve. When Denise was fifteen, she moved with her mother from Yakima, Washington, to San Diego, California, when Denise's mother remarried. Shortly after that, she met John Marroquin. "His parents lived next door. I was sixteen, and he had just returned from Vietnam. I had a tremendous crush on him and used to hang around watching him design and build a 41-foot sailboat," she said. "When my mom moved back to Washington, I moved in with John. I was only seventeen. We got married when I was nineteen and he was twenty-eight."

Denise worked as a secretary for an engineering firm and helped John build his boat. "We were about three-fourths of the way done when John went to Alaska to help his friend Ray get a commercial abalone fishing venture started," Denise said. "I had gone on a business trip to Hawaii for a week, and when I got back to work, I was called in to the president's office. I was terrified and thought I must have done something wrong. When I got to the office, Ray's mother was there, and I knew right away something horrible had happened. She said, 'Denise, there's been an accident. John's dead.'"

"For several days I didn't know what had happened. It was a pretty rough time, and I was only twenty-four. I learned that John and Ray were scuba diving in 35 feet of water. Ray came back up to the boat, and when John didn't surface after forty-five minutes, he went back down. John was on the bottom. His mask was filled with blood. He had had a massive embolism. He went up too fast, and they didn't know why. His airhose was disconnected, one of his fins was off, and his face was bruised. The Coast Guard investigated but never did find out what happened," Denise explained.

The loss devastated Denise, and she spent the next several months surviving in a thick fog of grief. "I had read that you don't do anything different for at least a year after you lose your spouse, because you could get into lots of problems by rebounding. I definitely wasn't looking for a relationship, so I stayed low and kept working very hard." She did leave her secretarial position to work as a waitress in a lobster and prime rib restaurant. "I made lots of money, and a year and a half later, in 1982, I sold everything I owned and bought a little Toyota truck and a fifth-wheel camper."

Denise spent the next few months traveling, visiting family in Washington and British Columbia, and eventually ended up in Arizona. "I fell in love with Arizona," Denise said. "I got a job doing boat tours at Canyon Lake east of Phoenix. In the evenings I would sit on the pier and watch the moon rise over the desert. It was so beautiful. This is where I met Charley, the man who taught me to backpack."

Charley was a musician from New Orleans who had left the music scene and was working in maintenance at the lake. "He did a lot of hiking and backpacking. Finally, I persuaded him to let me go on a backpacking trip with him. He taught me all the things to do to make it nice. He would set up a shower and make camp very comfortable," Denise explained. "I love doing things that are physical and seeing what is beyond the roads, but still, I want to be comfortable. I don't want to go out there and not brush my teeth for two weeks. I want to go out there and enjoy myself and live in style!"

Denise spent the next few years working at Canyon Lake in the winters and at a resort in the Verde Valley in the summer months, always finding time for solo backpacking trips. She first hiked the Grand Canyon in 1988. "The women I worked with were going to hike to Phantom Ranch, spend the night, and hike out, and

I went along. I got dehydrated and sick. I didn't even get a chance to enjoy the cabin. I had a headache and couldn't eat dinner or breakfast. I was sick for two days after hiking out. I said I was never coming back to the Grand Canyon as long as I lived!"

Denise did not return until she began working at the Canyon. "I kept having people say to me that as much as I liked the outdoors and liked to backpack that I should be a ranger, so I filled out an application to work as a 'seasonal.'" Denise was hired; she spent most of 1989 at Mather Campground Fee Collection. "I wasn't meant to be in fee collection," she laughed. "On my days off I would backpack alone in the Canyon, just on the corridor trails that first summer. On lunch hours I volunteered in the Backcountry Office and eventually joined Search and Rescue." In her search and rescue work, Denise met Patty Thompson, the supervisor at Phantom Ranch Ranger Station, who mentioned that there would be an opening the next year at Cottonwood Campground, Denise's favorite place in the Inner Canyon. Denise went to Santa Rosa Ranger Academy, where she got her commission and learned advanced first aid, and in spring 1990 became the ranger in residence at Cottonwood Campground.

Cottonwood Campground is 7 miles from the North Rim down the North Kaibab Trail. Named for the tall cottonwoods that shade the area, the campground is a favorite stopping place for hikers on cross-canyon trips. The small ranger station there, built in 1934, had no electricity but did have running water with propane lights, a refrigerator, and water heater. Denise thrived there.

"At Cottonwood you can be an old-fashioned ranger," she said. Unlike many rangers, whose jobs are primarily to enforce regulations, Denise spent her days and nights at Cottonwood involved in the more traditional tasks people associate with park rangers. "Law enforcement was such a small part of what I did at Cottonwood. I worked on campground revegetation, painted the ranger station, made curtains, and even crocheted." She visited with people staying at the campground, answering questions while checking permits.

"Some wanted to know [about the park's] geology or had

questions about backpacking. Because of the effort required to get there, the people that come to Cottonwood tend to be more prepared and experienced than the people that come down to Indian Garden," she recalled.

There were exceptions to this, though. One night at midnight Denise got a call from the North Rim night dispatcher concerning a husband and wife who had not shown up for dinner with his parents at the lodge at the North Rim. The woman was six weeks pregnant, and the man had bad knees, yet they were hiking down to the Colorado River and back in one day—a total of 28 miles. Denise put on her clothes and headed up the narrow ledges of the North Kaibab Trail calling the couple's names every few minutes.

"At the top, I called the dispatcher and told her I had not found anyone, but that I would rest for two hours and go back down to the river," Denise said. "After taking a quick nap, I called to see if anything had been found out about the couple. The dispatcher was incredulous as she told me they were on the South Rim! They had gone down to the river and were talking to someone who told them they should do the Bright Angel Trail instead of the Kaibab because it wasn't as steep and had water. Now these were educated people, but they didn't know that the Bright Angel took them to the wrong rim!" Their confusion may have occurred because there are two Kaibab Trails—North and South. They had come down the *North* Kaibab Trail to the Colorado River, but their well-meaning adviser was talking about the *South* Kaibab Trail.

Denise enjoyed being at Cottonwood. "I would work nine days on and be off for five days. On my days off I would go rock climbing, hiking, backpacking, or kayaking. I'd been widowed for eleven years, and I had no intention of getting married or even getting into a serious relationship. I was just having fun."

Fun, that is, until a chronic bout with tick fever proved dangerous her first year at Cottonwood. "I felt tired all the time towards the end of the summer," Denise explained. "The nurse at the North Rim diagnosed my tiredness as relapsing tick fever. After a course of tetracycline I finally got better."

That Labor Day weekend, Denise was sent to Thunder River on patrol. She drove out to Monument Point and began to hike down the Bill Hall Trail. "I really got tired, but I thought I was just out of shape," she said. "It was raining by the time I got to Upper Tapeats Creek, and I had to ford the creek." The tick fever had relapsed, and Denise quickly became very sick. "I spent the night in the Upper Tapeats Campground and then started back up to Thunder River. I sat under a boulder to keep out of the rain, and I was so sick. There were rockslides all around me, and I kept thinking this boulder would go too, but I was so miserable, I almost wished it would."

Denise struggled to get to Surprise Valley, nearly a mile above Thunder River. She didn't make it. "I set my tent up partially on the trail and spent the night. My radio couldn't get out. The next morning, I dragged myself up the trail, and I found a cave near the top," Denise remembered with a shudder. "I stayed there all day. I didn't know what I was going to do. My radio didn't reach anyone, and I was wishing I would die in that cave."

Just when Denise had almost given up, she saw two people coming up the trail from Thunder River. "You are not going to believe this," she told them, "but I'm a ranger here and I am very sick." One of the hikers, who turned out to also be a ranger, took Denise's radio up to Surprise Valley and was able to make contact. "He called for a helicopter and got me out of there. That experience killed all my pride as a backcountry ranger!" Denise was prescribed another series of tetracycline. "By the time I went back down to Cottonwood for my second season, I was much better."

Early that season Denise had some unexpected visitors. "I'd been suggesting that solar power might work at Cottonwood," Denise explained, "and a group of division chiefs were hiking through the Canyon, checking on projects that needed to be done. Jim Hutton, the corridor supervisor, said, 'If you want solar power here, Brad Traver is the one to talk to.'" Denise went over to talk to Brad. "He blushed so easily that I loved ribbing him," Denise said. "The next day the group walked down to Ribbon Falls and a few went to Upper Ribbon Falls, including me and Brad. We realized that we had common interests, and as he left, he shocked me with a hug. I said he would have to come down to dinner sometime."

A couple of weeks later a helicopter came down with a bunch of people to check on mouseproofing Denise's living quarters. It had been determined that all the people suffering from relapsing tick fever lived in the old buildings around the Canyon. Park officials wanted to mouseproof them without destroying their historic value.

"I was watching the helicopter land, and there in the front seat was Brad. I had no idea he was coming down," Denise remembered. "We talked, and he was considering building a solar-powered, self-contained house, and I was fascinated. Before he left, he pulled out a brown bag with a bottle of Bailey's Irish Cream. When I first met him, someone had said they wanted a beer, and I had remarked that I preferred Bailey's Irish Cream, and he had remembered. I said, 'I'll open this when you come and help me drink it.'"

Denise didn't have to wait long. Brad hiked in on a July full moon. "We had a nice dinner and walked in the moonlight to Ribbon Falls. It was very romantic, and we talked all night long. It was quite an experience, and I fell in love." Once again, the Canyon and the moon had worked their exquisite magic, helping two souls find each other.

A Canyon courtship is always a bit unusual, and Brad and Denise's was no exception. Logistics and accessibility make getting together in the Canyon something of a challenge. Brad worked on the South Rim while Denise continued her work at Cottonwood Camp. Thursday night after work, Brad would hike down from the South Rim to Phantom Ranch. Denise would hike the 7 miles down to Phantom Ranch, and together they would hike back to Cottonwood. Brad would stay for the weekend. On her days off, Denise would hike out to the South Rim.

After a year of this strenuous dating effort, the two decided to marry. But even after they wed, they still spent time apart so each could work at the Canyon. Denise accepted a position as an interpretive ranger at Phantom Ranch, which got her 7 miles closer to Brad.

But, she said, "It didn't work out, because I finished my last talk at 9:00 P.M., and it was too late to hike out," Denise said, "so I [transferred] up to the rim and worked in fee collection." She subsequently met John Frazier, director of the Grand Canyon Field Institute, who asked her to teach backpacking for the institute. "You know," Denise replied, "I would love to teach *women's* backpacking classes."

Frazier thought a separate backpacking class for women was an excellent idea, and he encouraged Denise to design a class. "I'd been thinking about it after observing people at Cottonwood," Denise explained. "Most women start out hiking with guys. Men hike differently than women. Men are out to conquer things—to be able to say that they did this; but women want to stop and see the flowers and stop in the creek and wiggle their toes. If you are talking to a man, they will say, 'How long did it take you?' and not 'What did you see?' Men don't take as many breaks."

Denise claims that women are excellent hikers if given a chance to go at their own pace and style. "Women are the mules of the human race," she explained. "We are slow, steady, and have the endurance. Don't make us go faster than we want. Let us do it in our own way, and we are very strong. Women are tough." She also thinks women are more relaxed on backpacking trips done without men. "Women together are very comfortable. There's no sexual tension. Women act differently around men. They worry about their make-up and how they look."

Denise described the typical woman who signs up for her course: "Most are in the 35–55 year range. Their children are grown, and they are looking for new challenges. Almost every class has at least one nurse. They tell me it is a way to release the stress from their jobs. Ninety-five percent of the participants are married. Most of their husbands are excited about it, and some of the women are doing it so they can go backpacking with their husbands."

Over the years, Denise has seen repeatedly that the women who take her backpacking trips get more than exercise and a chance to make friends while exploring an incredible place. Time and again, women gain confidence, self-esteem, and spiritual re-

DENISE TRAVER (SEATED ON GROUND) WITH HER BACKPACKING CLASS. (Photo by Mike Buchheit.)

newal. In a rugged and unassuming environment, the women learn to challenge themselves, and their expectations are their own. It's often a life-changing experience, and Denise is thrilled by the chance to offer such an experience to women.

"I spend the first day just getting acquainted and orienting them to the Canyon. First we introduce ourselves and tell why we are taking the class. I help fit their packs. Most of the weight has to be on the hips," Denise explained. "Then we go through what they have brought, and invariably they have too much, even though I have sent them a list of things they need. I tell them that I will stay with the slowest person." This policy once resulted in a seven-hour hike to do the 4 miles up from Indian Garden to the rim. "One lady was so worn out, but determined to make it on her own," Denise said, "that it took her seven hours. I actually crocheted while I was walking."

Denise says that staying behind prevents any conflict or any feeling of inadequacy. "If the fast people had to stay slow, or the slow people had to try and keep up with the fast ones, it just wouldn't work. I tell them of spots where we should all meet, and this works real well. I like to be alone at times and understand someone else's need to be alone for a while. Allowing people to hike at their own pace gives them the opportunity to be alone if they wish." She always includes a layover day on her hikes. "Women like to set up home for a couple of nights and not have to carry a pack."

Evenings in camp are wonderful as the light leaves the Canyon and the backpackers relax around dinner. "I don't do backpacking foods," Denise said. "I fix mashed potatoes and gravy, angel hair pasta with pesto sauce, and refried beans and tortillas. You can eat all you want when you are out backpacking because you are working so hard."

Denise feels that backpacking is often like a retreat of sorts, where women can resolve personal problems or come to terms with some inner conflict. "One of my backpackers was raped thirteen years before, and she was still dealing with it," Denise explained. "It has helped me as well. I didn't used to be nearly as confident as I am now. About twice a year I go on a solo backpacking trip. I'll go off for two weeks at a time, and you can't believe what that does to your confidence. I feel strong and good when I come back."

Denise's classes through the Grand Canyon Field Institute

TRAVER AT HUALAPAI HILLTOP, MARCH 1997. (Photo by Betty Leavengood.)

have grown in number and popularity. From seven-day treks across the Grand Canyon to short forays into the Havasupai Reservation, Denise has shown countless women her Canyon. It teaches them, as it did her, to face life with confidence.

D E N I S E   T R A V E R

Mothers and Daughters: An Epilogue

*F*INALLY, BOOK FINISHED, I could go back and enjoy the Canyon. I arranged a three-day camp-out on the South Rim with my two daughters—Cheryl, thirty-five, an artist living and working in Tucson, and Christy, twenty-seven, an intern with the Dusseldorf, Germany, opera, home for a short stay. We drove to the South Rim to Mather Campground. Because we all have different sleeping habits, we had quite a compound: a tent each for the girls, and me comfortable in the back of my Jeep.

The first day we just barely got there and got set up before sunset. "Let's get a bottle of wine and some cheese and watch the sunset," Cheryl suggested, and off we went to Babbit's General Store to carry out the plan. We would drink no wine cheaper than six dollars a bottle! As we sat, drinking wine out of the bottoms of plastic water bottles that Cheryl prepared with her Swiss Army knife, I marveled that by some miracle I had managed in my haphazard way to produce these two fine human beings who shared my love of the Canyon.

We moved inside to the Yavapai Lodge to begin the Grand Canyon Scrabble Championship. Cheryl, the avid reader, easily won the first game. Round two, the next morning over breakfast, I saw my chance. If no one blocked me, I could make a major score on a triple word. I used to always win, but now the girls nearly always win, their revenge for years of defeat. I said a little prayer, "Dear Lord, I've been pretty good this year, and I deserve to win just this one game." I spelled "crazy" on the triple space and scored 45 points. My next play I owe to the Honorable Fife Symington, then governor of Arizona. I placed "fife" on another triple space, scoring 32 points. Round two was a smashing victory for me.

SCRABBLE ON YAKI POINT, A FAVORITE FAMILY PASTIME FOR SISTERS CHRISTY AND CHERYL GRAHAM. (Photo by Betty Leavengood.)

The next day we hiked a mile down Hermit Trail, stopping often to inspect the view. Three youngish hikers, two of them obviously unhappy, shared the trail with us. We overheard one, a young woman in sandals, say, "We have better trees than this on Long Island." We agreed that she should go back to Long Island.

Sunset that evening was glorious. We shared our space at Yavapai Point with at least fifty people and could see folks all around on other points poised with their cameras, waiting for the sunset. The light plays magnificently on the temples and buttes of the Canyon, and it is a time worth waiting for.

Our last full day, we drove to the Watchtower, Mary Colter's tremendous structure along the east rim drive. On the porch of the cafe we had round three of the Grand Canyon Scrabble Tournament. With people all around us, we played Scrabble while enduring looks that said, "They're at the Grand Canyon and they're playing Scrabble?" Round three went to Christy. That evening we took the Scrabble board, the wine, and the plastic bottoms of the water bottles, and went to Yaki Point. There, on a flat rock high above the South Kaibab Trail, we played the final round. Christy won again and earned the title of Grand Canyon Scrabble Champion. The next day we left the Canyon with a vow to return again someday and stay longer.

And we will. For three years now, I'd been so busy researching the lives of women of the Canyon that I hadn't had time to enjoy it much myself. Now, I'm studying maps and planning trips. I want to camp where Ada Bass spent the winter at Shinumo Creek, see the light on the Canyon walls so beautifully described by Louise Teal, and find Gale Burak's route to the lone ponderosa pine in the Inner Canyon. With each step I take in the Canyon, I honor the women profiled in this book. Their groundbreaking efforts and passionate wills have made it easier for me and my daughters—and generations of women to come—to embrace this remarkable place and to explore it without fear or masculine intimidation. I am grateful for their stories. Some day, when I'm old and feeble, I want some young whippersnapper to call me up and say, "I'm writing a book about women hikers of the Canyon. Could I come talk to you?"

Notes

Chapter 1 — A Lady's Rough and Tumble Life: Ada Bass

1. Ada Bass, "My First Trip to Grand Canyon," Composition Book, Box 2, Folder 10, W. W. Bass Collection, Manuscript Number 1065, Arizona Historical Society, Tucson, Arizona; hereafter referred to as Bass Collection.

2. *Ibid.*

3. Ada Bass Diary, 1895, Box 2, Folder 11, Bass Collection. Folder 11 contains transcripts of all Ada Bass's diaries and is hereafter referred to as Ada Bass Diary.

4. Ada Bass, "My Second Trip to Grand Canyon," Composition Book, Box 2, Folder 10, Bass Collection.

5. *Ibid.*

6. *Ibid.*

7. *Ibid.*

8. *Ibid.*

9. Ada Bass Diary, 1895.

10. *Ibid.*

11. Ada Bass, "Stranded on the Cataract," Composition Book, Box 2, Folder 10, Bass Collection.

12. *Ibid.*

13. *Ibid.*

14. *Ibid.*, 1896.

15. *Ibid.*

16. *Ibid.*, 1900.

17. *Ibid.*

18. *Ibid.*, 1903.

19. *Ibid.*

20. *Ibid.*, 1904.

21. *Ibid.*

22. *Ibid.*, 1905.

23. Mrs. William Guy Bass, telephone interview with author, Wickenburg, Arizona, June 16, 1996.

Chapter 2 — Building a Legacy: Mary Elizabeth Jane Colter

1. Virginia L. Grattan, *Mary Colter: Builder Upon the Red Earth* (Grand Canyon, Arizona: Grand Canyon Natural History Association, 1992), p. 22.

2. *Ibid.*, p. 26.

3. Gale Burak, interview with author, North Woodstock, New Hampshire, September 5–8, 1995.

4. Elizabeth Kent Meyer, interview with author, Phoenix, Arizona, March 27, 1996.

5. Fred Kabotie and Bill Belknap, *Fred Kabotie: Hopi Indian Artist* (Flagstaff, Arizona: Northland Press, 1977), p. 50.

6. Grattan, *Mary Colter,* p. 78.

7. *Ibid.,* p. 76.

8. *Ibid.,* p. 88.

9. Ruth Stephens Baker, interview with author, Tucson, Arizona, July 30, 1996.

10. Grattan, *Mary Colter,* p. 108.

CHAPTER 3—A HARVEY GIRL: ELIZABETH KENT MEYER

1. Leslie Poling-Kempes, *The Harvey Girls: Women Who Opened the West* (New York: Paragon House, 1989), p. 42.

2. *Ibid.,* p. 43.

3. Here and following, unless otherwise cited, Elizabeth Kent Meyer, interview with author, Phoenix, Arizona, March 27, 1996.

CHAPTER 4—A FACE IN THE RAIN: BESSIE HALEY HYDE

1. *Parischan,* 1924 Parkersburg High School Annual, Parkersburg, West Virginia, p. 14.

2. Otis R. Marston Collection at the Huntington Library, San Marino, California, Box 96, Folder 1; hereafter referred to as Marston Collection.

3. *Ibid.,* Folder 9.

4. *Ibid.,* Folder 8.

5. *Ibid.,* Folder 3.

6. Fred Harvey Collection, University of Arizona Library Special Collections, Manuscript AZ326, v. 19.

7. Marston Collection, Box 96, Folder 2.

8. *Denver Post,* Denver, Colorado, November 20, 1928, as quoted by Tessman, Norm, in " 'I wonder if I shall ever wear pretty shoes again': The Disappearance of Glen and Bessie Hyde," *The Sharlot Hall Gazette,* Sharlot Hall Museum, Prescott, Arizona, March 1986.

9. Barry Goldwater, *Delightful Journey* (Tempe, Arizona: Arizona Historical Foundation, 1970), p. 189.

10. Marston Collection, Box 223, Folder 26.

11. Correspondence with Ronald L. Warren, August 19, 1995. Mr. Warren is researching southwest aviation history.

12. "Search by Air, Water for Pair," *Prescott Evening Courier,* Prescott, Arizona, December 18, 1928, p. 1.

13. Emery Kolb Collection, Northern Arizona University Cline Library Special Collections, Manuscript 197, Series 1, Box 3, Folders 814 and 815; hereafter referred to as Kolb Collection.

14. Marston Collection, Box 96, Folder 10.

15. Kolb Collection, Folder 841.

16. *Ibid.*

17. Marston Collection, Box 96, Folder 10.

18. *Ibid.*

19. David Lavender, *River Runners of the Grand Canyon* (Tucson, Arizona: University of Arizona Press, 1986), p. 83.

20. Martin J. Anderson, "A Perfect Place to Hyde," Martin J. Anderson Collection, Northern Arizona University, Cline Library Special Collections, Manuscript 77.

CHAPTER 5—A RANGER IN RIDING HABIT: POLLY MEAD PATRAW

1. Here and following, unless otherwise cited, Pauline Mead Patraw, interview with Mike Quinn, Santa Fe, New Mexico, September 4, 1995, Grand Canyon National Park Museum Collection, Catalog #GRCA 65559.

2. Pauline Mead Patraw, interview with Julie Russell, Santa Fe, New Mexico, August 3, 1981, Grand Canyon National Park Museum Collection, Catalog #GRCA 35736; hereafter referred to as Russell interview.

3. Merriam, C. Hart, *Results of a Biological Survey of the San Francisco Mountain Region and Desert of the Little Colorado, Arizona* (Washington: Government Printing Office, 1890), p. 36.

4. Russell interview.

5. *Nature Notes,* December 1930. This series of nature articles started by naturalist Glen Sturdevant has been edited and combined into a book; see Susan Lamb, ed., *The Best of Grand Canyon Nature Notes* (Grand Canyon: Grand Canyon Natural History Association, 1994).

6. Pauline Mead Patraw, *Flowers of the Southwest Mesas* (Globe, Arizona: Southwestern Monuments Association, 1953).

7. Russell interview.

Chapter 6—Race to Shiva Temple: Ruth Stephens Baker

1. Here and following, unless otherwise cited, Ruth Stephens Baker interview with Julie Russell, Tucson, Arizona, November 3 and 5, 1978, National Park Service Museum Collection, Catalog #GRCA 36152.

2. Ruth Stephens Baker, interview with author, Tucson, Arizona, July 30, 1996.

3. *Ibid.*

4. "Scientists to Seek Mountain Secrets," *New York Times*, August 27, 1937, p. 17; Meyer Berger, "Hunting the Secrets of the Awesome Colorado Canyon," *New York Times Magazine*, September 19, 1937, p. 14.

5. Kolb had been "in charge" at the Canyon before the National Park Service gained responsibility to oversee it, and over the years the two had been in conflict with one another. The Park Service had the power to kick out Kolb, but didn't. Instead, they built the Lookout Studio to compete with Kolb's gift shop.

6. Ruth Stephens Baker, interview with Karen Underhill, Grand Canyon, Arizona, May 29, 1994, Grand Canyon National Park Museum Collection, Catalog #GRCA 63378; hereafter referred to as Underhill interview.

7. *Ibid.*

8. *Ibid.*

9. *Ibid.*

10. *Ibid.*

11. *Ibid.*

12. "Scientists Reach Top of Sky Island," *New York Times*, September 17, 1937.

13. "Treasureless Island," *Time*, October 4, 1937, p. 45.

14. Harold E. Anthony, "Scientist Describes Visit to Unknown Island in the Sky," *Science News Letter*, October 16, 1937, pp. 245–254.

15. Underhill interview.

16. *Ibid.*

17. *Ibid.*

Chapter 7—Two Women, Three Boats, and a Plant Press: Elzada Clover and Lois Jotter

1. Stan Swinton, "Faculty Women to Face Danger on Stormy Colorado for Science," *Michigan Daily* University of Michigan (Ann Arbor), June 5, 1938, p. 1.

2. William Cook, *The* Wen, *the* Botany, *and the* Mexican Hat (Orangevale, California: Callisto Books, 1987), p. 25.

3. Elzada Clover Diary, Elzada Clover Collection, Bentley Historical Library, University of Michigan, Part 1, p. 2; hereafter referred to as Clover Diary. (Copy also at Grand Canyon National Park Museum Collection, Catalog #GRCA 58957.)

4. Cook, *The Wen,* p.32.

5. Clover Diary, Part 1, p. 26.

6. Lois Jotter Collection, Northern Arizona University, Cline Library Special Collections, Manuscript 69, Series One, Literary Productions, Box 1, Folder 2, Part l, p. 12; hereafter referred to as Jotter Diary.

7. Norm Nevills Diary, University of Utah, Marriott Library Special Collections, June 23; hereafter referred to as Nevills Diary. (Copy in *Some Colorado River Journals and Diaries* by Otis Marston at the Grand Canyon National Park Museum Collection, Catalog #GRCA 54981.)

8. Nevills Diary, June 23.

9. Clover Diary, Part 1 , p. 30.

10. *Ibid.,* p. 35.

11. Cook, *The Wen,* p. 37.

12. Clover Diary, Part 1, p. 33.

13. *Ibid.,* p. 14.

14. Jotter Diary, p. 26.

15. Nevills Diary, June 29.

16. *Ibid.*

17. Jotter Diary, p. 39.

18. "Planes Seek Six Explorers," *Los Angeles Herald,* July 5, 1938, p. 1.

19. Clover Diary, Part 1, p. 108.

20. Cook, *The Wen,* p. 62.

21. Nevills Diary, July 8.

22. *Ibid.,* July 13.

23. Clover Diary, Part 2, p. 9.

24. *Ibid.,* p. 10.

25. *Ibid.,* p. 12.

26. Cook, *The Wen,* p. 89.

27. Clover Diary, Part 2, p. 55.

28. *Ibid.,* p. 103.

29. Nevills Diary, July 29.

30. *Ibid.,* July 30.

31. Lois Jotter Cutter, personal correspondence with the author, March 25, 1998.

CHAPTER 8—IN POWELL'S WAKE: DORIS NEVILLS

1. Here and following, unless otherwise cited, Doris Nevills journal published in installments, *Daily Sentinel,* Grand Junction, Colorado, June 15, 1940, et. seq.

2. Nancy Nelson, *Any Time, Any Place, Any River* (Flagstaff, Arizona: Red Lake Books, 1991), pp. 3–4.

3. J. W. Powell, *The Exploration of the Colorado River and Its Canyons* (New York: Dover Publications, 1961), p. 119. First published in 1895 as *Canyons of the Colorado.*

4. *Ibid.,* p. 160.

5. *Ibid.,* p. 215.

6. *Ibid.,* pp. 230–231.

7. Norm gave the original *Mexican Hat,* the boat used in the 1938 Clover trip, to Don Harris.

CHAPTER 9—A CANYON TRAILBLAZER: GALE BURAK

1. Here and following, unless otherwise cited, Gale Burak, interview with author, North Woodstock, New Hampshire, September 5–8, 1995.

CHAPTER 10—WOMAN OF THE RIVER: GEORGIE WHITE CLARK

1. Many early river runners referred to the Colorado River as the Grand.

2. Georgie White Clark, interview with Karen Underhill of Northern Arizona University Cline Library Special Collections, Grand Canyon, Arizona, November 6, 1991, Tape 2, p. 14; hereafter referred to as Underhill interview.

3. *Ibid.,* Tape 1, p. 17.

4. Divorce certificate, May 8, 1941, Rosalyn Jirge Collection, Box 4, Folder 99, Northern Arizona University, Cline Library Special Collections.

5. Underhill interview, Tape 1, p. 22.

6. *Ibid.*

7. Here and following, unless otherwise cited, Georgie White

Clark and Duane Newcomb, *Thirty Years of River Running* (San Francisco: Chronicle Books, n.d.).

8. Underhill interview, Tape 1, p. 25.

9. Harry Aleson, "Colorado River Raft Drift," *Southern Sierran,* August 1946, p. 3.

10. Underhill interview, Tape 1, pp. 27-28.

11. *Ibid.,* pp. 37–38.

12. Dan Davis, interview with author, Tucson, Arizona, May 5, 1995.

13. Delphine Mohrline Gallagher Collection, "Colorado River Trips," Northern Arizona University, Cline Library Special Collections, PH.93.5.1-196, p. 5.

14. *Ibid.*

15. Joel Sayre, "The Average Can't Imagine," *Sports Illustrated,* June 16, 1958, pp. 61–72.

16. Underhill interview, Tape 1, p. 43.

17. *Ibid.,* pp. 41–44.

18. *Ibid.,* pp. 47–48.

19. *Ibid.,* Tape 3, p. 38.

20. Georgie Clark Collection, Northern Arizona University, Cline Library Special Collections, Subgroup Two, Friends of Georgie, Series Eight, Robert Atherton, 1958–1992, Box 4, Folder 86, Correspondence with Georgie Clark.

CHAPTER II — CATALOGING A CANYON: LOUISE HINCHLIFFE

1. Louise Hinchliffe, interview with author, Sedona, Arizona, November 1, 1995; hereafter cited as Author interview: Hinchliffe.

2. *Ibid.*

3. Here and following, unless otherwise noted, Louise Hinchliffe, interview with Julie Russell, Grand Canyon, Arizona, November 18, 1980, Grand Canyon National Park Museum Collection, Catalog #GRCA 35957.

4. Author interview: Hinchliffe.

5. *Ibid.*

6. *Ibid.*

7. *Ibid.*

8. *Ibid.*

9. *Ibid.*

10. *Ibid.*

11. *Ibid.*
12. *Ibid.*
13. *Ibid.*
14. *Ibid.*

CHAPTER 12—MY HEART KNOWS WHAT THE RIVER KNOWS: KATIE LEE

1. Copyrighted material reprinted with permission of Katie Lee.

2. Katie Lee, interview by Roy Webb, Jerome, Arizona, April 14, 1984, p. 22, University of Utah, Marriott Library Special Collections; hereafter referred to as Webb interview.

3. J. W. Powell, *The Exploration of the Colorado River and Its Canyons* (New York: Dover Publications, 1961), pp. 232–233. First published in 1895 as *Canyons of the Colorado.*

4. Katie Lee, interview with author, Jerome, Arizona, October 31, 1995; hereafter referred to as Author interview: Lee.

5. Katie Lee's name for the Bureau of Reclamation; Webb interview, p. 23.

6. Webb interview, pp. 6–7.

7. "Journal of Katie Lee, made during the traverse of the Grand Canyon from Bright Angel Creek to Temple Bar, July, 1955," Otis T. Marston Collection, Huntington Library, San Marino, California, Box 116, Folder 5.

8. Webb interview, p. 11.

9. Author interview: Lee.

10. Copyrighted material reprinted with permission of Katie Lee.

11. Katie Lee, "Glen Canyon Diary, 1956," *Journal of Arizona History*, Spring 1976, pp. 54–56.

12. *Ibid.*

13. Author interview: Lee.

14. Webb interview, pp. 14–15.

15. Author interview: Lee.

16. Russell Martin, *A Story That Stands Like a Dam* (New York: Henry Holt and Company, 1989), p. 239.

17. Katie has re-recorded her songs of the river. The cassette, *Colorado River Songs,* is available from Katydid Books and Music, Jerome, AZ 86331.

18. Webb interview, p. 14.

19. *Ibid.,* pp. 29–30.

20. Underhill interview, Tape 3, p. 38.

21. Webb interview, p. 23.

22. *Ibid.,* p. 29.

23. *Ibid.,* pp. 31–32.

24. Copyrighted material reprinted with the permission of Katie Lee.

25. Greg Hanscom, "Reclaiming a Lost Canyon," *High Country News,* Paonia, Colorado, November 10, 1997, p.10.

CHAPTER 13—ROWING A RIVER, ROWING A LIFE: LOUISE TEAL

1. Here and following, unless otherwise cited, Louise Teal, interview with author, Durango, Colorado, May 23, 1995, and subsequent correspondence.

2. Louise Teal, *Breaking into the Current* (Tucson:: University of Arizona Press, 1994), p. 53.

3. Complete account in Teal, *Breaking into the Current,* pp. 55–58.

4. See p. 98.

CHAPTER 14—SADDLE UP! LADY MULE WRANGLERS

1. "Grand Canyon Mule Ride," video, Don Briggs Productions, 398 11th Street, San Francisco, California, n.d.

2. Ron Clayton, interview with author, Grand Canyon, Arizona, July 11, 1996.

3. Here and following, unless otherwise cited, Patty Knox, interview with author, Grand Canyon, Arizona, July 11, 1996; Bernice Reeves, interview with author, Grand Canyon, Arizona, July 14, 1996; Kitty Marr, interview with author, Grand Canyon, Arizona, July 14, 1996.

CHAPTER 15—WITH A PACK ON HER BACK: DENISE TRAVER

1. Denise Traver, interview with author, Rock Springs, Arizona, June 18, 1996.

2. Here and following, unless otherwise cited, Denise Traver, interview with Mike Quinn, Grand Canyon, Arizona, May 12, 1996, Grand Canyon National Park Museum Collection, Catalog #GRCA 66189.

Bibliography

I. PRIMARY SOURCES

Interviews

Baker, Ruth Stephens. Interview by author, Tucson, Arizona, July 30, 1996.

Baker, Ruth Stephens. Interview with Julie Russell, Tucson, Arizona, November 3 and 5, 1978, National Park Service Museum Collection, Catalog #GRCA 36152.

Baker, Ruth Stephens. Interview with Karen Underhill, Grand Canyon, Arizona, May 29, 1994, Grand Canyon National Park Museum Collection, Catalog #GRCA 63378.

Burak, Gale. Interview by author, North Woodstock, New Hampshire, September 5–8, 1995.

Clayton, Ron. Interview by author, Grand Canyon, Arizona, July 11, 1996.

Davis, Dan. Interview by author, Tucson, Arizona, May 5, 1995.

Hinchliffe, Louise. Interview by author, Sedona, Arizona, November 1, 1995.

Hinchliffe, Louise. Interview with Julie Russell, Grand Canyon, Arizona, November 18, 1980, Grand Canyon National Park Museum Collection, Catalog #GRCA 35957.

Knox, Patty. Interview by author, Grand Canyon, Arizona, July 11, 1996.

Lee, Katie. Interview by author, Jerome, Arizona, October 31, 1995.

Lee, Katie. Interview with Roy Webb, Jerome, Arizona, April 14, 1984, University of Utah, Marriott Library Special Collections.

Marr, Kitty. Interview by author, Grand Canyon, Arizona, July 14, 1996.

Meyer, Elizabeth Kent. Interview by author, Phoenix, Arizona, March 27, 1996.

Patraw, Pauline Mead. Interview with Julie Russell, Santa Fe, New Mexico, August 3, 1981, Grand Canyon National Park Museum Collection, Catalog #GRCA 35736.

Patraw, Pauline Mead. Interview with Mike Quinn, Santa Fe, New Mexico, September 4, 1995, Grand Canyon National Park Museum Collection, Catalog #GRCA 65559.

Reeves, Bernice. Interview by author, Grand Canyon, Arizona, July 14, 1996.

Teal, Louise. Interview by author, Durango, Colorado, May 23, 1995, and subsequent correspondence.

Traver, Denise. Interview by author, Rock Springs, Arizona, June 18, 1996.

Traver, Denise. Interview with Mike Quinn, Grand Canyon, Arizona, May 12, 1996, Grand Canyon National Park Museum Collection, Catalog #GRCA 66189.

Diaries and Journals

Bass, Ada. Diaries and Manuscripts. W. W. Bass Collection, Manuscript Number 1065, Arizona Historical Society, Tucson, Arizona.

Clover, Elzada. Diary, Elzada Clover Collection, Bentley Historical Library, University of Michigan. (Copy also at Grand Canyon National Park Museum Collection, Catalog #GRCA 58957.)

Cutter, Lois Jotter. Diary, Lois Jotter Collection, Northern Arizona University, Cline Library Special Collections, Manuscript 69.

Lee, Katie. "Journal of Katie Lee, made during the traverse of the Grand Canyon from Bright Angel Creek to Temple Bar, July, 1955," Otis T. Marston Collection, Huntington Library, San Marino, California, Box 116, Folder 5.

Nevills, Doris. Journal published in installments, *Daily Sentinel,* Grand Junction, Colorado, June 15, 1940, et. seq.

Nevills, Norm. Diary, University of Utah, Marriott Library Special Collections. (Copy in *Some Colorado River Journals and Diaries* by Otis Marston at the Grand Canyon National Park Museum Collection, Catalog #GRCA 54981.)

Collections

Martin J. Anderson Collection, Northern Arizona University, Cline Library Special Collections, Flagstaff, Arizona.

Georgie Clark Collection, Northern Arizona University, Cline Library Special Collections, Flagstaff, Arizona.

Delphine Mohrline Gallagher Collection, Northern Arizona University, Cline Library Special Collections, Flagstaff, Arizona.

Fred Harvey Collection, University of Arizona Library Special Collections, Tucson, Arizona.

Emery Kolb Collection, Northern Arizona University, Cline Library
Special Collections, Flagstaff, Arizona.
Otis R. Marston Collection, Huntington Library, San Marino,
California.

II. Secondary Sources

Books

Babbit, Bruce, ed. *Grand Canyon: An Anthology.* Flagstaff, Arizona:
Northland Press, 1978.

Brower, David, ed. *The Place No One Knew.* San Francisco: Ballantine
Books, 1968.

Brian, Nancy. *River to Rim.* Flagstaff, Arizona: Earthquest Press, 1992.

Clark, Georgie White, and Duane Newcomb. *Georgie Clark: Thirty
Years of River Running.* San Francisco: Chronicle Books, n.d.

Cook, William. *The Wen, the Botany, and the Mexican Hat.* Orangevale, California: Callisto Books, 1987.

Fradkin, Philip L. *A River No More.* Tucson, Arizona: University of
Arizona Press, 1981.

Goldwater, Barry. *Delightful Journey.* Tempe, Arizona: Arizona Historical Foundation, 1970.

Grattan, Virginia L. *Mary Colter: Builder Upon the Red Earth.* Grand
Canyon, Arizona: Grand Canyon Natural History Association,
1992.

Inskip, Eleanor, ed. *The Colorado River Through Glen Canyon Before
Lake Powell.* Moab, Utah: Inskip Ink, 1995.

Kabotie, Fred, and Bill Belknap. *Fred Kabotie: Hopi Indian Artist.*
Flagstaff, Arizona: Northland Press, 1977.

Lamb, Susan, ed. *The Best of Grand Canyon Nature Notes.* Grand Canyon, Arizona: Grand Canyon Natural History Association, 1994.

Lavender, David. *River Runners of the Grand Canyon.* Tucson, Arizona: University of Arizona Press, 1986.

Lee, Katie. *All My Rivers Are Gone.* Boulder, Colorado: Johnson
Books, 1998.

Martin, Russell. *A Story That Stands Like a Dam.* New York: Henry
Holt and Company, 1989.

Maurer, Stephen G. *Solitude and Sunshine: Images of a Grand Canyon
Childhood.* Boulder, Colorado: Pruett Publishing Company,
1983.

Merriam, C. Hart. *Results of a Biological Survey of the San Francisco*

Mountain Region and Desert of the Little Colorado, Arizona (Washington: Government Printing Office, 1890), p. 36.

Nelson, Nancy. *Any Time Any Place Any River: The Nevills of Mexican Hat.* Flagstaff, Arizona: Red Lake Books, 1991.

Parischan. Parkersburg High School Annual, Parkersburg, West Virginia, 1924.

Patraw, Pauline Mead. *Flowers of the Southwest Mesas.* Globe, Arizona: Southwestern Monuments Association, 1953.

Poling-Kempes, Lesley. *The Harvey Girls.* New York: Paragon House, 1989.

Powell, J. W. *The Exploration of the Colorado River and Its Canyons.* New York: Dover Publications, 1961. First published in 1895 as *Canyons of the Colorado.*

Sadler, Christa, ed. *There's This River: Grand Canyon Boatman Stories.* Flagstaff, Arizona: Red Lake Books, 1994.

Teal, Louise. *Breaking Into the Current: Boatwomen of the Grand Canyon.* Tucson, Arizona: University of Arizona Press, 1994.

Webb, Robert H. *Grand Canyon: A Century of Change.* Tucson, Arizona: University of Arizona Press, 1996.

Webb, Roy. *Call of the Colorado.* Moscow, Idaho: University of Idaho Press, 1994.

Westwood, Richard. *Woman of the River.* Logan, Utah: Utah State University Press, 1997.

Zwinger, Ann Haymond. *Down Canyon.* Tucson, Arizona: University of Arizona Press, 1995.

Newspaper Articles

Denver Post, Denver, Colorado, November 20, 1928.

"Reclaiming a Lost Canyon," *High Country News,* Paonia, Colorado, November 10, 1997.

"Planes Seek Six Explorers," *Los Angeles Herald,* July 5, 1938.

"Search by Air, Water for Pair," *Prescott Evening Courier,* Prescott, Arizona, December 18, 1928.

"Scientists Reach Top of Sky Island," *New York Times,* September 17, 1937.

"Scientists to Seek Mountain Secrets," *New York Times,* August 27, 1937.

Swinton, Stan. "Faculty Women to Face Danger on Stormy Colorado for Science," *Michigan Daily* (University of Michigan, Ann Arbor), June 5, 1938.

Magazine and Journal Articles

Aleson, Harry. "Colorado River Raft Drift," *Southern Sierran,* August 1946.

Anthony, Harold E. "Scientist Describes Visit to Unknown Island in the Sky," *Science News Letter,* October 16, 1937.

Berger, Meyer. "Hunting the Secrets of the Awesome Colorado Canyon," *New York Times Magazine,* September 19, 1937.

Lee, Katie. "Glen Canyon Diary, 1956," *Journal of Arizona History,* Spring 1976.

Sayre, Joel. "The Average Can't Imagine," *Sports Illustrated,* June 16, 1958.

"Treasureless Island," *Time,* October 4, 1937.

Videos

Briggs, Don. *Grand Canyon Mule Ride,* Don Briggs Productions, 398 11th Street, San Francisco, California, n.d.